The Effective Management of Parkinson's Disease

The Effective Management of Parkinson's Disease

Edited by

Leslie Findley MD FRCP
Consultant Neurologist, Essex Neurosciences Centre and
Professor, South Bank University, UK

Brian Hurwitz MA MSc MD FRCP FRCGP
Professor of Medicine and the Arts, King's College, London
and General Practitioner NHS Principal, London, UK

Andrew Miles MSc MPhil PhD
Professor of Public Health Sciences and Editor-in-Chief, Journal of Evaluation
in Clinical Practice, Barts and The London, Queen Mary's School of Medicine
and Dentistry, University of London, UK

European
Parkinson's Disease
Association

Parkinson's
Disease Society

AESCULAPIUS MEDICAL PRESS
LONDON SAN FRANCISCO SYDNEY

Published by

Aesculapius Medical Press (London, San Francisco, Sydney)
PO Box LB48, London EC1A 1LB, UK

© Aesculapius Medical Press 2004

First published 2004

British Library Cataloguing in Publication Data
A CIP catalogue record for this book is available from the British Library

ISBN: 1 903044 32 4

While the advice and information in this book are believed to be true and accurate at the
time of going to press, neither the authors nor the publishers nor the sponsoring institutions
can accept any legal responsibility or liability for errors or omissions that may be made.
In particular (but without limiting the generality of the preceding disclaimer) every effort
has been made to check drug usages; however, it is possible that errors have been missed.
Furthermore, dosage schedules are constantly being revised and new side effects recognised.
For these reasons, the reader is strongly urged to consult the drug companies' printed
instructions before administering any of the drugs recommended in this book.

Further copies of this volume are available from:

Claudio Melchiorri
Aesculapius Medical Press
PO Box LB48, Mount Pleasant Mail Centre, Farringdon Road, London EC1A 1LB, UK

Fax: 020 8525 8661
Email: claudio@keyadvances4.demon.co.uk

Copy edited by The Clyvedon Press Ltd, Cardiff, UK

Typeset, printed and bound in Britain
Peter Powell Origination & Print Limited

Contents

Contributors

Madhavi Bajekal PhD, Honorary Research Fellow, Department of Primary Health Care and General Practice, Faculty of Medicine, Imperial College of Science, Technology and Medicine, London

Clive Bowman FRCP, Medical Director, BUPA Care Services, Leeds

Richard Brown BA MPhil PhD CPsychol, Reader in Cognitive Neuroscience, Department of Psychology, Institute of Psychiatry, London

David Burn MB BS MA MD FRCP, Consultant and Senior Lecturer in Neurology, Regional Neurosciences Centre, Newcastle General Hospital, Newcastle upon Tyne

Carl E Clarke BSc MD FRCP, Reader in Clinical Neurology, City Hospital and University of Birmingham

K Ray Chaudhuri MD FRCP(Edin) FRCP(Lond.), Consultant Neurologist, Honorary Senior Lecturer and Co-Director, Movement Disorders Unit, King's College and Lewisham Hospitals

Adrian Cook MSc, Research Analyst, Department of Primary Health Care and General Practice, Faculty of Medicine, Imperial College of Science, Technology and Medicine, London

Leslie Findley MD FRCP, Consultant Neurologist, Essex Neurosciences Centre, Oldchurch Hospital, Romford, Essex and Professor, University of the South Bank

Clare Fowler FRCP, Professor in Uro-neurology, National Hospital for Neurology and Neurosurgery, London

Donald Grosset BSc MB ChB MD FRCP(Glas), Consultant Neurologist and Honorary Senior Lecturer, Department of Neurology, Institute of Neurological Sciences, Southern General Hospital, Glasgow

Christopher Hawkes MD FRCP, Consultant Neurologist, Essex Neuroscience Centre, Oldchurch Hospital, Romford, Essex

Max Henderson MB BS MRCP MRCPsych, Clinical Research Fellow, Institute of Psychiatry, Denmark Hill, London

Brian Hurwitz MSc MD FRCP FRCGP, Professor of Medicine and the Arts, King's College, London, and Visiting Professor of Primary Health Care and General Practice, Faculty of Medicine, Imperial College of Science, Technology and Medicine, London

Sir Brian Jarman PhD FRCP FRCGP, Emeritus Professor of Primary Health Care and General Practice, Faculty of Medicine, Imperial College of Science, Technology and Medicine; currently Visiting Professor, Institute for Healthcare Improvement, Boston, USA

Diana Jones BA MCSP, Research Fellow, Institute of Rehabilitation, Hunters Moor Regional Neurological Rehabilitation Centre, Newcastle upon Tyne

Douglas MacMahon MB BS FRCP, Consultant Physician, Royal Cornwall Hospitals NHS Trust

Lynne Osborne BSc RGN, Parkinson's Disease Nurse Specialist, Hammersmith Hospitals NHS Trust

Rowena Plant PhD MSc MSCP PGCED, Professor of Rehabilitation Therapy, Institute of Rehabilitation, Hunters Moor Regional Neurological Rehabilitation Centre, Newcastle upon Tyne

Malcolm J Steiger MD FRCP, Consultant Neurologist, Walton Centre for Neurology and Neurosurgery, Liverpool

Rebecca Stowe BMedSc PhD, Information Scientist, University of Birmingham Clinical Trials Unit, Edgbaston, Birmingham

Sue Thomas BA(Hons) CRT DN RGN RM, Nursing Practice and Policy Adviser, Royal College of Nursing

Brian K Toone MB BS MPhil FRCP FRCPsych, Consultant Neuropsychiatrist, Maudsley Hospital, London

Ian Whittle MD PhD FRACS FRCSE(SN) FRCPE, Forbes Professor of Surgical Neurology, Department of Clinical Neurosciences, Western General Hospital, Edinburgh

Kristian Winge MD, Research Fellow, Department of Neurology, Bispebjerg Hospital and University of Copenhagen, Denmark

Preface

Parkinson's disease and its allied disorders are the cause of much suffering and collectively constitute an enormous burden of illness on patients and their carers. Despite a low prevalence, the longevity and complex physical and psychological morbidities associated with the conditions impose a considerable disease burden on health services, which is set to increase further as the population ages and as patients rightly demand better, more effective health care.[i] As this volume demonstrates, good health care for these patients requires committed multi-disciplinary working supported by specialists and practitioners with particular interests and training in evidence based care of these conditions.[ii] This volume offers an up-to-date synthesis, by leading clinical academics and researchers, of evidence informed practices in the care of PD, based on studies spanning pathology, diagnosis, pharmacological, surgical and physiotherapy treatments, physical and psychological complications, health services organisation and patient quality of life assessments.

In spite of advances in the understanding of the pathophysiology and aetiology of Parkinson's disease (PD), the diagnosis of this condition remains largely clinical and is often related to the clinical expertise of the physician. A typical case of PD presenting with a classical rest tremor, bradykinesia and gait difficulties, for example, is easy to recognise, but problems arise when patients do not develop tremor, may have vascular pseudo-parkinsonism or parkinsonism secondary to multiple system atrophy, Lewy body dementia or progressive supranuclear palsy. Early and accurate diagnosis, as Chaudhuri emphasises in the opening chapter of Part One of this volume, is important for counselling, appropriate therapy, neuroprotection and the inclusion of patients in research studies and the author proceeds to present a particularly thorough review of the current basis on which we should aim to establish a definitive diagnosis.

It has been suggested that abnormalities in mood and olfaction may predate the diagnosis of PD and it is to olfaction in Parkinson's disease that Hawkes turns in Chapter Two in a stimulating account of current research as it relates to the measurement of olfactory function in parkinsonian syndromes. It is now recognised, as the author points out, that the olfactory system is damaged to varying degrees in the presence of clinically evident parkinsonism with the most severe changes seen in the idiopathic, Guamanian and Lewy body disease varieties and these observations as Hawkes describes, are of relevance to diagnosis. Thus, if a patient is suspected to have PD, the presence of normal olfaction should prompt review of the diagnosis. Anosmia in corticobasal degeneration (CBD), progressive supranuclear palsy (PSP) or vascular parkinsonism would similarly be unexpected. In Chapter Three, the final chapter of

---

[i] European Parkinson's Disease Association. www.epda.eu.com (accessed Jan 04)

[ii] Kale R, Menken M. (2004).Who should look after people with Parkinson's disease? *BMJ* **328**, 62–3.

Part One, Grosset completes the section on diagnosis with a review on the clinical applications of functional cerebral imaging and shows how DaTSCAN using single photon emission computed tomography can assist in the differential diagnosis of Parkinson's disease from other movement disorders.

Part Two of the volume is dedicated to a thorough review of the current scientific evidence and expert opinion base for medical and surgical intervention in PD. Levodopa, as Clarke discusses in Chapter Four, remains the 'gold standard' treatment for Parkinson's disease and although there are concerns that the toxicity of levodopa in tissue culture may occur *in vivo*, no convincing evidence has yet been accumulated to support this contention. The drug is, however, associated with the generation of motor complications and so it may be preferable to delay its introduction, at least in younger patients with early disease; he similarly recommends avoiding the use of anticholinergics and amantidine given their side effects and accumulated experience which seems to show that they are probably less effective than levodopa. Turning to the dopamine agonists, Clarke details the debate that has surrounded the role of selegiline in early PD, noting that the trials of the dopamine agonists in early disease have suggested their beneficial effect in delaying the onset of the motor complications of PD but that there remains a paucity of information to date on their effects on quality of life. In later PD the standard approach, as the author describes, is to administer a dopamine agonist given disease progression and motor complications. In this context, Cochrane reviews of placebo-controlled trials with adjuvant agonist therapy have shown that the 'modern' agonists pergolide, ropinirole, cabergoline and pramipexole can reduce off time, reduce levodopa dose and improve motor impairments albeit at the expense of some adverse dopaminergic events. The novel catechol-O-methyltransferase inhibitor entacapone can also reduce off time and improve motor impairments. In terms of the place of selegiline as an adjuvant in later disease, Clarke notes that, although trials were small, the agent demonstrated benefical effects on motor function. No trials have directly compared agonists with entacapone and selegiline but the PD MED trial will do so using quality of life and health economics as the main outcome measure. For patients with severe off periods which are not responding to the addition of an oral agent, apomorphine injections or continuous infusion can be useful.

Many patients with Parkinsons disease suffer from intractable tremor, drug induced dyskinesia, and severe motor fluctuations that are characterised by "on" and "off" periods. Since these symptoms are either refractory to therapy or partly caused by it, and are disabling, functional neurosurgery is often considered. However, clinical surgical research has been described, as Whittle notes in Chapter Five, as "comic opera...with results but no answers". This is pertinent to neurosurgery for PD since, as the author explains, there is no randomised, controlled evidence that any procedure is definitely beneficial. Furthermore, surgical attempts at altering either the course of the disease or ameliorating symptoms have been caught up in the enormous biological and technical advances that characterised the decade of the brain. We therefore have a large amount of descriptive studies of functional neurosurgical procedures, either ablative or neurostimulatory, to various meso-diencephalic targets, as well as experimental treatments involving neurotransplantation of various neural tissues into varying diencephalic targets.

The explosion in publications describing case series of surgical procedures is paralleled by numerous reviews of the topic and consensus statements from various august bodies that have a direct interest in the management of Parkinsonian patients. From this enormous body of literature it is possible to conclude that for patients still responsive to levodopa therapy neurostimulation is safer than ablative procedures to the thalamus (for tremor) and globus pallidus (for drug induced dyskinesia and tremor); bilateral ablative surgery is hazardous; bilateral stimulation of the subthalamic nuclei (STN) appears a promising treatment for many motor features as well as enabling reduction of medication dosage; subthalamic nucleotomy is currently being evaluated. Clearly, many scientific hurdles need to be overcome prior to successful use of neurotransplantation. Relative contraindications to surgery include advanced age, cognitive dysfunction, voice dysfunction, and hypertension. The major surgical unknowns at this stage, as Whittle notes, are who are the best candidates for surgery; which target (pallidal or STN) is best and safest to stimulate; how long do the beneficial effects of surgery last; and whether results from centres of excellence, with their multidisciplinary well resourced facilities, can be reproduced at the average UK neuroscience unit.

Answering these questions requires randomized, multicentre, controlled trials, and a national minimal database on outcome for Parkinsonian patients treated at the various centres performing functional neurosurgery. Without adequate planning and investment, to provide the necessary infrastructure, the UK will not make significant contributions to solving these questions. Chapter Six, the final chapter of this part, forms a particularly useful conclusion to Part Two of the text, in providing an 'evidence-based' overview of the studies employing stereotactic neurosugery conducted over the last decade or so; and Stowe finds herself in essential agreement with Whittle in concluding that current evidence is essentially based on a substantial number of uncontrolled case series and that, as yet, no definitive evidence has been generated by adequately performed randomised controlled trials.

Part Three of the volume is devoted to an in-depth study of the neuropsychiatric elements of PD, specifically to the management of depression in Chapter Seven, the mangement of psychosis in Chapter Eight and the management of cognitive dysfunction and dementia in Chapter Nine. The variation in the levels of depression in different studies described by Henderson and Toone in Chapter Seven, bears testament to the difficulties in making the diagnosis. Forty percent has been described as a consensus prevalence figure but recent evidence suggests that 'major' depression is seen less commonly. Depression as a reaction to the disability of PD may account for a proportion but evidence particularly from functional neuroimaging suggests that least some patients suffer depression as a direct consequence of parkinsonian neurodegeneration and subsequent monoaminergic dysfunction although the precise risk factors for depression have still to be fully elicited. Cognitive impairment and motor fluctuations are associated with depression, as the authors describe, although there is little evidence that age, sex, illness duration or levodopa dose are relevant. Symptom overlap is the reason for depression in PD being a classical clinical conundrum. Sleep disturbance, loss of energy and "slowness" are poor discriminators and guilt and a negative cognitive triad appear less common than in a non-PD depressed population. A number of syndromes which overlap with depression and can lead to further diagnostic dilemmas are explored by the authors and these include apathy, fatigue, anxiety and pain. In terms of treatment, Henderson and Toone are clear that antidepressant drugs represent effective treatments and that the newer drugs appear better tolerated and interestingly they discuss the possible place of physical treatments such as electroconvulsive therapy. As they point out, good evidence exists to pinpoint depression as a key factor in the quality of life of the PD patient and it must be remembered that its presence is strongly associated with depression in carers. For these reasons they are clear that the effective treatment of depression in PD is of considerable significance and that it may also act to slow progression of disease and cognitive impairment.

Henderson and Toone continue their discussion of the neuropsychiatric elements of PD with a review of the nature and management of psychosis in PD in Chapter Eight, noting the conflicting evidence regarding risk factors for psychosis in PD and observing that Parkinsonian psychosis is generally seen as secondary to medication. However, the limitations of a simple cause and effect model, as they emphasize, must be borne in mind, particularly in the context of the widespread neurotransmitter abnormalities in PD. The prevalence of psychosis in PD, as Henderson and Toone describe, has varied with different populations studied and different definitions of psychosis. A commonly quoted figure is 20–30%, and this has been validated in community studies. Parkinsonian psychosis classically involves visual hallucinations, though these can vary in complexity and intensity with hallucinations in other modalities being rare and delusions notably less common than visual hallucinations. A distinction between hallucinosis occurring in clear consciousness and delirium is drawn by the authors, together with the implications for management.

Chapter Nine, the final chapter of Part Three of the text, is concerned with the management of cognitive dysfunction and dementia in PD. Cognitive dysfunction, as Brown discusses, is one of a range of non-motor problems associated with Parkinson's disease and particularly Parkinson-plus syndromes. Its pathological and pathophysiological substrate is complex and poorly understood, but is likely to involve multiple transmitter systems at both cortical and subcortical levels. In most cases, the primary emphasis on motor symptom control means that cognitive problems may be ignored, particularly when they are relatively mild. As a result, the evidence base for the clinical management of cognitive dysfunction is small and weak, based often on clinical impression or small scale studies.

In its more severe forms, cognitive impairment is inextricably linked with other neuropsychiatric features of the disease including depression, apathy and psychosis and the author goes on to observe that the management of these problems may conflict with the control of the motor symptoms. Indeed, existing anti-parkinsonian drugs may cause or exacerbate cognitive impairment and psychosis and in such cases, drug switching or dose reduction is the most obvious strategy, with the clinician seeking to maintain an optimum balance between motor symptom control and the minimization of non-motor complications. More recently, advances have been made in the direct drug management of non-motor problems. Here, Brown points out, some of the new neuroleptics and cognitive enhancers can be combined with anti-parkinsonian drugs, enabling the direct management of both psychosis and cognitive dysfunction with less need to compromise motor-symptom control. Even when mild, cognitive dysfunction may limit the activities of some patients, for example, those still in work. Again, a balance may need to be sought between the control of motor and non-motor symptoms. The potential role of direct drug treatment of mild cognitive impairment has yet to be determined. However, he concludes that far greater use could be made of cognitive or behavioural remediation approaches to help such patients.

Part Four of the volume is concerned with the uroneurology of PD. Winge and Fowler discuss the cause and nature of bladder symptoms in patients with genuine PD which may be difficult to establish and treatment is often unsatisfactory. Many male patients with PD will be in the age group in which bladder outflow obstruction due to benign prostatic disease is a common co-existent factor and this should be excluded before considering neurological causes. There are however, as the authors describe, several possible neurogenic causes of bladder symptoms in PD and it is important in patients with parkinsonism and urinary symptoms to be alert to the diagnosis of Multiple System Atrophy (MSA). MSA affects the central nervous system at many different sites which are concerned with the neurological control of micturition, and because of this the onset of urinary symptoms in relation to other neurological symptoms tends to be much earlier. The cause of erectile dysfunction (ED) in PD is unclear but it may be due to a central deficiency of dopa agonists and, typically, the problem affects men only some years after the neurological disease has been established unlike in MSA when the onset of ED may be a premonitory symptom. The authors discuss the various treatments available and their likely efficacies.

We have dedicated Parts Five and Six of this volume to a detailed examination of the measures which may be taken to develop the efficiency and effectiveness of clinical services for Parkinson's disease. In Part Five we focus specifically on the roles of the PD clinical nurse specialist and physiotherapist. Given that Parkinson's disease is a complex, chronic, incurable, and disabling disease it is reasonable to seek to mitigate its effects by assessing the efficacy of a variety of interventions from a range of health and social agencies. With this approach follows the need to ensure an effective liaison between patients, doctors and other health professionals in both primary and secondary health care, and social services. For MacMahon and his colleagues, writing in Chapter Eleven, Parkinson's Disease Nurse Specialists (PDNS) are crucial in effecting this liaison, and their effects on other professional and lay interventions are becoming clearer with recent research. The application of the skills and knowledge of a specialist nurse has the potential to be a cost-effective way to enhance patient care and can effect appropriate referral for interventions from other therapists particularly physiotherapists, occupational therapists, speech and language therapists and dieticians. The authors outline the development of the PDNS role and review the published results of trials of their interventions, discussing also the basis and recommendations of the most recent treatment guidelines. They use case histories as examples of PDNS interventions and, while being clear that the levels of evidence for the effectiveness of the PDNS are not scientifically incontrovertible, they note that the evidence of effect at an anecdotal, 'district and societal' level, has stimulated the appointment of over 100 nurses in the UK in the last decade.

The study of the role of the specialist nurse in the care of PD patients continues in Chapter Twelve. Noting that few definitive evaluations of the effectiveness of nurse specialists in patient care have been undertaken, Hurwitz and associates describe their study of the effectiveness of community-based PDNSs working with GPs in a randomised controlled trial design. The formal null hypothesis tested was that there were no differences in health outcome, or in net healthcare costs, between patients who receive community-based PDNS care and those who receive standard GP care. As the authors describe, their study found no significant differences in health outcome between PDNS and control patients except in the subjective well-being of PD patients. which significantly benefited from care by recently trained community-based PDNSs. This is indeed a noteworthy observation because the trial was of sufficient size to detect important changes and the measured decline of health in the group as a whole confirmed that the research instruments employed to measure PD health status were sensitive and appropriate. Hurwitz and co-workers therefore conclude that the finding of benefit in subjective well-being is an important observation of direct relevance to the care of PD patients given that the course of the disease is usually relentless and that the benefit observed was achieved without an increase in healthcare costs.

Having considered rhe role of the nurse specialist in the care of PD patient in Chapter Twelve we move, in Chapter 13, to an evaluation of the evidence base for physiotherapy. The evidence base relating to physiotherapy and Parkinson's disease is, as Jones and Plant describe, composed of a relatively small number of studies, using a range of experimental and non-experimental research methodologies, in addition to the opinion of experts in the field. Attempts to synthesise the evidence of randomised controlled trials have been hampered by, amongst other factors, the wide range of physiotherapy techniques and outcome measures used. The authors usefully categorise the types of studies that have been employed to assess the effectiveness of physiotherapist intervention into two distinct groups – one evaluating the conventional eclectic treatment approach composed of a range of techniques, and a more recent second group evaluating specific treatment techniques. They note that a greater congruence exists between the aims of the studies, the techniques employed and the outcome measures used in the evaluation of specific treatment techniques. A relatively recent study of best practice physiotherapy in Parkinson's disease in the UK has articulated a model of physiotherapy which defines the purpose of physiotherapy intervention as the promotion of meaningful movement. The model, as the authors describe, links the four core areas of physiotherapy practice – gait, balance, posture (including range of movement) and transfers, with the treatment concept of Movement Enablement Through Exercise Regimens and Strategies – METERS, which encapsulates the treatment techniques most commonly used and they conclude that use of the physiotherapy model identified as a baseline for future evaluations should enable the development of a more cohesive and accurate scientific knowledge base and guidelines for clinical practice.

Part Six of the volume addresses the study of two areas of fundamental significance to the clinical governance of PD services: health economics and clinical errors/service deficiencies. For Bowman and Findley, writing in Chapter Fourteen, current management patterns of PD are essentially 'haphazard'. They argue that the disease and its management are variably under the aegis of primary or secondary care and, even within secondary care, specialist or general neurological, medical or geratological clinics may be providing management guidance that may or may not be part of an interdisciplinary service facilitated by a Parkinson's disease specialist. This state of affairs, the authors argue, obfuscates variations in standards and the cost of care and contrasts starkly with the standards of organisation and care for other medical conditions such as diabetes or chronic renal failure. The economic burden of Parkinson's disease has been investigated by a prospective evaluation in the UK which has demonstrated that the direct costs of the disease (those pertaining to health service treatment and personal care) rise steeply with disease stage and age and are heavily influenced by nursing care home fees. The most expensive patients, collectively, are therefore the PD residents in nursing home care and they conclude that these patients represent the most clinically overlooked cases.

In Chapter Fifteen, Burn considers the common errors and service deficiencies that can occur in the management of PD. For Burn, an error may be defined as "a mistake, wrong opinion or a sin", while a deficiency is "to be wanting or falling short in something". Errors are linked inextricably with adverse events, clinical risk and clinical negligence and in the context of errors and deficiencies in Parkinson's disease he finds that there are a number of factors specific to the condition itself which need to be borne in mind. These problems may occur at a number of levels of care, and may affect both newly diagnosed and established patients. Burn argues that errors may be classified as either 'permanent' or 'temporary', depending upon their consequences and that deficiencies may be 'absolute' or 'relative'. Common errors in PD include diagnostic mistakes, the poor giving of the diagnosis, inappropriate drug treatment and failure to detect co-existing depression, while common deficiencies in the system pertaining to PD include delay to referral and lack of ancillary investigations, a PD nurse specialist and access to a multidisciplinary team. Current frameworks provided through clinical governance may therefore, the author contends, provide an opportunity to reduce both error and deficiency in the modern investigation and management of PD, and he is in no doubt that a principal aim of care of the PD patient should be to move the overall standard of service provided for the disease across the UK up the "quality curve".

Part Seven of the current volume, the final Part, is concerned with study of the scientific and clinical factors which govern the quality of life of PD patients and with the impact of ongoing therapeutic innovation in increasing the effectiveness of clinical practice. In Chapter Sixteen, Findley and Bowman define 'quality of life' as "a perceived state of well being which is influenced by physical, mental, functional, social and emotional factors." It is axiomatic, in their view, that improvement in quality of life must be the ultimate and desirable outcome of any medical or surgical intervention. Likewise, they emphasize, it must be an important measure in healthcare outcomes when planning optimal use of scarce health care resources. The authors describe how recent studies using disease specific health status measure (PDQ39) alongside generic general health status scales are allowing exploration of factors which impact on quality of life of those with PD. Current research has confirmed, perhaps not surprisingly, the importance of disease stage (disability) as a factor influencing quality of life and it is now recognised that the emotional status of the patient, in particular the presence of depression, frequently unrecognised, has a major impact on quality of life as, indeed, Henderson and Toone have earlier outlined in Chapter Seven. A further factor in improving quality of life is, for Findley and Bowman, satisfaction with the explanation of the condition given at the time of diagnosis. But Findley and Bowman are clear that without an in-depth knowledge of the factors influencing quality of life in PD and the magnitude of their effects, comprehensive management guidelines, other than drug focused protocols, cannot be drawn up, a fact that surely emphasizes the need for urgent research into this increasingly important index of the quality of clinical care.

The final chapter of the volume, Chapter Seventeen, is concerned to discuss the likely impact of ongoing research and therapeutic innovation on the prevention and management of PD. Steiger is clear that the next decade will see the development of therapies for Parkinson's disease on a broad front. He acknowledges that while we have, over the last thirty years, witnessed the beginning of effective pharmacological manipulation of denervated striatum with the use of dopaminergic compounds, currently available treatments fall short of our expectations for optimal management. Indeed, the quality of life of many patients prescribed symptomatic treatment regimens needs to be urgently improved, particularly in those patients who have had the illness for ten years or more and who are therefore likely to have developed impairment of postural reflexes with increasing tendency to fall, disorders of speech, autonomic disturbances (particulary urinary urgency and urge incontinence) and increasing neuropsychiatric manifestations. As Steiger points out, the last of these are particularly distressing and destructive to the personality of the individual, affecting self-confidence and influencing the relationships of those who care for the patient. The optimal therapeutic options that are set to become available with time may well, initially, be viewed as costly but, increasingly, the socioeconomic costs of illness are being recognised and included within the economic evaluations that will determine treatment availability. There are, then, grounds for therapeutic optimism, as more focused studies begin to address, more intensively, the biological, pharmacological and societal complexity of this disabling disease.

In the current age, where doctors and health care professionals are increasingly overwhelmed with clinical information, we have aimed to provide a fully detailed and extensively referenced text which is as succinct as possible but as comprehensive as necessary. Consultants in Neurology, Medicine for the Elderly, General Medicine and General Practitioners and their registrars, are likely to find the volume invaluable in contributing to their continuing professional development and specialist training, and we advance the book explicitly as an excellent tool for this purpose. We anticipate, however, that clinical nurse specialists, physiotherapists, occupational therapists and speech and language therapists as well as hospital pharmacists are likely to find it of considerable use as a reference text, as part of their own professional education and development, and in supporting the development of effective multi-disciplinary approaches to the management of the patient with Parkinson's disease.

Leslie Findley TD OLJ MD FRCP FACP
Brian Hurwitz MA MSc MD FRCGP FRCP
Andrew Miles MSc MPhil PhD

PART 1

Diagnosis and imaging

Chapter 1

Can we establish a definitive diagnosis of Parkinson's disease in life?

K Ray Chaudhuri

Introduction

James Parkinson described the features of Parkinson's disease (PD) based on the assessment of six cases in 1817. His original description of 'paralysis agitans' remains a classic and valid essay, although he did not refer to typical cogwheel rigidity and possibly referred to bradykinesia as paralysis. Parkinson's disease is now defined as a slowly progressive neurodegenerative condition with a worldwide distribution, which affects the basal ganglia and produces an akinetic rigid syndrome in late or middle life although young patients are not exempt. The symptoms are usually those of rest tremor and bradykinesia accompanied by a variety of motor disturbances, including flexed posture, difficulty in turning, a shuffling gait and postural instability. The distinctive pathology of PD consists of degeneration of the pigmented brain-stem nuclei, including the dopaminergic pars compacta of the substantia nigra. Lewy bodies (intracytoplasmic eosinophilic inclusion bodies staining deeply with haematoxylin and eosin) are usually present in areas of neuronal degeneration in PD (Fearnley & Lees 1990).

Diagnosis of Parkinson's disease
What is the need for early or accurate diagnosis?

Many clinicians take the view that early and accurate diagnosis may be an academic exercise, given the lack of effective treatment strategies for parkinsonian syndromes apart from PD, and the similarity of treatment approaches in PD and parkinsonism. Some clinicians may also delay treatment of early PD until the disability becomes more pronounced. However, these views are being increasingly challenged because of the following:

- Inaccurate diagnosis may lead to inappropriate prescribing of dopaminergic therapy for patients without nigrostriatal dysfunction such as essential tremor or vascular pseudo-parkinsonism. This may be harmful, costly and ineffective for patients and society.
- Similarly, patients with PD may be erroneously diagnosed as having frozen shoulder, psychiatric illnesses or stroke, and treated accordingly.

- Inaccurate diagnosis leads to improper counselling, planning strategies for patient and carer, and delay in obtaining disability benefits where appropriate.
- Some clinicians would strongly argue the case for treating very early PD patients with dopaminergic therapy, based on the hypothesis that delayed treatment (1) may predispose to early dopaminergic side effects, (2) reduce the chance of neuroprotection and, although currently unproven, such therapies potentially are available and (3) may adversely affect the quality of life even of patients with very mild disability, particularly in relation to work and socialising.
- Inaccurate diagnosis and inappropriate prescribing may become medicolegal issues

Diagnostic dilemmas

Diagnosis of PD is clinical and there are no specific tests to confirm diagnosis. A typical patient with PD may be relatively easy to diagnose when the classic 'pill rolling' rest tremor, bradykinesia and shuffling gait at a frequency of 4–6 Hz are present. However, the diagnosis becomes difficult when there is little or no tremor (30% of cases), presentation with atypical signs and subtypes of PD (Tables 1.1 and 1.2), or when slowing of performance is compounded by ageing. Subtle extrapyramidal signs may occur in up to 32–35% of those aged over 65 years (Bennett et al. 1996) and up to two-thirds of patients diagnosed with PD are aged over 70 years. However, the prevalence of PD in this age group is about 3%, suggesting that diagnosis of PD continues to be imprecise.

Table 1.1 Atypical presenting symptoms and signs of PD

Facial	Impassivity, poverty of blinking, seborrhoea
Speech	Monotonous, low volume, repetition of words
Movement	Reduction of manual dexterity, rigid arm (mimicking 'frozen shoulder')
Micrographia	
Dribbling of saliva and swallowing difficulties	
Olfactory abnormalities: could predate development of PD	
Dysautonomia	Constipation, postural hypotension, urinary frequency/urgency, nocturia, impotence, hyperhidrosis
Neuropsychiatric	Depression, apathy
Pain	
Sleep disabilities	Nocturia, difficulty in turning, fragmented sleep, early morning freezing
Dystonia (striatal hand)	
Motor	Dragging foot, limping

Table 1.2 *International Classification of Disease*: clinical subtypes of PD

G120-0	Classic PD	Akinesia/tremor/rigidity
G120-1	Akinetic PD	Akinesia dominant
G120-2	Tremulous PD	Tremor dominant
G120-3	Postural instability gait difficulties	Postural instability, gait difficulty
G120-4	Hemi-parkinsonism	
G120-X0	Sporadic	
G120-X1	Familial	

The symptoms of parkinsonism may also be experienced by patients with other movement disorders such as essential tremor (ET), vascular pseudo-parkinsonism, multiple system atrophy (MSA) or progressive supranuclear palsy (PSP), or could be medication induced (antipsychotics, vestibular sedatives). Making an accurate premortem diagnosis of true idiopathic PD is, therefore, difficult even in expert hands. The published error rate of diagnosis ranges from 12% to 15% (Hughes *et al.* 1992) up to 20–25 % within the neurological and general medical communities (Meara *et al.* 1999; Jankovic *et al.* 2000). In a study involving 74 general practices, Meara and colleagues (1999) could confirm a diagnosis of PD in only 74% of those initially labelled as having PD. Among the rest (103 subjects), 48% had ET, 36% vascular pseudo-parkinsonism and 16% Alzheimer's disease (Figure 1.1). Approximately 25% of subjects labelled as having PD in this community would thus be receiving inappropriate therapy, most notably dopaminergic therapy for ET, Alzheimer's disease and vascular pseudo-parkinsonism with few or occasionally adverse effects.

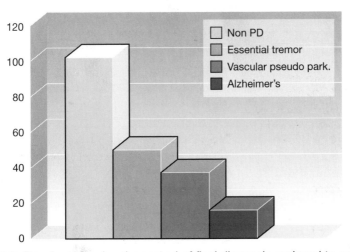

Figure 1.1 Bar chart showing the spread of final diagnosis assigned to patients originally thought to have Parkinson's disease (PD) in the community. Non PD, total number of patients wrongly diagnosed to have PD. From Meara *et al.* (1999)

Litvan and colleagues (1998) have also examined the accuracy of clinical diagnosis of PD using six clinical raters in a series of cases with neuropathologically proven diagnosis of parkinsonian syndromes. Their results suggest a low positive predictive value and high sensitivity for diagnosis of PD, whereas dementia with Lewy bodies (DLB) appears to be under-diagnosed. However, a recent paper by Jankovic and colleagues (2000) reported improved clinical accuracy of diagnosis among movement disorders experts. After an average follow-up of 7.6 years, only 65 of 800 early PD patients (8.1%) with an initial diagnosis of PD had an alternative diagnosis. This optimism is clouded by the fact that, of the 13 cases that were found *post mortem*, nine had an alternative diagnosis to PD. It has also been reported that the accuracy of diagnosis of PD improves with time from the first consultation, the implication being that there may be considerable delay in the diagnosis. In a retrospective study, MacMahon *et al.* (1999) reported that there was a delay of 1.6 ± 1.5 years in reaching a diagnosis of clinically definite PD within a UK general hospital clinic.

Diagnostic criteria and helpful clinical clues

To improve diagnostic accuracy, based on postmortem histopathological appearances, the UK Parkinson's Disease Society Brain Bank has devised revised diagnostic criteria with a predictive accuracy of up to 90% (Table 1.3). These criteria are now widely used and thus it must be accepted that the diagnosis of PD continues to be imprecise. Formal confirmation of disease is only possible *post mortem*. There are, however, several clues to aid diagnosis of PD. Studies by Litvan *et al.* (1998) suggested that several features distinguished PD from the three other parkinsonian disorders (MSA, PSP and DLB) commonly confused with PD. These are as follows:

- Asymmetrical onset of parkinsonism (bradykinesia, rest tremor, rigidity)
- Response to levodopa (moderate to excellent) and development of dyskinesias
- Absence of pyramidal or oculomotor symptoms
- Absence of early (usually within 2 years of onset) memory disturbances, hallucinations, confusional episodes not related to treatment
- Absence of early postural instability, particularly falls.

Additional features that may aid correct diagnosis of PD are listed in Table 1.4.

Clinical test battery

To aid early diagnosis of PD, Montgomery and colleagues (2000a, 2000b) have devised a diagnostic test battery comprising:

- Motor function test using an electronically monitored measurement of wrist flexion and extension movements

- Measurement of olfactory function using the University of Pennsylvania Smell Identification Test (UPSIT) which consists of 40 standardised encapsulated odours
- Measurement of mood using the Beck Depression Inventory (BDI).

Using a regression model by combining the three tests, Montgomery *et al.* report that this test battery distinguishes between normal controls and very early PD where considerable diagnostic inaccuracy may occur. Application of this diagnostic battery in 212 patients with signs suggestive, but not diagnostic, of PD shows a 92% specificity and 68% sensitivity for PD at 1-year follow-up. These tests are simple and could be widely available, and thus might be of clinical importance in the wider field of neurology and care of elderly people.

Table 1.3 Diagnostic Clues of PD (UK PD Brain Bank Criteria) (Hughes *et al.* 1992, 2001)

Bradykinesia (slowness and progressive decrease of amplitude of movement) plus at least one of:

    Resting tremor (4–6 Hz & frequently 'pill rolling') or
    Rigidity (plastic or 'lead pipe', 'cog wheeling' if additional tremor) or
    Disorders of posture (flexion of neck and trunk):
        balance (loss of righting reflexes)
        gait (short steps, shuffling, festination and freezing)

None of the following:
    Recent neuroleptic, toxin, designer drug exposure
    Past history of encephalitis/oculogyric crisis
    Stepwise progression of stroke
    Cerebellar or pyramidal signs
    Early severe autonomic failure
    Supranuclear downgaze paresis
    Cerebellar/frontal tumours/communicating hydrocephalus

Table 1.4 Features doubting diagnosis of idiopathic PD

Early and prominent eye movement disorders
Early dementia (particularly frontal)
Early non-drug-related hallucinations
Early bulbar disturbance (speech and swallowing)
Lower body parkinsonism (severe gait apraxia)
Early dysautonomia: bladder, sexual dysfunction, postural hypotension
Patients confined to wheelchairs

Can we make pre-symptomatic diagnosis of PD?

By definition it is impossible to recognise preclinical PD, although retrospective analysis would suggest the presence of pre-morbid signs that reflect underlying disease process. Neuropathological and functional imaging studies using positron emission tomography (PET) would suggest that cell loss in the ventrolateral tier of the pars compacta of substantia nigra may occur 6 years or more before disease onset. However, Morrish (1997), based on ^{18}F-labelled fluorodopa (^{18}F-dopa) studies and the variable clinical rate of progression of PD, argues that PD is not a long latency disorder. The precise onset of the disease is often difficult to ascertain, although prodromal manifestations such as depression, shoulder pain or dysautonomia can be identified retrospectively (Gonera *et al.* 1997). The reality of the prodromal period of PD is exemplified by the archival videotape of the Liverpool footballer Ray Kennedy showing signs of parkinsonism 8 years before diagnosis (Lees 1992). Several features (Table 1.5) have been proposed to identify an 'at-risk' group of people who may develop PD, although such features overlap with other unrelated disorders such as ulcerative colitis. Of these, reduced olfaction appears to be a strong predictive factor for development of PD and may correlate with Lewy bodies in the anterior olfactory nucleus (see Chapter 2).

Table 1.5 Individual groups who may be 'at risk' for developing PD

Ageing (> 60 years)
Habitual non-smokers
Rural living and drinking well water
Chronic exposure to insecticides and pesticides
Low resting blink rate (12/min or less)
Positive glabellar tap in individuals < 60 years age
Reduced unilateral arm swing
Depressive illness
Olfactory impairment particularly for pizza and oil of wintergreen smell
Obsessional, introspective and inflexible behavioural traits

Differential diagnosis of Parkinson's disease

The conditions most commonly confused with PD include ET, vascular pseudo-parkinsonism (VP), drug-induced parkinsonism and the parkinsonian syndromes such as MSA, PSP and DLB (see Figure 1.1). Differentiation between early PD and MSA (particularly the parkinsonian variant, MSA-P, or DLB) may be impossible. This diagnostic difficulty is further compounded by the fact that some patients with MSA, particularly the striatonigral degeneration variant, or Lewy body dementia may have a good initial response to levodopa similar to PD (Fearnley & Lees 1990; Wenning *et al.* 1997). Clinical clues help (Tables 1.6 and 1.7), although increasingly ancillary investigations are proving to be useful.

Table 1.6 Differential diagnoses

Essential tremor	Bilateral postural dominant 8–10 Hz tremor often worse on drawing spirals or action, no significant bradykinesia or rest tremor, alcohol sensitivity, titubation
Vascular pseudo-parkinsonism	Cognitive impairment, significant vascular disease (often visible on brain imaging), absent levodopa response, lower limb involvement and gait initiation problems
	Parkinsonism plus
Multiple system atrophy: MSA-C, MSA-P	Cerebellar, pyramidal, autonomic (postural hypotension, Shy–Drager phenotype) or urogenital features
	Moderate to good but falling response to levodopa
	Early falls, minimal cognitive impairment
Progressive supranuclear palsy	Early eye movement disorders (diminished saccadic down- and up-gaze, supranuclear gaze palsy)
	Falls
	Axial dominance of rigidity (extended fixed neck)
	Frontal type dementia
	Falling or no levodopa response
Dementia with Lewy body	Early drug-unrelated hallucinations (within 2 years)
	Early cognitive impairment
	Often early good levodopa response with waning of response
	Sensitivity to neuroleptics
Corticobasal degeneration	Asymmetrical disease
	Presentation with rigid dystonic hand/arm
	Apraxic hand (alien limb)
	Absent levodopa response
	No dysautonomia
Dystonia–parkinsonism	Juvenile onset ± family history
	Early dystonia
	Early levodopa-induced dyskinesias

Symptoms and signs

Tremor

The initial complaint of tremor is seen in about 70–75% of patients with PD and tremor will occur eventually in most patients. The characteristic tremor is present at rest, at a frequency usually of 4–6 Hz, and occurs commonly in the upper limbs to produce the so-called 'pill-rolling' or 'drum-beating' movements. The tremor may be conducted to the jaw, head and legs, and is usually intensified by mental or emotional stress but disappears during deep sleep. There may occasionally be tremor of the outstretched hands and posture as well, at a frequency of 5–12 Hz (Findley *et al.* 1981).

Table 1.7 Best clinical criteria for a diagnosis of multiple system atrophy

Sporadic adult onset
Dysautonomia
Parkinsonism
Pyramidal signs
Cerebellar signs
No levodopa response
No cognitive dysfunction
No downward gaze supranuclear palsy

Six out of these eight enhance possibility of correct diagnosis of MSA.
Litvan *et al.* (1998)

Atypical tremor

In PD, a postural tremor may be more obvious after the hand is kept outstretched for a prolonged period and has been called 'the re-emergent tremor' (Jankovic *et al.* 1998). Essential tremor is dominantly bilateral and postural in the absence of resting tremor at complete relaxation. It is important to differentiate between essential tremor and parkinsonian tremor because the former carries a more benign prognosis and appears to be twice as common as parkinsonian tremor. Some patients with tremor without bradykinesia may turn out to have nigrostriatal dysfunction on functional imaging (Brooks 1992). These patients are therefore unlikely to have ET and are likely to develop tremulous PD. Clinically, such patients often present with a unilateral postural and occasionally resting tremor (Pal *et al.* 2002). Similarly, some patients with a postural tremor may not satisfy standard criteria for diagnosis of ET (Findley & Koller 1995) and the final diagnosis may be aided by description of the history and physical signs rather than assigning an incorrect definitive diagnosis (Schrag *et al.* 2000).

Bradykinesia/akinesia

Bradykinesia indicates slowness of movement and difficulty in performing and initiating movement. This is the critical sign of PD and initially would often affect fine movements involving manual dexterity such as undoing buttons, knitting, writing or tying shoelaces. Handwriting shows a typical characteristic of becoming small and tailing off, known as micrographia. Associated movements also suffer and one of the early signs is loss of arm swing on the affected side. Later on both arms may stop swinging when the patient is walking. Akinesia also affects walking and gait with difficulty in initiating walking, turning and shuffling as a result of taking small steps. Festination occurs and refers to hurrying; this can be interrupted by sudden arrest, as if the patient were nailed to the floor. This phenomenon of freezing may be provoked by a stimulus such as anxiety or surprise, or visual stimuli such as unopened doorways, corners or narrow passages. Akinesia would also account for many of the other parkinsonian features such as facial impassivity, reduction in blinking, soft monotonous hypophonic speech disorder and nocturnal disabilities, e.g. difficulty in turning in bed at night.

Rigidity

Rigidity of muscles is often picked up by physicians and is detected clinically by resistance to passive manipulation of the limbs. The patient may sometimes complain of stiffness and pain, which can be diffuse and localised to one limb or the trunk. Rigidity is detected by moving the body parts slowly and gently, in contrast to the quick movement needed to elicit clasp knife rigidity of pyramidal origin. Uniform resistance is seen throughout the range of passive movements, so the term 'lead pipe rigidity', equal in agonist and antagonist muscles, is applied. When tremor is added, the pattern of rigidity appears to be broken up and is referred to as 'cog-wheel' rigidity.

Additional symptoms and signs frequently occur in PD and are outlined in Table 1.1. A lot of these symptoms are the result of the illness itself, but factors such as side effects of drug therapy and concurrent illnesses also play a part. Mental illnesses are particularly common and, although in the initial stages of the condition intellect and senses are well preserved, many patients develop a degree of intellectual deterioration as the disease advances. Global dementia may occur in up to 15–20% of cases. (Mayeux *et al.* 1990; Biggins *et al.* 1992).

Investigations

There are no specific tests for diagnosing PD. Pharmacological challenge tests and specialised neuroimaging may help distinguish between PD and parkinsonism, particularly MSA, as can sphincter electromyography (SEMG).

Pharmacological challenge tests

The pharmacological challenge tests can be differentiated into the following:

* Outpatient or ward-based tests: levodopa and apomorphine challenge tests.
* Laboratory-based tests: clonidine and meal challenge tests.

Levodopa challenge test

This is an oral challenge test usually performed in the morning after overnight fasting and withdrawal of anti-parkinsonian drugs by administering a single levodopa with a decarboxylase inhibitor (DCI) tablet (usually 250 mg) (Albanese *et al.* 2002). This is otherwise known as a practically defined 'off' condition, as opposed to naturally occurring 'off' periods such as at the end of dose or in the afternoon. The purpose of levodopa challenge is to:

- support clinical diagnosis of PD
- predict chronic response to levodopa or dopamine agonists
- aid direct assessment of levodopa-related dyskinesias in PD (latency, magnitude, duration and characterisation).

The outcome measure is usually assessed using validated clinical scales such as tremor scales, UPDRS (Unified Parkinson's Disease Rating Scale) part III, or clinical measures such as finger tapping speed or walking time. The motor effects after levodopa challenge commence 30 min after oral dose with peak efficacy being at 45–120 min. A positive response is defined as a greater than 20% improvement in motor scores compared with baseline, although in chronically levodopa-treated patients, the cut-off figure is likely to be 30% (Gasser *et al.* 1992).

Clinical issues and problems related to acute levodopa challenge test

Acute challenge tests are useful for clinical research protocols, although in clinical practice there are concerns because levodopa challenge may prime a drug-naïve patient to development of dyskinesias (Chase 1998) and may be time-consuming. Higher doses of levodopa may be required to observe improvements in (1) severe tremor, (2) freezing of gait and (3) handwriting compared with akinesia or rigidity. Furthermore, lack of a positive response to levodopa in drug-naïve or recently treated patients may not exclude a positive chronic response to levodopa (which can extend up to 2 weeks), and as such levodopa challenge test should not be used as routine clinical practice in such patients (Nutt *et al.* 1995). Ideally, chronic response to levodopa can be assessed by administration of maximally tolerated levodopa (up to 800–1,500 mg), given three or four times a day for a period of 3 months.

Apomorphine challenge test

Apomorphine is a rapidly acting, potent, parenteral dopamine agonist with a comparable potency to levodopa (Chaudhuri & Clough 1998). The subcutaneous administration reduces variability of gastrointestinal absorption and repeat challenges are possibly the result of the very short half-life of apomorphine (10–30 min). Apomorphine is usually administered subcutaneously (anterior abdomen or thigh) with a starting dose of 1–1.5 mg followed by stepwise increments of 1.5–3 mg every 30–45 min up to 10 mg or maximal tolerated dose. The onset of effect is usually seen within 5–10 min and motor effect may last for 60 min. Apomorphine test has been introduced because:

- apomorphine is similar in potency to levodopa
- there is reduced variability of absorption using the subcutaneous route
- the short half-life allows repeat challenges in the same sitting
- the test is less time-consuming
- compared with levodopa, apomorphine has a theoretical advantage of not priming for dyskinesias

- apomorphine challenge can be performed in the outpatient department with prior planning.

However, apomorphine challenge needs to be supervised because the drug is less well tolerated (adverse events in up to 50%) and may cause severe nausea and vomiting if domperidone (a peripheral dopamine antagonist) is not administered for 3 days before the test (20 mg three times daily); domperidone is not universally available. Postural hypotension may be unmasked and may cause occasional syncope/pre-syncope, particularly in elderly people and those with pre-existing postural hypotension. Needle phobia or local skin site pain may distress patients. Furthermore, the anti-parkinsonian effect of apomorphine is not mediated by dopamine and evidence suggests that, in drug-naïve patients, the levodopa challenge test has a better negative predictive value for chronic dopaminergic response compared with apomorphine (Gasser *et al.* 1992).

Summary of possible indications for levodopa/apomorphine challenge tests (Albanese et al. 2001)

- In levodopa-treated PD patients, apomorphine challenge correctly predicts response to levodopa in approximately 90%, although the specificity for clinical diagnosis of PD is less than that with levodopa (Hughes *et al.* 1990a).
- In untreated PD patients, a single oral levodopa challenge test predicts subsequent response to levodopa in approximately 80% of cases compared with about 70% with apomorphine (Hughes *et al.* 1991).
- In patients with atypical rest tremor, apomorphine challenge is a useful test for clarifying dopaminergic response and the diagnosis. Apomorphine challenge can predict dopaminergic response in approximately 75% of cases with isolated tremor (Hughes *et al.* 1990b).
- A negative response to apomorphine challenge may not rule out a positive response to levodopa challenge.
- Approximately 50% of drug-naïve patients with a negative apomorphine or levodopa challenge test develop abnormal/atypical signs suggestive of a Parkinson plus syndrome.

Clonidine challenge test

Clonidine is a central acting α_2-receptor agonist and, given intravenously, it stimulates release of growth hormone. Intravenous clonidine infusion (2 μg/kg body weight over 10 min) causes a sequential rise in growth hormone levels in normal individuals, but not in MSA as a result of central autonomic dysfunction, possibly affecting the hypothalamic growth hormone-secreting centre in the latter (Thomaides *et al.* 1992). Distinction of PD from early MSA (a common diagnostic issue) has been proposed on the basis that clonidine-induced growth hormone release will occur in PD but not in MSA (Kimber *et al.* 1997). This is controversial because other workers have suggested that there may be a trend towards increased growth hormone levels after clonidine infusion in chronic PD patients and that this test may not distinguish between the cerebellar form of MSA and PD (Clarke *et al.* 1999). Furthermore, factors such as depression may affect the interpretation of the clonidine challenge test and as such the role of this test in the diagnosis of parkinsonian syndrome remains to be established. In selected cases, the clonidine challenge test may be undertaken in established laboratories with careful explanation of the procedure to the patient. Sedation, local (arm) discomfort and availability of a specialised laboratory may limit the usefulness of this test.

Meal challenge test

Challenge with a test meal may be required if a PD patient feels unusually tired, sleepy, dizzy or stiff after a midday meal or in the afternoon. Postprandial hypotension (PPH) may be implicated and if PPH is clinically suspected then a standard meal test using a liquid meal (100 g glucose, one sachet of Complan [a dietary supplement] in 300 ml milk is used in the UK laboratories) with measurements of blood pressure and heart rate every 15 min for 60 min after the meal may confirm significant PPH (Mathias *et al.* 1991; Chaudhuri *et al.* 1995). However, PPH is not unique to PD and may also be observed in MSA.

Imaging

PET studies

PET provides a means of studying regional metabolism and neurotransmitter function in vivo, having a functional resolution of between 3 and 8 mm. PET studies may enable distinction of the functional effects of the various parkinsonian syndromes, in particular PD and MSA.

Presynaptic dopaminergic function

Presynaptic function of the nigrostriatal dopaminergic projections can be assessed in PET using the ligands ^{18}F-dopa, ^{11}C-labelled nomifensine and tropane-based tracers such as ^{11}C-CFT. Given intravenously, ^{18}F-dopa is taken up by the nigrostriatal dopaminergic terminals and converted to ^{18}F-dopamine and its metabolites (see Chapter 3). The rate of striatal accumulation of ^{18}F-dopa reflect (1) transport of ^{18}F-dopa to striatal vesicles and (2) decarboxylation by dopa decarboxylase. Both striatal and nigral ^{18}F-dopa uptake have been shown to correlate with clinical disease severity and asymmetry. PET studies show that MSA patients have uniformly depressed striatal fluorodopa uptake affecting both putamen and caudate in contrast to PD, where there appears to be relative sparing of the caudate (Brooks *et al.* 1990; Brooks 1992). Using fluorodopa PET, workers were able to discriminate normal individuals from those with PD in up to 100% of cases, but this investigation was less reliable in distinguishing PD from MSA patients, agreeing with the clinical categorisation in only 60% of cases (Salmon *et al.* 1990; Brooks 1992; Burn *et al.* 1994). In early hemi-parkinsonian patients, recent three-dimensional PET studies show reductions in fluorodopa uptake in the contralateral and ipsilateral putamen, with smaller reductions in the contralateral caudate (Rakshi *et al.* 1996).

Other PET studies

PET studies of resting cerebral glucose utilisation using [^{18}F]fluorodeoxyglucose suggest that approximately 80% of MSA-P cases may be differentiated from PD cases based on striatal metabolism, although this finding remains controversial (Eidelberg *et al.* 1990, 1993). Opiate binding, vesicular monoamine transporter and muscarinic acetylcholine receptor (mAChR) function have also been studied and the last may help differentiate PD from PSP, although these techniques remain research tools (Asahina *et al.* 1998). Imaging of postsynaptic dopamine D_2-receptors is also possible but, in PD, the D_2-receptor density is generally unchanged and thus this test is unlikely to identify PD positively.

Single photon emission tomography studies

Single photon emission tomography (SPET) is an alternative imaging modality to PET, providing a more widely accessible means of studying striatal function and metabolism; it is increasingly available in nuclear medicine departments of district general hospitals. Spatial resolution is between 8 and 12 mm, compared with 3 and 8 mm for PET. The cocaine analogues [^{123}I]-labelled β-carbomethoxy-3β-(4-iodophenyl)-tropane (β-CIT) and [^{123}I]-fluoropropyl (FP)-CIT have a high affinity for the striatal dopamine transporter, giving a measure of presynaptic striatal dopaminergic function similar to the PET [^{18}F]-dopa ligand which correlates well with motor disability in PD (Booij *et al.* 1997; Brucke *et al.* 1997) (Figure 1.2a,b). Putamen uptake has been shown to be consistently decreased on the contralateral and, to a lesser extent, the ipsilateral side to the worst affected limb, whereas the caudate is relatively spared. (Asenbaum *et al.* 1997; Booij *et al.* 1997). β-CIT technique requires a 2-hour procedure where the patient is injected with the ligand the day before the scan, to return 24 hours later for imaging, and the data can be expressed as ratios between a relatively unaffected (cortex or cerebellum) and the affected (stratum) area. FP-CIT (DaTSCAN) can be performed 3–6 hours after injection using a gamma camera and so investigations can be completed in a day. Local validation of acquisition of images is required. Studies have reported the high accuracy of the use of FP-CIT imaging and visual assessment in the differentiation of essential tremor from tremulous PD (Benamer *et al.* 2000). CIT SPET scans can therefore be used to differentiate ET from PD because striatal CIT uptake would be normal in ET but reduced in PD.

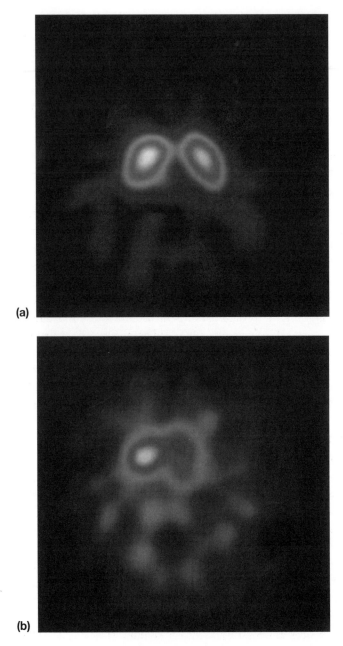

(a)

(b)

Figure 1.2 (a) ^{123}I-β-CIT images from a normal subject, showing symmetrical uptake of the ligand in both striatum (lit up like a comma). **(b)** ^{123}I-β-CIT images from a subject with Parkinson's disease showing virtually complete absence of uptake of ^{123}I-β-CIT in the left striatum. Patient has dominantly right-sided parkinsonian signs.

Images courtesy of Dr M Buxton-Thomas, King's College Hospital.

Studies using the same ligands in patients with MSA show a reduction of dopaminergic function in both the caudate and the putamen (Brucke *et al.* 1997). SPET studies using the [^{123}I]-IBZM (see Figure 1.2c) and [^{123}I]-epidepride ligands, which have a high affinity for striatal D$_2$-receptors, have shown significant reductions in striatum to cerebellum ratios in MSA patients, whereas these ratios are unchanged in PD (Schulz *et al.* 1994; Pirker *et al.* 1997) and thus may aid differentiation of PD from MSA.

Cardiac SPET/PET studies

A SPET scan with *meta*-[^{123}I]iodobenzyl-guanidine (MIBG) allows assessment of the functional integrity of postganglionic cardiac adrenergic neurons, and the ratio of MIBG uptake of the heart and the mediastinum is thought to serve as an index of cardiac innervation (Braune *et al.* 1998). MIBG SPET of cardiac neurons may help discriminate between PD with or without autonomic failure and MSA, where the MIBG SPET appears to be normal, because the pathogenesis of dysautonomia in MSA involves central and preganglionic autonomic neurons (Braune *et al.* 1998). Parkinson's disease with autonomic failure, however, shows impaired cardiac uptake of MIBG, suggesting a postganglionic involvement. PET studies measuring interventricular septal ^{18}F-dopamine uptake and cardiac noradrenaline spillover have confirmed that cardiac sympathetic denervation appears to occur in most patients with PD but not in MSA (Goldstein *et al.* 2000). Both MIBG and SPET are widely available and thus measurement of cardiac MIBG uptake using SPET may offer a useful method for differentiating between PD and MSA (Chaudhuri and Hu, 2000).

Proton magnetic resonance spectroscopy

Proton magnetic resonance spectroscopy (^{1}H MRS) is a non-invasive technique that studies metabolism of several endogenous brain chemicals, principally *N*-acetylaspartate (NAA – an amino acid contained almost exclusively within neurons and their processes within adult brain), choline (Cho – a metabolite involved in membrane synthesis and degradation) and creatinine and phosphocreatine (Cr + Pcr – involved in neuronal energy status in vivo) (Howe *et al.* 1993; Urenjak *et al.* 1993) (Figure 1.3). Significant striatal reductions in NAA/Cr ratios, thought to reflect neuronal loss, have been demonstrated in patients with both MSA (Davie *et al.* 1995; Aotsuka *et al.* 1997; Federico *et al.* 1997) and PSP (Federico *et al.* 1997; Tedeschi *et al.* 1997). Most studies comparing striatal metabolism in PD patients with normal controls have found no significant differences in NAA/Cr and NAA/Cho ratios (Davie *et al.* 1995; Holhouser *et al.* 1995; Clarke *et al.* 1997). One study found reduced NAA/Cho ratios in drug-naïve PD patients, but not in the levodopa-treated PD group, possibly reflecting neuronal dysfunction secondary to loss of nigrostriatal dopamine terminals (Ellis *et al.* 1997). A second study found reductions in NAA/Cho ratios in an elderly subgroup of PD patients aged 51–70 years, and in the PD group untreated with levodopa

(Holhouse *et al.* 1995).The role of ¹H MRS in distinguishing between MSA and PD is unclear and current evidence from our group and others suggests that MRS alone may not be sufficient to distinguish reliably between MSA and PD (Ellis *et al.* 1997; Davie 1998).

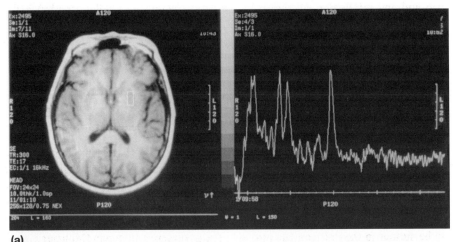

(a)

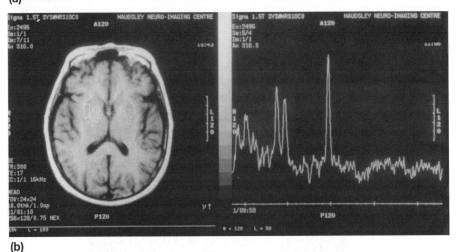

(b)

Figure 1.3 Magnetic resonance spectroscopic images showing proton spectrum from the striatum of a parkinsonian individual. **(a)** The voxel centred on the putamen with reduced NAA peak on proton spectrums; **(b)** corresponding proton spectrum from the normal putamen. Note raised NAA peak.

Magnetic resonance imaging

Magnetic resonance imaging (MRI) scanning of the brain may be helpful in some cases of MSA and may indeed show cerebellar atrophy, but often cerebellar signs in these patients are evident clinically by this stage. The presence of putaminal atrophy and hypointensity relative to the globus pallidus on 1.5 tesla T2-weighted MRI or a slit hyperintensity of the lateral putaminal margin may suggest MSA (Drayer *et al.* 1986). A recent study reported that the presence of putaminal atrophy, hyperintense rim and any infratentorial abnormality (most commonly cerebellar atrophy) had a 93% specificity to differentiate between MSA and PD on a 1.0 T scan. The sensitivity of MRI to detect any abnormalities in MSA was 88% on a 1.5 T scan in this series of 44 MSA patients and 47 PD patients (Schrag *et al.* 1998). An interesting sign is the 'hot-cross bun' sign in the pons because of atrophy of the brain stem and prominence of the transverse pontine fibres (Figure 1.4).

Neurophysiological tests

Several abnormal autonomic neurophysiological tests in MSA have been reported and include interneuronal sympathetic recording, sympathetic skin responses, intradermal histamine test, thermoregulatory sweat test and quantitative pseudomotor axon reflex test (Mathias & Bannister 1992; Fealey 1997). In up to 50% of cases of MSA, there may be a selective fibre type atrophy seen on muscle biopsy. This has been thought to be similar to the muscle fibre atrophy seen in myasthenia gravis (Montagna *et al.* 1983). Sleep disorders may accompany dysautonomia and laboratory tests include polysomnographic studies (PSG) for excessive daytime sleepiness and REM sleep behaviour disorder (RBD). A multiple sleep latency test preceded by PSG, video-PSG and pulmonary function tests may be required in some cases (Chokroverty 1994)

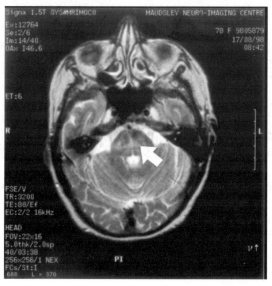

Figure 1.4 Magnetic resonance image of a typical 'hot-cross bun' appearance of the pons secondary to pontine atrophy in multiple system atrophy and resultant prominence of the transverse pontine fibres

However, none of these tests are robust enough to distinguish reliably between early PD and parkinsonian syndromes, and thus aid diagnosis.

Sphincter electromyography

Patients with MSA have selective loss of a group of anterior horn cells in the sacral spinal cord called Onuf's nucleus, which innervates the striated muscles of the urethral and anal sphincter (Palace *et al.* 1997). The resulting changes of chronic reinnervation in the motor units of the striated anal and urethral sphincter can be shown using electromyographic (EMG) techniques (Sakuta *et al.* 1978; Kirby *et al.* 1986). In PD, the anterior horn cells of Onuf's nucleus are not affected, hence sphincter EMG (SEMG) has been proposed as a means of differentiating PD and MSA in patients with bladder symptoms (Eardley *et al.* 1989). Studies have reported abnormal SEMG in MSA patients to range from 75% to 90% (Wenning *et al.* 1994; Pramstaller *et al.* 1995; Stocchi *et al.* 1997), although only 40% had abnormal nerve conduction or skeletal muscle EMG studies (Chaudhuri, 2001). In patients with the cerebellar presentation of MSA, SEMG was abnormal in 93% of patients (Wenning *et al.* 1997). However, the ability of SEMG to discriminate PSP from MSA has been questioned, because studies have reported involvement of Onuf's nucleus and abnormal SEMG results in patients with PSP that do not differ from patients with MSA (Sakakibara *et al.* 1993; Tolosa *et al.* 1994; Scaravilli *et al.* 2000). Furthermore, the value of this test has also been recently questioned in two studies that suggest that SEMG may not be accurately able to distinguish between PD (particularly late PD) and MSA (Giladi *et al.* 2000; Libelius & Johansson 2000).

Conclusion

In spite of the emergence of a wide range of pharmacological/biochemical, imaging and neurophysiological tests, the diagnosis of PD remains clinical and observer dependent. In classic cases with typical signs, accurate diagnosis is possible without any investigations. The problem arises when the clinical signs are subtle, not present in combination or the clinician is inexperienced in the area of movement disorders. In such situations PD may be misdiagnosed as ET or, more commonly, ET, vascular pseudo-parkinsonism, LBD and MSA/PSP may be misdiagnosed as PD. This can be avoided by carefully choosing investigations with high specificity and sensitivity to aid correct diagnosis, treatment and counselling. In this respect, dopaminergic challenge tests using levodopa or apomorphine, SEMG, specialised imaging of presynaptic dopaminergic terminals (^{18}F-dopa PET or CIT SPET) or cardiac sympathetic terminals (MIBG SPET) may be helpful (Figure 1.5). Although sometimes expensive and of limited availability, such tests may be justified to help accurate diagnosis. Accurate diagnosis is essential for good clinical practice, appropriate prescribing of drugs that are likely to be used lifelong and proper counselling of patients and carers. Wrong diagnosis is costly to society, may be harmful to patients and traumatic for carers.

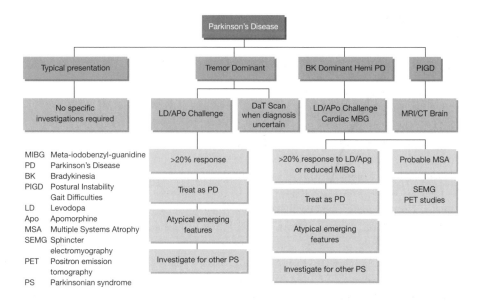

Figure 1.5 A suggested flow chart to aid diagnosis of Parkinson's disease (PD) in atypical cases. Apo, apomorphine; BK, bradykinesia; LD, levodopa; MSA, multiple systems atrophy; PET, positron emission tomography; PIGD, postural instability gait difficulties; PS, parkinsonian syndrome; SEMG, sphincter electromyography

Acknowledgements

I wish to acknowledge the excellent editorial and technical assistance of Linda Appiah-Kubi. I am also indebted to Professor David Brooks, Dr J Jarosch for much of the information within the imaging section.

References

Albanese A, Bonuccelli U, Brefel C, Chaudhuri KR, Colosimo C *et al.* (2001). Consensus statement on the role of acute dopaminergic challenge in Parkinson's disease. *Movement Disorders* **16**(2), 197–201

Aotsuka, A, Shinotoh H, Hattori T (1997). Magnetic resonance spectroscopy in PD and multiple system atrophy. *Nippon Rinsho. Japanese Journal of Clinical Medicine* **55**, 249–254

Asahina M, Suhara T, Shinotoh H, Inoue O, Suzuki K, Hattori T (1998). Brain muscarinic receptors in progressive supranuclear palsy and PD: a positron emission topographic study. *Journal of Neurology, Neurosurgery, and Psychiatry* **65**, 155–163

Asenbaum S, Brucke T, Pirker W *et al.* (1997). Imaging of dopamine transporters with iodine-123 – CIT and SPECT in PD. *Journal of Nuclear Medicine* **38**, 1–6

Benamer H, Patterson J, Grosset D & The [123I]FP-CIT Study Group (2000). Accurate differentiation of parkinsonism and essential tremor using visual assessment of [123I]FP-CIT SPECT imaging. *Movement Disorders* **15**, 503–510

Bennett DA, Beckett LA, Murray AM *et al.* (1996). Prevalence of parkinsonian signs and associated mortality in a community population of older people. *New England Journal of Medicine* **334**, 71–76

Biggins CA, Boyd JL, Harrop FM *et al.* (1992). A controlled longitudinal study of dementia in PD. *Journal of Neurology, Neurosurgery, and Psychiatry* **55**, 566–571

Booij J, Tissingh G, Winogrodzka A *et al.* (1997). Practical benefit of [123I]FP-CIT SPET in the demonstration of the dopaminergic deficit in PD. *European Journal of Nuclear Medicine* **24**, 68–71

Braune S, Reinhardt S, Bathmann J, Kraine T, Lehmann M, Lucking CH (1998). Impaired cardiac uptake of meta[123I]iodobenzylguanidine in PD with autonomic failure. *Acta Scandinavica Neurologica* **97**, 307–314

Brooks DJ (1992). Positron emission tomography (PET) studies. In Bannister R & Mathias CJ (eds) *Autonomic Failure. A textbook of clinical disorders of the autonomic nervous system.* Oxford: Oxford University Press, pp 548–553

Brooks DJ, Ibanez V, Sawle GV *et al.* (1990). Differing patterns of striatal ^{18}F-dopa uptake in PD, multiple system atrophy, and progressive supranuclear palsy. *Annals of Neurology* **28**, 547–555

Brucke T, Asenbaum S, Pirker W *et al.* (1997). Measurement of the dopaminergic degeneration in PD with [123I] beta-CIT and SPECT. Correlation with clinical findings and comparison with multiple system atrophy and progressive supranuclear palsy. *Journal of Neural Transmission* **50**(suppl), 9–24

Burn DJ, Sawle GV, Brooks DJ (1994). Differential diagnosis of PD, multiple system atrophy, and Steele-Richardson-Olszewski syndrome: discriminant analysis of striatal ^{18}F-dopa PET data. *Journal of Neurology, Neurosurgery, and Psychiatry* **57**, 278–284

Chase TN (1998). Levodopa therapy: consequences of the nonphysiologic replacement of dopamine., *Neurology* 50, S17–S25

Chaudhuri KR (2001). Autonomic dysfunction in movement disorders. *Current Opinion in Neurology* **14**, 505–511

Chaudhuri KR, Clough C (1998). Subcutaneous apomorphine for Parkinson's disease. Effective yet underused. *British Medical Journal* **316**, 641

Chaudhuri KR, Thomaides T, Watson L, Mathias CJ (1995). The somatostatin analogue 'octreotide' reduces alcohol induced hypotension and orthostatic symptoms in primary autonomic failure. *Quarterly Journal of Medicine* **88**, 719–725

Chaudhuri KR, Hu M (2000). Central autonomic dysfunction. In Appenzeller O, Vinken PJ & Bruyn GW (eds) *Handbook of Clinical Neurology, vol. 75(31), The Autonomic Nervous System. Part II. Dysfunctions.* Amsterdam: Elsevier, pp 161–202

Chokroverty S (1994). Sleep, breathing and neurological disorders. In Chokroverty S (ed.) *Sleep Disorders Medicine: Basic science, technical considerations and clinical aspects.* Boston: Butterworth-Heineman, pp 295–335

Clarke CE, Lowry M, Horsman A (1997). Unchanged basal ganglia *N*-acetylaspartate and glutamate in idiopathic PD measured by proton magnetic resonance spectroscopy. *Movement Disorders* **12**, 297–301

Clarke CE, Ray PF, Speller JM (1999). Failure of the clonidine growth hormone stimulation test to differentiate multiple system atrophy from early or advanced idiopathic Parkinson's disease. *The Lancet* **353**, 1329–1330

Davie CA (1998). The role of spectroscopy in Parkinsonism. *Movement Disorders* **13**, 2–4

Davie CA, Wenning GK, Barker GJ *et al.* (1995). Differentiation of multiple system atrophy from idiopathic PD using proton magnetic resonance spectroscopy. *Annals of Neurology* **37**, 204–210

Drayer BP, Olanow W, Burger PEA (1986). Parkinson plus syndrome: diagnosis using high field imaging of brain iron. *Radiology* **159**, 493–498

Eardley I, Quinn NP, Fowler CJ *et al*. (1989). The value of urethral sphincter electromyography in the differential diagnosis of parkinsonism. *British Journal of Urology* **64**, 360–362

Eidelberg D, Moeeler JR, Dhawan V *et al*. (1990). The metabolic anatomy of PD: complimentary 18F-fluorodeoxyglucose and 18F-fluorodopa positron emission tomography studies. *Movement Disorders* **5**, 203–213

Eidelberg D, Takikawa S, Moeller *et al*. (1993). Striatal hypometabolism distinguishes striatonigral degeneration from PD. *Annals of Neurology* **33**, 518–27

Ellis CM, Lemmens G, Williams SCR *et al*. (1997). Changes in putamen N-acetylaspartate and choline ratios in untreated and levodopa-treated PD: A proton magnetic resonance spectroscopy study. *Neurology* **49**, 438–444

Fealey R (1997). Disorders of sweating, In Robertston D, Low P, Polinsky R (eds) *Primer on the Autonomic Nervous System 59*. New York: Academic Press, pp 293–299

Fearnley JM & Lees AJ (1990). Striatonigral degeneration. A clinicopathological study. *Brain* **113**, 1823–1842

Federico F, Simone IL, Lucivero V *et al*. (1997). Proton magnetic resonance spectroscopy in PD and atypical parkinsonian disorders. *Movement Disorders* **12**, 903–909

Findley LJ & Koller WC (eds) (1995). Definitions and behavioural classifications. In Findley LJ & Koller WC (eds) *Handbook of Tremor Disorders*. New York: Marcel Dekker, pp 1–5

Findley LJ, Gresti MA, Hammaggi GM (1981). Tremor, the cogwheel phenomenon and clonus in PD. *Journal of Neurology, Neurosurgery, and Psychiatry* **44**, 534–546

Gasser T, Schwarz J, Arnold G, Trenkwalder C, Oertel WH (1992). Apomorphine test for dopaminergic responsiveness in patients with previously untreated Parkinson's disease. *Archives of Neurology* **49**, 1131–1134

Giladi N, Simon ES, Korczyn AD *et al*. (2000). Anal sphincter EMG does not distinguish between multiple system atrophy and Parkinson's disease. *Muscle and Nerve* **23**, 731–734

Goldstein DS, Holmes C, Li S-T, Bruce S, Metman LV, Cannon RO (2000). Cardiac sympathetic denervation in Parkinson's disease. *Annals of Internal Medicine* **133**, 338–347

Gonera EG, van't Hof M, Berger HJC, van Weel C, Horstink MWIM (1997). Symptom and duration of the prodromal phase in Parkinson's disease. *Movement Disorders* **12**, 871–876

Holhouse BA, Komu M, Moller HE *et al*. (1995). Localized Proton NMR spectroscopy in the striatum of patients with idiopathic PD: a multicenter pilot study. *Magnetic Resonance Medicine* **33**, 589–594

Howe FA, Maxwell RJ, Saunders DE, Brown MM, Griffiths JR (1993). Proton spectroscopy in vivo. *Magnetic Resonance Quarterly* **9**, 31–59

Hughes AJ, Lees AJ, Stern GM (1990a). Apomorphine test to predict dopaminergic responsiveness in parkinsonian syndromes. *The Lancet* **336**, 32–34

Hughes AJ, Lees AJ, Stern GM (1990b). Apomorphine in the diagnosis and treatment of parkinsonian tremor. *Clinical Neuropharmacology* **13**, 312–317

Hughes AJ, Lees AJ, Stern GM (1991). Challenge tests to predict the dopaminergic response in untreated Parkinson's Disease. *Neurology* **41**, 1723–1725

Hughes AJ, Daniel SE, Kilford L, Lees A J (1992). Accuracy of clinical diagnosis of idiopathic PD: a clinico-pathological study of 100 cases. *Journal of Neurology, Neurosurgery, and Psychiatry* **55**, 181–184

Hughes AJ, Daniel SE, Lees AJ (2001). Improved accuracy of clinical diagnosis of Lewy body Parkinson's disease. *Neurology* **57**, 1497–1499

Jankovic J, Schwartz K, Ondo WG (1998). Re-emergent tremor of PD. *Neurology* **50**(suppl 4), A348 (abstract)

Jankovic J, Rajput AH, McDermott MP, Pert DP (2000). The evolution of diagnosis in early Parkinson's Disease. *Archives of Neurology* **57**, 369–372

Kimber J, Watson L, Mathias C (1997). Distinction of multiple system atrophy from idiopathic PD by stimulation of GH release with clonidine. *The Lancet* **349**, 1877–1881

Kirby RS, Fowler C, Gosling J, Bannister R (1986). Urethro-vesical dysfunction in progressive autonomic failure with multiple system atrophy. *Journal of Neurology, Neurosurgery, and Psychiatry* **49**, 554–562

Lees J (1992). When did Ray Kennedy's Parkinson's disease begin? *Movement Disorders* **7**, 110–116

Libelius R & Johansson F (2000). Quantitative electromyography of the external anal sphincter in Parkinson's disease and multiple system atrophy. *Muscle and Nerve* **23**, 1250–1256

Litvan I, Booth V, Wenning GK *et al.* (1998). Retrospective application of a set of clinical diagnostic criteria for the diagnosis of multiple system atrophy. *Journal of Neural Transmission* **105**, 217–227

MacMahon DG, Thomas S, Campbell S (1999). Validation of pathways paradigm for the management of Parkinson's Disease. *Parkinsonism and Related Disorders* 5(suppl), S53

Mathias CJ & Banister R (1992). Postural hypotension in autonomic disorders. In Bannister R & Mathias CJ (eds) *Autonomic Failure. A textbook of clinical disorders of the autonomic nervous system.* Oxford: Oxford University Press, pp 489–509

Mathias CJ, Holly E, Armstrong E, Shareef M, Bannister R (1991). Influence of food on postural hypotension in 3 groups with chronic autonomic failure – clinical and therapeutic indications. *Journal of Neurology, Neurosurgery, and Psychiatry* **54**, 726–737

Mayeux R, Chen J, Mirabello E (1990). An estimate of the incidence of dementia in idiopathic PD. *Neurology* **40**, 1513–1517

Meara J, Bhowmick BK, Hobson P (1999). Accuracy of diagnosis in patients with presumed Parkinson's Disease. *Age and Ageing* **28**, 99–102

Montagna P, Maribinelli P, Rizzuto N, Salviati A, Rasi F, Lugaresi E (1983). Amyotrophy in Shy–Drager syndrome. *Acta Neurologica Belgica* **83**, 142–157

Montgomery EB, Koller WC, LaMantia TJK *et al.* (2000a). Early detection of probable idiopathic Parkinson's disease: I. Development of a diagnostic test battery. *Movement Disorders* **15**, 467–473

Montgomery EB, Lyons K, Koller WC (2000b). Early detection of probable idiopathic Parkinson's disease: II. A prospective application of diagnostic test battery. *Movement Disorders* **15**, 474–478

Morrish PK (1997). Parkinson's disease is not a long latency illness. *Movement Disorders* **12**, 849–854

Nutt JG, Carter JH, Woodward WR (1995). Long duration response to levodopa. *Neurology* **45**, 1613–1616

Pal S, Peng R, Brooks DJ, Rao CS, Chaudhuri KR (2002). Isolated symmetric dominantly postural tremor with or without resting tremor: a variant presentation of long latency tremulous Parkinson's disease? A clinical follow up study. *Journal of Neurology, Neurosurgery, and Psychiatry* **73**, 213 (abstract)

Palace J, Chandiramani VA, Fowler CJ (1997). Value of sphincter electromyography in the diagnosis of multiple system atrophy. *Muscle and Nerve* **20**, 1396–403

Pirker W, Asenbaum S, Wenger S *et al.* (1997). Iodine-123-epidepride-SPECT: studies in PD, multiple system atrophy and Huntington's disease. *Journal of Nuclear Medicine* **38**, 1711–1717

Pramstaller P, Wenning G, Smith S, Beck R, Quinn N, Fowler C (1995). Nerve conduction studies, skeletal muscle EMG, and sphincter EMG in multiple system atrophy. *Journal of Neurology, Neurosurgery, and Psychiatry* **58**, 618–621

Rakshi JS, Bailey DL, Morrish PK (1996). Implementation of 3D acquisition, reconstruction and analysis of dynamic ^{18}F-Fluorodopa studies. In Myers R, Cunningham V, Bailey D (eds) *Quantification of Brain Function using PET*. San Diego: San Diego Academic, p 82

Sakakibara R, Hattori T, Tojo M, Yamanishi T, Yasuda K, Hirayama K (1993). Micturitional disturbance in progressive supranuclear palsy. *Journal of the Autonomic Nervous System* **45**, 101–106

Sakuta M, Nakanishi T, Tohokura Y (1978). Anal muscle electromyograms differ in amyotrophic lateral sclerosis and Shy–Drager syndrome. *Neurology* **28**, 1289–1293

Salmon EP, Brooks DJ, Leenders KL *et al.* (1990). A two-compartment description and kinetic procedure for measuring regional cerebral ^{11}C-nomifensine uptake using positron emission tomography. *Journal of Cerebral Blood Flow and Metabolism* **10**, 307–316

Scaravilli T, Pramstaller PP, Salerno A *et al.* (2000). Neuronal loss in Onuf's nucleus in three patients with progressive supranuclear palsy. *Annals of Neurology* **48**, 97–101

Schrag A, Kingsley D, Phatouros C *et al.* (1998). Clinical usefulness of magnetic resonance imaging in multiple system atrophy. *Journal of Neurology, Neurosurgery, and Psychiatry* **65**, 65–71

Schrag A, Munchau A, Bhatia KP, Quinn NP, Marsden CD (2000). Essential tremor: An over-diagnosed condition? *Journal of Neurology* **247**, 955–959

Schulz J B, Klockgether T, Petersen D *et al.* (1994). Multiple system atrophy: natural history, MRI morphology, and dopamine receptor imaging with ^{123}IBZM-SPECT. *Journal of Neurology, Neurosurgery, and Psychiatry* **57**, 1047–1056

Stocchi F, Carbone A, Inghilleri M *et al.* (1997). Urodynamic and neurophysiological evaluation in PD and multiple system atrophy. *Journal of Neurology, Neurosurgery, and Psychiatry* **62**, 507–11.

Tedeschi G, Litvan I, Bonavita S *et al.* (1997). Proton magnetic resonance spectroscopic imaging in progressive supranuclear palsy, PD and corticobasal degeneration. *Brain* **120**, 1541–1552

Thomaides TN, Chaudhuri KR, Maule S, Watson L, Marsden CD, Mathias CJ (1992). Growth hormone response to clonidine in central and peripheral primary autonomic failure. *The Lancet* **340**, 263–266

Tolosa E, Valldeoriola F, Marti M (1994). Clinical diagnosis and diagnostic criteria of progressive supranuclear palsy (Steele–Richardson–Olszewski syndrome). *Journal of Neural Transmission* **42**(Gen Sect suppl), 15–31

Urenjak J, Williams SR, Giadian DG, Noble M (1993). Proton nuclear magnetic resonance spectroscopy unambiguously identifies neural cell types. *Journal of Neuroscience* **13**, 981–989

Wenning GK, Ben Shlomo Y, Magalhaes M, Daniel SE, Quinn NP (1994). Clinical features and natural history of multiple system atrophy. An analysis of 100 cases. *Brain* **117**, 835–845

Wenning GK, Tison F, Ben Shlomo Y, Daniel SE, Quinn NP (1997). Multiple system atrophy: a review of 203 pathologically proven cases. *Movement Disorders* **12**, 133–147

Chapter 2

Olfactory disorder in parkinsonian syndromes

Christopher Hawkes

Introduction

This is a review of research relating to measurement of olfactory function in parkinsonian syndromes. Under this heading are included idiopathic Parkinson's disease (IPD), diffuse Lewy body disease (LBD), progressive supranuclear palsy (PSP), multisystem atrophy (MSA), corticobasal degeneration (CBD), familial forms of parkinsonism, Guamanian PD, X-linked dystonia-parkinsonism (Lubag), drug-induced parkinsonism (DIPD) and vascular parkinsonism.

Table 2.1 Relative degree of olfactory dysfunction in various parkinsonian syndromes on an arbitrary scale

Disease	Severity of smell loss
Idiopathic Parkinson's disease	++++
Guam PD–dementia complex	++++
Lewy body disease	++++
Familial Parkinson's disease: affected/at risk	+++/+
X-linked dystonia-parkinsonism (Lubag)	++
Multiple system atrophy	++
Drug-induced PD	++
Progressive supranuclear palsy	0/+
Vascular parkinsonism	0
MPTP parkinsonism	0
Corticobasal degeneration	0

++++, marked damage; + mild; 0, normal. Note that most of the above values are based on relatively small patient numbers except for idiopathic Parkinson's disease.

When testing olfaction, it is insufficient just to ask a patient about their sense of smell. Many do not realise they have any defect and although there have been few systematic studies, at least one-third of subjects are unaware of their problem (Hawkes *et al.* 1997) and others complain of loss of taste instead. Local nasal disease has to be excluded by clinical examination, endoscopy and ideally computerised tomography/magnetic resonance imaging (CT/MRI), but a useful clue is that when anosmia is intermittent the problem is probably conductive, i.e. air cannot reach the olfactory neurons in the nose. Conversely, continual anosmia is characteristic of sensorineural loss.

Sniffing enhances smell detection and apart from redirection of airflow to the olfactory neuroepithelium, functional MRI studies have shown that it activates the pyriform and orbitofrontal cortices (Sobel *et al.* 1998). In a meticulous study of sniffing in patients with IPD, Sobel and colleagues (Sobel *et al.* 2001) showed that sniffing was impaired in IPD and this caused slight reduction in their performance on identification and detection threshold tests. This equates to a mean reduction of around 2–3 points on the UPSIT-40 test (see below). Increasing sniff vigour improved olfactory scores. Studies that have not allowed for this effect (which includes the majority) may tend to exaggerate slightly the severity of any smell defect especially where bulbar function is involved.

Simple bedside tests of smell appreciation are of four types: detection threshold, discrimination, odour memory and identification. Identification tests are rapid and simple to perform and correlate well with threshold and discrimination score and for this reason most workers have preferred identification tests unless there is a possibility of cognitive impairment. Many assessments have involved small groups and test odours have had significant trigeminal effects (Mesholam *et al.* 1998). Prior assessment of cognitive function is clearly important for tests of smell identification and memory. Mild depression and use of antidepressant drugs probably have no important effect on smell identification ability (Amsterdam *et al.* 1987) but not all agree with this (Serby *et al.* 1990) and it is better to screen out depressed patients in any research programme. The most popular and probably the most suitable identification procedure for research work is the 40-odour University of Pennsylvania Smell Identification test (UPSIT-40; Doty *et al.* 1984). This uses microencapsulated odorants that are released on scratching an impregnated strip with a pencil. There are 40 different odours and a forced choice is made from four answers. Possible answers include the smell of skunk, root beer and pumpkin pie – substances with which non-Americans may be unfamiliar. This may be circumvented by undertaking a large control sample so that cultural differences will be balanced out. Local control data are essential research prerequisites in any event. Another workaround is to employ the smaller International UPSIT-12 kit which has a good cultural cross-platform but it is less sensitive for research work because of the large variance associated with just 12 test samples. An alternative method of assessing olfactory identification is by 'Sniffin' Sticks'. This consists of a collection of felt-tip pens impregnated with various smells. Subjects make a forced choice from 4 alternatives and variously 7 or 16 odours may be used. Published normative data are available for over 1000 German people (Kobal *et al.* 1990) and may be expressed as a threshold, discrimination and identification score ('TDI index'). Sniffin' sticks will be more time consuming to use if the TDI score is required, but in the longer term they are inexpensive.

Idiopathic Parkinson's disease

It is now well established that patients with IPD have a profound disorder of olfactory function (Doty *et al.* 1988; Hawkes *et al.* 1997). This observation is based on pathological abnormality, psychophysical tests and evoked potential studies.

Pathology

The rhinencephalon has not been investigated systematically in Parkinson's disease (PD) without dementia. In a preliminary study we examined, blind to clinical information, the olfactory bulbs and tracts from formalin-fixed brains of eight control individuals and eight patients with a clinical and pathological diagnosis of IPD taken from the UK Parkinson's Disease Brain Bank (Daniel & Hawkes 1992). By inspecting the olfactory bulb and tract, all eight cases were correctly diagnosed as 'probable PD'. Lewy bodies were most numerous in the anterior olfactory nucleus but they were also found in mitral cells. The morphology of Lewy bodies at this site resembled their cortical counterparts and inclusions showing a classic trilaminar structure were rare. In two cases Lewy bodies were plentiful and associated with distended ubiquitin-immunoreactive neurites. Cortical Lewy bodies, mainly in the anterior cingulate gyrus and parahippocampus, were also plentiful in these two patients. There were large numbers of distended neurites in the CA2 region of the hippocampus which is said to be characteristic for LBD. It was subsequently shown that loss of anterior olfactory neurons correlated with disease duration (Pearce *et al.* 1995).

The pathological evidence therefore confirms the presence of cellular damage characteristic of PD in the olfactory bulb, although the relative degree of central versus peripheral involvement has not yet been determined pathologically.

Psychophysical tests

Simple bedside tests of smell appreciation are of four types: detection threshold, discrimination, odour memory and identification. The most popular identification procedure for research work is the University of Pennsylvania Smell Identification Test (UPSIT) involving 40 odours (Doty *et al.* 1984), described above. The first sizeable olfactory study in PD by Doty *et al.* (1988, 1992b), using UPSIT-40, showed that olfactory dysfunction did not relate to odour type, was independent of disease duration, and did not correlate with motor function, tremor or cognition. They also demonstrated that the deficit was of the same magnitude in both nostrils, and uninfluenced by anti-parkinsonian medication. Further studies in subtypes of presumed IPD showed that women with mild disability and tremor-dominant disease had a significantly higher UPSIT-40 score than men with moderate-to-severe disability and little or no tremor. Age of disease onset was irrelevant (Stern *et al.* 1994). We undertook a comparable survey (Hawkes *et al.* 1997) using UPSIT in healthy controls (Figure 2.1). All patients had clinically defined IPD, although the fallibility of such classification is acknowledged to be about 25% (Hughes *et al.* 1992). There were 155 cognitively intact, non-depressed IPD patients aged 34–84 years, and 156 control individuals aged 17–90 years. The UPSIT scores for PD patients were significantly lower than those for controls. Only 19% (30/155) of the PD patients had a score within the level expected for 95% of our age-matched healthy controls. There were 65 (42%) who were anosmic, i.e. scoring < 17. There was no correlation between disease duration and UPSIT score ($r = 0.074$) in keeping with earlier work (Doty *et al.* 1988). We analysed individual odours in the UPSIT and showed that pizza was the single most difficult smell for patients to identify and that a combination of pizza and wintergreen was the best discriminator, with a sensitivity of 90% and specificity of 86%.

An alternative method of assessing olfactory identification is by 'sniffin' sticks' which is basically a collection of felt-tipped pens impregnated with various odours. Impairment of smell sense has been documented in IPD patients using this approach (Daum *et al.* 2000). According to the most recent study by Tissingh *et al.* (2001), there was a significant negative correlation between odour discrimination and disease severity, suggesting as far as psychophysical tests go that there is some correlation between olfactory testing and disease severity.

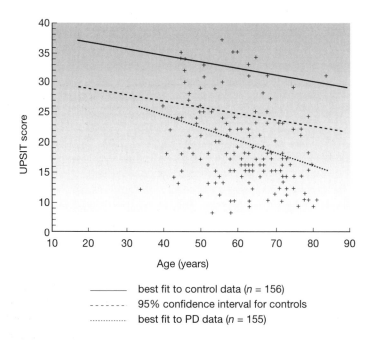

Figure 2.1 UPSIT scores in Parkinson's disease compared with healthy controls. The continuous line is the best fit by age for controls. The long dotted line represents the 95% confidence limit for controls. The fine dotted line is the best fit for Parkinson's disease patients by age. Each + represents the actual UPSIT score for one patient.

Neurophysiological tests

One of the most informative and validated objective measurements of the sense of smell is the olfactory (chemosensory) evoked response pioneered by Kobal (1978). We tested 73 patients with IPD by recording olfactory evoked potentials (OEPs) (Figure 2.2) (Hawkes *et al.* 1997). In 36 (49%), responses were either absent or unsatisfactory for technical reasons. Regression analysis on the 37 with a measurable trace showed that for hydrogen sulphide (H_2S) a highly significant latency difference existed between diagnostic groups (i.e. control or PD). Assuming that the 36 of the 73 who had no detectable OEP were abnormal and combining this with the abnormal 12 of 37 (32%), 81% have abnormality on OEP which is the same as for UPSIT measurements. In 10 patients with *normal* UPSIT-40 scores there was one with absent H_2S responses and three with significantly prolonged latency to H_2S, suggesting that the prevalence of olfactory disorder may be higher still.

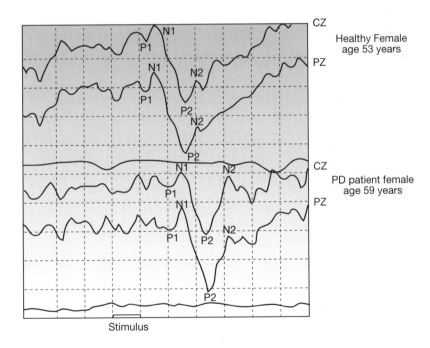

Stimulus

Figure 2.2 Sample of olfactory evoked response in normal person. Upper pair of traces are derived from CZ and PZ in a healthy woman aged 53 years. The third tracing is an eye artefact monitor. The next pair of tracings is from a 59-year-old woman with idiopathic Parkinson's disease. There is clear delay of responses at CZ and PZ. Note the slightly larger response from PZ in both cases. Bottom trace is again the eye movement channel. The stimulant was a 200-mS pulse of H2S at a concentration of 20 p.p.m. in both cases. Filters are set at 1–50 Hz. Squares represent 6.25 μV on the vertical axis and 200 mS on the horizontal axis.

We used only one odour whereas the UPSIT implements 40. If a large number of different gases were used, the sensitivity of the OEP might well increase. Similar results were obtained in 31 patients with PD tested by OEP to vanillin and H_2S (Bartz et al. 1997). Responses were found to both stimulants in all patients. Prolonged latencies were seen in the PD patients whether or not they were taking medication for the disease. More marked changes were seen in those on treatment, however, possibly because they were more disabled. The same group demonstrated for the first time a correlation between disability (as measured by Webster score) and latency to the H_2S OEP. This observation complements the recent findings of Tissingh et al. (2001), mentioned above. To date the issue of correlation of clinical status and olfactory test score has not been resolved, but it would appear that the original contentions of Doty et al. (1988, 1992b) may not be correct.

Familial and presymptomatic parkinsonism

The first study of familial parkinsonism was by Markopoulou et al. (1997). They used the UPSIT-40 in six kindreds of whom three had typical PD and three had a 'parkinsonism-plus' syndrome. In the typical families there were four apparently healthy individuals at 50% risk, of whom three were microsmic. In the PD-plus families there were eight at risk and two had an abnormal UPSIT score. Clearly this situation opens the potential for premorbid disease detection. A follow-up study has not yet been published so the findings must be regarded as provisional. Montgomery et al. (1999) administered a test battery to first-degree relatives of IPD patients. The battery included tests of motor function, olfaction and mood. There were significant differences in first-degree relatives (both sons and daughters), particularly where the affected parent was the father.

Berendse et al. (2001) studied subclinical dopamine dysfunction in asymptomatic IPD patients' relatives who were hyposmic. Single photon emission computed tomography (SPECT) with β-CIT was used to label the dopamine transporter. Abnormal dopamine transporter binding was found in 4 of 25 hyposmic relatives, 2 of whom subsequently developed IPD. None of the 23 normosmic relatives developed IPD. The authors suggested that olfactory dysfunction preceded clinical motor signs of the disease.

The question of olfaction and its relation to the basic aetiology is discussed in depth elsewhere (Hawkes et al. 1999). It remains possible that the olfactory system is the site of initial damage in IPD and the motor component is a late manifestation of what is basically a primary olfactory disorder. The results of large ongoing prospective studies in relatives of PD patients will probably resolve this question.

Parkinsonism

This will include guam PD–dementia complex, DLBD, MSA, PSP, CBD, MPTP-induced PD and drug-induced PD (DIPD). All data in this group have been obtained by psychophysical measurement and in most cases the number of patients studied has been relatively small.

Guam PD–dementia complex

This is typified by coexistence of Alzheimer-type dementia and sometimes motor neuron disease. Pathologically the presence of neurofibrillary tangles and the absence of Lewy bodies place this disorder well apart from idiopathic PD. Severe impairment of olfactory function was found of a magnitude comparable to that seen in idiopathic PD (Ahlskog *et al.* 1988; Doty *et al.* 1991), although a few had cognitive impairment.

X-linked dystonia-parkinsonism ('Lubag')

This is an X-linked disorder affecting Filipino male adults with maternal roots from the Philippine Island of Panay. A single study of 20 affected males using UPSIT-40 showed that olfaction is moderately impaired in Lubag even early on in the disorder and that it is independent of phenotype (i.e. degree of dystonia or rigidity) severity or duration of disease (Evidente *et al.* 2002).

Lewy body disease

In comparison to idiopathic PD, this disorder is characterised by a more rapid course, early onset of confusion, hallucinations, drug sensitivity and dementia. The pathology differs only quantitatively from typical PD. In one study of clinically defined LBD, severe impairment of olfactory identification and detection threshold was observed. Test scores were independent of disease stage and duration (Liberini *et al.* 1999, 2000) as found by Doty and co-workers (1988, 1992b). In another study by McShane *et al.* (2001) smell perception to one odour (lavender water) was examined in 92 patients with LBD confirmed *post mortem* and compared with age-matched controls and patients with Alzheimer's disease. The main finding was of impaired smell perception in the LBD group and little or no defect in the Alzheimer's disease patients. Although just one odorant was used for perception tests, this study confirms, at clinical and pathological levels, the conclusions of Liberini *et al.* (1999, 2000) that there is significant impairment of smell in LBD. For those who consider LBD to be no more than severe IPD, this observation would not be surprising. Their finding of normal values in Alzheimer's disease is at variance with those of all other workers and may be the effect of small sample size.

Multiple system atrophy

This is also a rapidly progressive form of parkinsonism in which autonomic dysfunction predominates, particularly affecting the bladder and orthostatic blood pressure control. Pathological changes characteristic of MSA can be seen in olfactory bulbs – as well as those typifying Alzheimer's and Pick's diseases (Daniel & Hawkes 1992). In the only study of identification in 29 patients with a clinical diagnosis of MSA, moderate impairment of UPSIT-40 score was demonstrated. The mean UPSIT score was 26.7 compared with the control mean of 33.5 (Wenning *et al.* 1993).

Corticobasal degeneration

Here parkinsonian features are supplemented by limb dystonia, ideomotor apraxia and myoclonus. In the only study of 7 patients with clinically suspected CBD, smell identification scores (UPSIT-40) were in the low normal range with a mean of 27.1 (Wenning *et al.* 1995), a value not significantly different from their controls.

Progressive supranuclear palsy

In this variety there is failure of voluntary vertical gaze, rapid course, marked problems with balance and dementia. Normal values have been found in two studies (Bonucelli *et al.* 1991; Wenning *et al.* 1995). In a study by Doty *et al.* (1993) there were no differences in the UPSIT-40 score. Threshold tests to phenylethylalcohol were not significantly different from control values ($p = 0.085$), but there was a trend to a higher threshold values which may have failed to reach significance because of the relatively small numbers used.

Drug-induced Parkinson's disease

In MPTP-induced PD, six participants were tested and found to be normal (Doty *et al.* 1992a). Although this is a small series, it implies that MPTP-induced PD is a poor model of its idiopathic counterpart. We undertook a small study of drug-induced PD in 10 cognitively normal patients (Hensiek *et al.* 2000). All had experienced parkinsonism in response to a variety of phenothiazine drugs which had been administered for at least 2 weeks. Of the 10 patients, 5 had abnormal UPSIT-40 score. The interpretation is difficult but it implies that patients with drug-induced PD may be those who are genetically predisposed to develop 'idiopathic' PD.

Vascular parkinsonism

A recently published study of UPSIT-40 in 13 patients fulfilling strictly defined criteria for vascular parkinsonism showed no significant difference compared with age matched controls, suggesting that identification tests may aid differentiation from idiopathic PD (Katsenschlager *et al.* 2002).

Conclusion

The olfactory system is damaged to varying degrees in the presence of clinically evident parkinsonism. The most severe changes are seen in the idiopathic, Guamanian and LBD varieties. The least involvement would be expected in CBD and PSP, and intermediate damage in MSA. These differences could aid diagnosis. For example, if a patient is suspected to have IPD, the presence of normal olfaction would prompt review of the diagnosis. Anosmia in CBD, PSP or vascular parkinsonism would also be unexpected. In a patient with predominant tremor, it is occasionally difficult to know whether the patient has tremor-dominant IPD or benign essential tremor. One study (Busenbark *et al.* 1992) and our own unpublished observations suggest that UPSIT score is normal in essential tremor, although this has been challenged recently (Louis *et al.* 2002). Patients with tremor-dominant PD, especially women, may have only a mildly affected ability to identify smells, so that smell testing in isolation may be less helpful in this context. There is need for a large long-term prospective study of patients with unexplained anosmia, especially those with a family history of IPD.

References

Ahlskog JE, Waring SC, Petersen RC *et al.* (1988). Olfactory dysfunction on Guamanian ALS, parkinsonism and dementia. *Neurology* **51**, 1672–1677

Amsterdam JD, Settle RG, Doty RL, Abelman E, Winokur A. (1987). Taste and smell perception in depression. *Biological Psychiatry* **22**, 1481–1485

Bartz S, Hummel T, Pauli E, Majer M, Lang CJG, Kobal G (1997). Chemosensory event-related potentials in response to trigeminal and olfactory stimulation in Parkinson's disease. *Neurology* **49**, 1424–1431

Berendse HW, Booij J, Francot CM *et al.* (2001). Subclinical dopaminergic dysfunction in asymptomatic Parkinson's disease patients' relatives with a decreased sense of smell. *Annals of Neurology* **50**, 34–41

Bonucelli U, Maremmani C, Piccini P, Del Dotto P, Nocita G, Muratorio A (1991). Parkinson's disease and progressive supranuclear palsy: differences in performance on an odour test. *10th International Symposium on Parkinson's Disease*, Tokyo, Japan

Busenbark KL, Huber SJ, Greer G, Pahwa R, Koller WC (1992). Olfactory function in essential tremor. *Neurology* **42**, 1631–1632

Daniel SE & Hawkes CH (1992). Preliminary diagnosis of Parkinson's Disease using olfactory bulb pathology. *The Lancet* **340**, 186 (letter)

Daum RF, Sekinger B, Kobal G, Lang CJ (2000). Olfactory testing with 'sniffin' sticks' for clinical diagnosis of Parkinson disease. *Nervenarzt* **71**, 643–650

Doty RL, Shaman P, Dann M (1984). Development of the University of Pennsylvania Smell Identification Test: A standardised microencapsulated test of olfactory function. *Physiology and Behavior* **32**, 489–502

Doty RL, Deems DA, Stellar S (1988). Olfactory dysfunction in parkinsonism: a general deficit unrelated to neurologic signs, disease stage or disease duration. *Neurology* **38**, 1237–44

Doty RL, Perl DP, Steele JC *et al.* (1991). Odour identification deficit of the parkinsonism-dementia complex of Guam: equivalence to that of Alzheimer's disease and idiopathic Parkinson's disease. *Neurology* **41**(suppl 2), 77–81

Doty RL, Singh A, Tetrud J, Langston JW (1992a). Lack of major olfactory dysfunction in MPTP-induced parkinsonism. *Annals of Neurology* **32**, 87–100

Doty RL, Stern MB, Pfeiffer C, Gollomp SM, Hurtig HI (1992b). Bilateral olfactory dysfunction in early stage treated and untreated idiopathic Parkinson's disease. *Journal of Neurology, Neurosurgery, and Psychiatry* **55**, 138–142

Doty RL, Golbe LI, McKeown DA, Stern MB, Lehrach CM, Crawford D (1993). Olfactory testing differentiates between progressive supranuclear palsy and idiopathic Parkinson's Disease. *Neurology* **43**, 962–965

Evidente VGH, Esteban R, Gwinn-Hardy K, Hardy J, Adam A, Singleton A (2002). Smell testing is abnormal in 'Lubag' or X-linked dystonia-parkinsonism. [Abstract.] *Neurology* (April Suppl.) P06.145

Hawkes CH, Shephard BC, Daniel SE (1997). Olfactory dysfunction in Parkinson's disease. *Journal of Neurology, Neurosurgery, and Psychiatry* **62**, 436–446

Hawkes CH, Shephard BC, Daniel SE (1999). Is Parkinson's disease a primary olfactory disorder? *Quarterly Journal of Medicine* **92**, 473–480

Hensiek AE, Bhatia K, Hawkes CH (2000). Olfactory function in drug induced parkinsonism. *Journal of Neurology* **247** (suppl 3), 303, III/82

Hughes AJ, Daniel SE, Kilford L (1992). Lees AJ. Accuracy of clinical diagnosis of idiopathic Parkinson's disease: a clinico-pathological study of 100 cases. *Journal of Neurology, Neurosurgery, and Psychiatry* **55**, 181–184

Katzenschlager R, Zijlmans, Lees AJ (2002). Olfactory function distinguishes vascular parkinsonism from Parkinson's disease. *European Journal of Neurology* **9**(suppl 2), SC 206, 27–28

Kobal G & Plattig KH (1978). Objective olfactometry: methodological annotations for recording olfactory EEG-responses from the awake human. *EEG EMG Z. Elektroenzephalogr. Verwandte Geb.* **9**, 135–145

Kobal G, Klimek L, Wolfensberger M, Gudziol H, Temmel A, Owen CM, Seeber H, Pauli E, Hummel T (2000). Multicenter investigation of 1,036 subjects using a standardized method for the assessment of olfactory function combining tests of odor identification, odor discrimination, and olfactory thresholds. *European Archives of Otorhinolaryngology* **257**, 205–211

Liberini P, Parola S, Spano PF, Antonini L (1999). Olfactory dysfunction in dementia associated with Lewy bodies. *Parkinsonism and Related Disorders* **5**, 30.

Liberini P, Parola S, Spano PF, Antonini L (2000). Olfaction in Parkinson's disease: methods of assessment and clinical relevance. *Journal of Neurology* **247**, 88–96

Louis ED, Bromley SM, Jurewicz EC, Watner D (2002). Olfactory dysfunction in essential tremor. *Neurology* **59**, 1631–1633

McShane RH, Nagy Z, Esiri MM *et al.* (2001). Anosmia in dementia is associated with Lewy bodies rather than Alzheimer's pathology. *Journal of Neurology, Neurosurgery, and Psychiatry* **70**, 739–743

Markoupoulou K, Larsen KW, Wszolek EK *et al.* (1997). Olfactory dysfunction in familial parkinsonism. *Neurology* **49**, 1262–1267

Mesholam RI, Moberg PJ, Mahr RN, Doty RL (1998). Olfaction in neurodegenerative disease: a meta-analysis of olfactory functioning in Alzheimer's and Parkinson's diseases. *Archives of Neurology* **55**, 84–90

Montgomery EB Jr, Baker KB, Lyons K, Koller WC (1999). Abnormal performance on the PD test battery by asymptomatic first-degree relatives. *Neurology* **52**, 757–762

Pearce RKB Hawkes CH, Daniel SE (1995). The anterior olfactory nucleus in Parkinson's disease. *Movement Disorders* **10**, 283–287

Serby M, Larson P, Kalkstein D (1990). Olfactory sense in psychosis. *Biological Psychiatry* **28**, 829–830

Sobel N, Prabhakaran V, Desmond JE, Glover GH, Goode RL, Sullivan EV, Gabrieli JD (1998). Sniffing and smelling: separate subsystems in the human olfactory cortex. *Nature* **392**, 282–286

Sobel N, Thomason ME, Stappen I, Tanner CM, Tetrud JW, Bower JM, Sullivan EV, Gabrieli JD (2001). An impairment in sniffing contributes to the olfactory impairment in Parkinson's disease. *Proceedings of the National Academy of Sciences of the USA* **98**, 4154–4159

Stern MB, Doty RL, Dotti M *et al.* (1994). Olfactory function in Parkinson's disease subtypes. *Neurology* **44**, 266–68.

Tissingh G, Berendse HW, Bergmans P *et al.* (2001). Loss of olfaction in de novo and treated Parkinson's disease: possible implications for early diagnosis. *Movement Disorders* **16**, 41–46

Wenning GK, Shephard B, Magalhaes M, Hawkes CH, Quinn NP (1993). Olfactory function in multiple system atrophy. *Neurodegeneration* **2**, 169–171

Wenning GK, Shephard BC, Hawkes CH, Petruckevitch A, Lees A, Quinn N (1995). Olfactory function in atypical parkinsonian syndromes. *Acta Neurologica Scandinavica* **91**, 247–250

Chapter 3

Clinical application of functional imaging in Parkinson's disease

Donald Grosset

Introduction

Functional cerebral imaging to aid diagnosis in Parkinson's disease has recently become a licensed treatment with the availability of DaTSCAN (also known as ^{123}I-fluoropropyl (FP)-CIT scanning). This test is much more widely available than some other functional imaging techniques that are of interest in Parkinson's disease, namely positron emission tomography (PET). Although PET has been largely a research tool and has added significantly to our understanding of the pathophysiology of Parkinson's disease, in both the dopamine system and elsewhere, it is restricted to a few centres and is predominantly considered a research technique. On the other hand, DaTSCAN uses single photon emission computed tomography (SPECT) which is available in most major hospital centres; accordingly, it is available for clinical use. This chapter analyses the application of this technique, and gives guidance about the type of results that can be obtained with it and how this can help in the differential diagnosis of Parkinson's disease from other movement disorders.

Clinical diagnosis of Parkinson's disease

The diagnosis of Parkinson's disease has always been a clinical one supported at times by some technical observations. Accordingly the standard accepted clinical criteria remain, namely the presence of bradykinesia in conjunction with tremor of a parkinsonian type, mainly rest tremor, but at times additional postural tremor and/or rigidity when testing tone at individual muscle groups, typically the wrist and other joints in the upper limbs and neck. The supporting feature of postural instability is relevant when there are no other clinical features that could lead to instability of posture. Even with the advent of new diagnostic supportive tests, the application of the basic clinical skills remains crucial. However, it should be recognised that the published criteria for diagnosis of Parkinson's disease and other movement disorders are in themselves imperfect, e.g. the Parkinson's Disease Society Brain Bank Criteria that were established after the study of 100 patients who carried a diagnosis of Parkinson's disease throughout life, and subsequently underwent postmortem examination, under-represents the more benign disorders such as essential tremor which at times can cause confusion in diagnosis (Hughes *et al.* 1992). Also, the refinement of diagnostic criteria improves the sensitivity of clinical criteria but at the expense of false-negative cases (Hughes *et al.* 1993; Gelb *et al.* 1999). In a clinical setting, this means that patients who have Parkinson's disease can fail to fulfil clinical diagnostic criteria. This is particularly so at early presentation when the full set of clinical features is not developed. Accordingly the use of clinical diagnostic criteria is a helpful framework but not an absolute guideline against which to test patients entering the clinic.

In considering a new diagnostic test for differential diagnosis of Parkinson's disease, it is appropriate to examine the level of diagnostic accuracy with present techniques. Hospital specialists with an interest in Parkinson's disease report a level of diagnostic uncertainty in between 10% and 20% of cases of parkinsonian-type movement disorders. This includes patients with one of the Parkinson's disease plus disorders such as multiple system atrophy (MSA) or progressive supranuclear palsy (PSP). It also includes patients with tremor-dominant disorders which can include a tremor-dominant variant of Parkinson's disease, and even the more recently recognised monosymptomatic rest tremor as a precursor to the development of true Parkinson's disease. Also under consideration are disorders that cause a tremor and a degree of slowness that may be physical, mental or both. In this group are patients with Alzheimer's disease, cerebrovascular disease and patients with essential tremor and coexisting disorders, which become more common in older patients such as those with arthritis. Non-structural nervous system disease such as depression can of course influence the interpretation of physical symptoms and signs. A recent community-based study shows that there is a high diagnostic error rate in patients receiving anti-parkinsonian medication with a presumptive diagnosis of idiopathic Parkinson's disease or at least levodopa-responsive parkinsonism (Meara *et al.* 1999). In this study, parkinsonism was confirmed in 74% of 402 cases examined by one observer and only 53% were felt to have clinically probable Parkinson's disease. The patients with alternative diagnoses according to the reassessment had essential tremor, Alzheimer's disease or vascular pseudo-parkinsonism.

Clinical features of parkinsonian and tremor disorders
Essential tremor

This is the most common of all the movement disorders and is at least ten times more common than idiopathic Parkinson's disease, although it is generally mild so that less than 10% of patients seek medical advice. In its pure form, it is present in other members of the family as it is a dominant condition; this consists of a mainly postural tremor sometimes associated with kinetic tremor, with an onset in the teens or 20s, and becoming worse as the decades progress. This worsening leads to clinical presentation, often in the 50s or 60s around the time of the average age of onset of Parkinson's disease. Supportive features for Parkinson's disease are a response to alcohol as well as positive family history, in conjunction with the clinical pattern of tremor, but it is clear that some patients do not fulfil the clinical diagnostic criteria and often this will result in difficulty distinguishing it from Parkinson's disease.

Vascular parkinsonism

The development of parkinsonism in patients with cerebrovascular disease, usually subcortical small vessel disease, was a concept initially introduced by Critchley in 1929 when patterns of parkinsonism in association with risk factors for vascular disease were noted. These patients had dementia, incontinence, and pyramidal or cerebellar signs as additional features. With the advent of structural cranial imaging, there was an initial challenge to the concept of vascular parkinsonism, because patients with Parkinson's disease were found to have normal structural images; however, there has been a revival of interest and recognition in the condition and accepted terms today include vascular parkinsonism and lower body parkinsonism. Recently published criteria demand the presence of at least two of the four cardinal features of parkinsonism and two or more points on a vascular rating scale, including a history or risk factors for stroke and structural imaging evidence of vascular disease (Winikates & Jankovic 1999).

Alzheimer's disease

This is the most common neurodegenerative disorder in the elderly population. Patients with Alzheimer's disease often have an associated movement disorder and the most common is a form of parkinsonism. This includes bradykinesia and rigidity. The Brain Bank study was a turning point in the recognition of this, with a number of patients either having Alzheimer's disease-type changes in the brain in conjunction with their Parkinson's disease, or having no evidence of Lewy body-positive Parkinson's disease but having Alzheimer's disease-type changes and accordingly a confirmed diagnosis of Alzheimer's disease. Tremor is much less common in Alzheimer's disease than the other parkinsonian features, but it can occur. It is thought that in some patients their Parkinson's disease may evolve to Alzheimer's disease, and rest tremor that is present initially then settles. Myoclonus is another movement disorder noted is some Alzheimer's disease patients.

Dementia with Lewy bodies

This is sometimes also referred to as diffuse Lewy body disease. Such patients typically have Lewy body pathology in cortical neurons as well as in the brain stem. Clinical diagnostic criteria for dementia with Lewy bodies emphasise the occurrence of progressive cognitive decline, fluctuating cognition with recurrent visual hallucination and parkinsonian features (McKeith 2000).

Multiple system atrophy

This and PSP are generally considered the two main types of Parkinson's plus disorder. In MSA there is involvement of the extrapyramidal system resulting in parkinsonism, in conjunction with cerebellar and/or autonomic dysfunction. The evolution of the condition varies between individuals, so that some patients present with cerebellar dysfunction and others have parkinsonism, although eventually most patients will have mixed features from each of the different areas of the nervous system affected. Inaccuracy of clinical diagnosis is well recognised. Clinical diagnostic criteria can be of some assistance (Quinn 1994; Consensus Committee 1996). The presence of parkinsonism with poor levodopa response, or parkinsonism with cerebellar features and/or autonomic dysfunction or autonomic failure, supports the diagnosis. An overlap with idiopathic Parkinson's disease will be evident because symptoms of postural or orthostatic hypotension do occur in Parkinson's disease itself and are worsened by dopaminergic therapy. Further, the autonomic dysfunction of the bladder is not unique to cases of autonomic failure with MSA and is a common component of idiopathic Parkinson's disease.

Progressive supranuclear palsy

In this condition, gait disturbance with falls early in the course of the illness, and the presence of changes in personality with mental and physical slowness, tend to precede the classic clinical features of gaze palsy, dysphagia or dysarthria. Rigidity tends to be more central proximal and there is often an erect posture with a degree of retrocollis of the neck. There is a poor response to dopaminergic treatment, probably at an even lesser rate than that for MSA.

DaTSCAN (123I-FP-CIT) imaging

^{123}I-FP-CIT works at the presynaptic dopamine system. It shows the level of functioning dopamine transporters, which are uptake sites on the presynaptic dopaminergic nerve terminals that have been shown to correlate with the quantity of striatal dopamine.

DaTSCAN imaging tests abnormal in patients with Parkinson's disease, Parkinson's plus disorders such as MSA and PSP, and dementia with Lewy bodies. It will test normal or negative in patients with Alzheimer's disease, essential tremor and at least in some cases of vascular parkinsonism.

It has long been recognised that there is a preclinical state of some years before the patient attends with early signs of Parkinson's disease. Therefore the patient reaches a level of 50–70% of their baseline dopamine before becoming sufficiently symptomatic to seek medical attention. The exact duration of the preclinical period has been the subject of much debate, but is certainly more than a few months – probably at least 2–3 years, and in some instances may be considerably longer. This means that DaTSCAN is sensitive to abnormalities early in the course of the clinical presentation, and present results indicate a far greater sensitivity of DaTSCAN to the pathological changes than relying on the clinical features alone. It has been possible to analyse this in individual patients because of the usual unilateral onset of Parkinson's disease. This means that a defect in dopamine is identified not only in the basal ganglia appropriate to the side of onset, but also on the other side of the brain. This suggests that DaTSCAN has high sensitivity and could be an alternative to PET in studies of pre-symptomatic detection such as in twins and family studies. This is of potential interest in relation to the recent increased understanding about the genetic contribution to Parkinson's disease, at least in some familial cases.

It would be expected intuitively that the degree of dopamine loss in patients with Parkinson's disease should correlate with the level of symptoms. This generally holds true but there is enormous individual variation. This means that some patients with modest loss of dopamine have much more severe symptoms than patients with a more marked dopamine loss. The correlation of clinical symptom severity to dopamine activity appears best for bradykinesia and rigidity, and is even quite good for activities of daily living scored by the Unified Parkinson's Disease Rating Scale (UPDRS) system, but is not so good for tremor. This adds to evidence from elsewhere that tremor may have significant contribution outwith the dopaminergic system, or at least elsewhere within the nigrostriatal systems than at the presynaptic dopamine receptor (Benamer *et al.* 2000).

The agreement between DaTSCAN imaging and clinical diagnosis according to available criteria discussed above was tested in patients with Parkinson's disease, Parkinson's plus disorders, and essential tremor. The overall level of diagnostic accuracy was 97%. The sensitivity of diagnosing parkinsonian syndrome (a combination of idiopathic Parkinson's disease, PSP and MSA) was 150 of 158 patients (95%). For essential tremor cases the specificity was 25 of 27 patients (92.5%) (Benamer *et al.* 2000a). The use of DaTSCAN within this large clinical trial has resulted in reclassification of patients as essential tremor or cerebrovascular disease where the prior clinical diagnosis was one of Parkinson's disease.

Of potentially even greater clinical significance is the application of DaTSCAN testing in patients with early signs and symptoms raising the possibility of Parkinson's disease. This is the subject of an ongoing study. It is clear from interim analysis that patients who carry a provisional label of possible or even probable Parkinson's disease may have no abnormality in their dopaminergic system. This highlights the issue of clinical differential diagnosis and in these patients special attention is required for examining the evolution of their disorder and the ongoing response to drug treatment.

Alternative presynaptic dopamine imaging techniques

In addition to ^{123}I-FP-CIT, ^{123}I-labelled β-carbomethoxy-3β-(4-iodophenyl)-tropane (β-CIT) is a similar agent to FP-CIT and shows evidence of early loss bilaterally in hemi-parkinsonism, and a correlation with clinical features. Similar to FP-CIT, it does not differentiate between Parkinson's disease and the Parkinson's plus disorders such as MSA and PSP. There is a difference in kinetics between FP-CIT and β-CIT so that imaging can be undertaken on the same day as injection for FP-CIT but on the following day for β-CIT. FP-CIT (DaTSCAN) has a product licence for use in the differential diagnosis of Parkinson's disease from tremor disorders but at present β-CIT remains a research tool.

Postsynaptic dopaminergic imaging

The D_2-receptors in the postsynaptic area can be imaged with SPECT using iodobenzamide (IBZM). This shows reduced uptake in patients with Parkinson's plus disorder such as PSP and MSA, but remains normal in Parkinson's disease because the degeneration in Parkinson's disease is only presynaptic. Results of IBZM SPECT and similar studies with PET suggest that the initial dopaminergic therapy response obtained in patients with the Parkinson's plus disorders relies on the initial survival of a small proportion of postsynaptic neurons, which deteriorates with time. By contrast, in Parkinson's disease itself the postsynaptic dopamine neurons remain intact, allowing continued life-long response to dopaminergic therapy, albeit punctuated by the severe fluctuations and dyskinesia that typify the later stages of the disease.

Conclusion

The appropriate application of DaTSCAN (FP-CIT) SPECT scanning as part of the diagnostic assessment of a patient with Parkinson's disease, parkinsonism or essential tremor is a worthy consideration. The clinical diagnosis alone may be adequate in some or even most patients but there is often a degree of uncertainty. Where this uncertainty is between Parkinson's disease and a tremor dominant disorder or other condition where presynaptic dopamine imaging would be expected to test normal, DaTSCAN imaging should be strongly considered. Another consideration is the uncertainty in the patient and family usually at the initial stages, when the examining physician may regard the symptoms as mild and not medically troublesome, but the possibility of Parkinson's disease is unsettling to the patient. This is another situation when DaTSCAN imaging my be of value, as confirming or refuting the presence of dopaminergic deficit provides useful prognostic information.

Recommendations

- Review the available clinical diagnostic criteria for Parkinson's disease and associated disorders.
- Consider the differential diagnosis of Parkinson's disease according to the site of neuronal degeneration, which is presynaptic for Parkinson's disease, pre- and postsynaptic for PSP and MSA, and which is outwith the dopaminergic system in essential tremor.
- Consider the application of DaTSCAN where it would aid differential diagnosis and remove diagnostic uncertainty in patients with early and/or atypical parkinsonism.

References

Benamer HT, Patterson J, Grosset DG *et al*. (2000a). Accurate differentiation of parkinsonism and essential tremor using visual assessment of [123I]-FP-CIT SPECT imaging: the [123I]-FP-CIT study group. *Movement Disorders* **15**, 503–510

Benamer HT, Patterson J, Wyper DJ, Hadley DM, Macphee GJ, Grosset DG (2000b). Correlation of Parkinson's disease severity and duration with [^{123}I]FP-CIT, *Movement Disorders* **15**, 692–698

Consensus Committee of the American Autonomic Society and the American Academy of Neurology (1996). Consensus statement on the definition of orthostatic hypotension, pure autonomic failure, and multiple system atrophy. *Neurology* **46**, 147

Gelb DJ, Oliver E, Gilman S (1999). Diagnostic criteria for Parkinson disease. *Archives of Neurology* **56**, 33–39

Hughes AJ, Daniel SE, Kilford L, Lees AJ (1992). Accuracy of clinical diagnosis of idiopathic Parkinson's disease: a clinico-pathological study of 100 cases. *Journal of Neurology, Neurosurgery, and Psychiatry* **55**, 181–184

Hughes AJ, Daniel SE, Blankson S, Lees AJ (1993). A clinico-pathological study of 100 cases of Parkinson's disease. *Archives of Neurology* **50**, 140–148

McKeith IG (2000). Clinical Lewy body syndromes. *Annals of the New York Academy of Sciences* **920**, 1–8

Meara J, Bhowmick BK, Hobson P (1999). Accuracy of diagnosis in patients with presumed Parkinson's disease, *Age and Ageing* **28**, 99–102

Quinn N (1994) Multiple system atrophy. In Marsden CD & Fahn S (eds) *Movement Disorders*, Vol. 3. London: Butterworth pp 262–281

Winikates J & Jankovic J (1999). Clinical correlates of vascular parkinsonism. *Archives of Neurology* **56**, 98–102

PART 2

Scientific evidence and expert clinical opinion for medical and surgical intervention

Scientific evidence and expert clinical opinion for medical intervention in early and late disease

Carl E Clarke

Introduction

Pharmacotherapy remains at the heart of the management of Parkinson's disease. Over the last few decades, much has been learnt about the newer anti-parkinsonian drugs during their development programmes. However, such information usually relates to placebo-controlled trials, with few data on comparisons with other active agents. Although clinicians feel that they can estimate which drug is better without such comparisons, this is based on experience not head-to-head class effect trials. Many more phase IV post-marketing studies are required to establish the optimum therapeutic regimen in Parkinson's disease.

In the meantime, recommendations for individual patients must be based on the best evidence available. Clinical evidence is usually classified using the hierarchies detailed in Tables 4.1 and 4.2. Wherever possible, this chapter documents the type of evidence on which statements are made so that the reader can gauge the strength of the recommendations being made. Some of these will necessarily be based on expert opinion only in view of the current lack of knowledge in certain areas.

Table 4.1 Categories of evidence for clinical decision-making

Ia	Evidence from systematic review of RCTs
Ib	Evidence from one or more RCT
IIa	Evidence from one or more controlled but non-randomised study
IIb	Evidence from one or more quasi-experimental study
III	Evidence from descriptive study(s) such as case–control study
IV	Evidence from expert committee reports or opinions or clinical experience of respected authorities

RCTs, randomised controlled trials.

Early Parkinson's disease

Levodopa

The dramatic therapeutic effect of levodopa in Parkinson's disease in the early 1970s and the desperate need of patients for such effective therapy meant that randomised

Table 4.2 Strength of recommendation for clinical decision-making

A	Directly based on category I evidence
B	Directly based on category II evidence or extrapolated recommendation from category I evidence
C	Directly based on category III evidence or extrapolated recommendation from category I or II evidence
D	Directly based on category IV evidence or extrapolated recommendation from category I, II or III evidence

controlled trials were not performed with the agent. The addition of the aromatic amino acid decarboxylase (AADC) (Figure 4.1) inhibitors benserazide and carbidopa improved tolerance and led to the widespread use of the combined preparations over the course of the 1980s (Clarke & Sampaio 1997). However, over the last decade, the realisation that levodopa is related to motor complications and may be toxic has led to a move away from its use as first-line monotherapy.

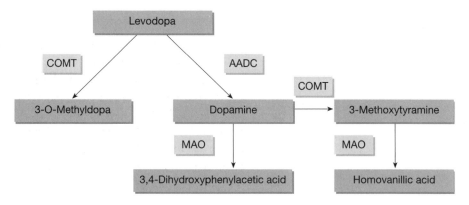

COMT   Catechol-O-methyltransferase
AADC   Aromatic amino acid decarboxylase
MAO   Monoamine oxidase

Figure 4.1 Catecholamine metabolism. COMT, catechol-O-methyltransferase; AADC, aromatic amino acid decarboxylase; MAO, monoamine oxidase.

The long-term motor complications associated with levodopa therapy include abnormal involuntary movements such as choreoathetoid dyskinesia (e.g. trunk and limb writhing and twisting movements) and dystonia (e.g. painful spasm of calf muscles leading to dorsiflexion and inversion of the foot). Response fluctuations constitute the other main motor complication of levodopa. These comprise a shortening response to each dose of medication (i.e. end-of-dose deterioration or wearing-off effect) and unpredictable switching between the mobile 'on' phase and relatively immobile 'off' phase (i.e. on/off fluctuations). Such complications affect around 10% of patients with each year of levodopa therapy, so that after around 5 years 50% will be suffering from them (Rajput *et al.* 1984; Quinn *et al.* 1986). In young onset patients (onset < 40 years), by 6 years of treatment 100% will suffer from motor complications (Quinn *et al.* 1986).

The hypothesis that levodopa may be toxic stems from tissue culture experiments in which supraphysiological doses of levodopa in the absence of glial cells have proved to be toxic to dopaminergic neurons (Fahn 1998). At present, there is no evidence to show that this occurs in humans but a North American trial is currently examining the issue (ELLDOPA Trial) (Fahn 1999).

These arguments have led to decreasing use of immediate-release levodopa preparations as monotherapy in early Parkinson's disease. The challenge has been to find alternative agents which are as efficacious as levodopa, but which cause less or no motor complications with an acceptable side-effect profile. Such alternatives are now considered in turn against these requirements.

Modified-release levodopa

One theory suggests that motor complications are generated by the pulsatile stimulation of dopamine receptors by immediate-release levodopa preparations. This led to the proposition that modified-release preparations of levodopa with longer half-lives may produce fewer complications than immediate-release forms. This has been examined in two 5-year trials, one with each of the modified-release levodopa preparations available (Sinemet CR and Madopar CR/HBS), which showed no significant differences in the incidence of motor complications between the two formulations of levodopa (Table 4.3). Therefore, there is no evidence to support the use of these more expensive formulations of levodopa as monotherapy in early disease.

Amantadine

Amantadine was initially examined as an antiviral agent but was coincidentally found to have anti-parkinsonian activity. A Cochrane systematic review of the trials with this agent in Parkinson's disease is under way but not yet available. As these studies were performed in the early 1970s when randomised controlled trials were in their infancy, these were small placebo-controlled studies with numerous different outcome measures, mainly centred on motor impairments, with little information on motor complication rates. As a result, no good evidence is available to support amantadine monotherapy in preference to levodopa. Coupled with this is the relatively high adverse event profile of the drug. Central side effects include confusion and hallucinations and peripheral reactions such as ankle oedema and livedo reticularis are not uncommon.

Table 4.3 Modified-release levodopa trials

Name	Year	Reference	Allowed prior medication	Design	Number MR	IR	Incidence of motor complications at 5 years Dyskinesia	Fluctuations
CR First Study	1997	Block et al. (1997)	Selegiline, amantadine and anticholinergics	Randomised triple-masked parallel group study	312	306	16% both groups	
Danish–Norwegian study	1996	Dupont et al. (1996)	Anticholinergics and bromocriptine	Randomised double-masked parallel group study	65	69	34% IR vs 41% CR	57% IR vs 59% MR

MR, modified-release levodopa; IR, immediate-release levodopa.

Over the last few years, a number of small trials have examined the use of amantadine as an anti-dyskinetic agent with some promising results (Verhagen-Metman *et al.* 1998). Further much larger trials will be required before the use of amantadine in the treatment of dyskinesia can be supported.

Anticholinergics

The anticholinergics were first used in the treatment of Parkinson's disease in the late nineteenth century after Charcot's work with hyoscine. However, it took until the mid-twentieth century for selective, centrally active, muscarinic receptor antagonists to be developed which have fewer peripheral side effects. Numerous agents are available but the most commonly used in the UK are benzhexol and orphenadrine.

As with amantadine, clinical trials with the anticholinergics were performed many years ago, so many do not stand up to modern scrutiny. A Cochrane systematic review is under way in this area but in the meantime recommendations are based mainly on clinical experience.

No good evidence is available on motor complication rates with the anticholinergics. Motor impairments, in particular tremor, improve with anticholinergics but probably not as much as with levodopa. It is their adverse event profile that has led to their declining use. Thus, confusion, hallucinations and cognitive impairment are common unwanted central effects. Peripheral side effects include nausea, dry mouth, constipation, dizziness, blurred vision, precipitation of closed-angle glaucoma and urinary retention in prostatic hypertrophy. These are all more common in elderly people in whom these drugs should be avoided but they can also occur in younger patients.

Selegiline

Selegiline was introduced as an adjuvant agent in later disease (see later) in view of its ability to inhibit monoamine oxidase (MAO) B both in neurons and in glial cells (see Figure 4.1). This reduces the degradation of dopamine and thus increases the amount available at the synapse. However, from a retrospective longitudinal study in 1985, Birkmayer *et al.* (1985) suggested that selegiline had reduced mortality when used in association with levodopa in Parkinson's disease. This raised the prospect for the first time of an agent that could not only treat the symptoms of the condition but also slow its progression. There then followed a series of small prospective monotherapy studies with selegiline alone versus placebo and selegiline combined with levodopa versus levodopa alone, to be followed by one large North American trial (the DATATOP study) and one from the UK. Cochrane systematic reviews of this work are awaited but in the meantime conclusions should be based on the results of the larger randomised controlled trials.

In the DATATOP (Deprenyl and Tocopherol Antioxidative Therapy of Parkinsonism) study, 800 previously untreated patients with Parkinson's disease were randomised to receive masked therapy with placebos, selegiline (deprenyl

10 mg/day), tocopherol (the biologically active component of vitamin E) or both (Parkinson Study Group 1989). At 12 months, 97 patients on selegiline reached the primary endpoint of requiring levodopa compared with 176 patients on placebo (hazard ratio 0.43; 95% confidence interval [95%CI] of 0.33, 0.55; $p < 10^{-10}$). In contrast, tocopherol was ineffective. The authors concluded that selegiline delayed the need for levodopa and the trial was stopped at this point, all patients being started on open-label selegiline. Whether this represented a symptomatic or a neuroprotective effect remained uncertain. The mortality rates after a mean of 8.2 years of follow-up in the DATATOP study showed no difference between the groups, although all patients received open-label selegiline for around 3.5 years after a mean period on double-masked medication of around 3 years (Parkinson Study Group 1998). The incidence of motor complications in the DATATOP study, in those who went on to levodopa early in the trial, was the same in selegiline-treated and -untreated patients (Parkinson Study Group 1996).

The SINDAPAR study randomised 101 untreated PD patients to selegiline and Sinemet, placebo and Sinemet, selegiline and bromocriptine, or placebo and bromocriptine (Olanow *et al.* 1995). After 12 months, selegiline had delayed progression in the motor and activities of daily living (ADL) scores of the Unified Parkinson's Disease Rating Scale (UPDRS), but after 2 months' wash-out of the selegiline or placebo, there was no difference between treatment groups in the deterioration in UPDRS scores, arguing against a neuroprotective effect. In a subset of 23 patients, Sinemet or bromocriptine was also withdrawn for 14 days. There was significantly less deterioration from baseline UPDRS scores for those randomised to selegiline, supporting a neuroprotective effect.

In the open-label UK Parkinson's Disease Research Group (PDRG) trial, 782 patients were randomised to receive Madopar, Madopar and selegiline, or bromocriptine. After a mean of 3 years, motor impairment was similar in the levodopa-treated groups but with more adverse events in the selegiline arm. The bromocriptine-treated patients were worse in terms of motor impairments but had fewer motor complications. It was concluded that the choice of first-line therapy in early disease may not be critical (Parkinson's Disease Research Group 1993). However, after 5.6 years, the mortality rate adjusted for all baseline factors was greater in the Madopar/selegiline-treated group than in the Madopar-alone group (hazard ratio 1.57; 95%CI 1.07, 2.31) (Lees and Parkinson's Disease Research Group of the UK 1995). Motor impairment was similar in both groups but motor complications were worse with selegiline. After this interim analysis all patients in the trial were withdrawn from selegiline. At a further analysis after 6.8 years, the excess mortality in the selegiline group, corrected for baseline co-variates, was 1.30 (95%CI 0.99, 1.72) which is probably not significant because the lower confidence interval overlaps unity.

It is unlikely that a systematic review of these data and the smaller studies will be able to resolve the uncertainties regarding any neuroprotective effect of selegiline and whether it can delay the onset of motor complications. Further even larger trials are required in this area.

Dopamine agonists

The agonists were originally developed as adjuvant therapy to reduce motor complications in later Parkinson's disease (see below). Having proved effective at this stage of the condition, it was then thought possible that they could be used either as monotherapy in place of levodopa or at least in combination therapy to reduce the initial dose of levodopa. The first monotherapy and combination therapy trials with bromocriptine were performed in the 1980s. Two Cochrane systematic reviews have assessed these studies (Ramaker & van Hilten 1999a, 1999b). The monotherapy review found six randomised controlled trials with follow-up for 1.5–5 years in about 850 patients. There was no reduction in response fluctuations but dyskinesia was reduced in one of the three studies in which this was measured. Motor impairment and disability rating scales were too diverse to reach any conclusions. Adverse events were worse in the bromocriptine arms of the studies. It was concluded that bromocriptine monotherapy could delay the onset of dyskinesia in those who were able to tolerate it. The combined bromocriptine/levodopa therapy versus levodopa alone Cochrane review found a further six trials with follow-up for 1.5–5 years in 898 patients. There was a trend for less dyskinesia in the combination therapy group with no difference in fluctuations, and impairment and disability scales were too diverse to interpret. There were more adverse events in the bromocriptine/levodopa arms of the trials. The conclusion was that there was no advantage in combination therapy with bromocriptine.

Long before the results of these Cochrane reviews were known, it had been decided that the adverse event profile of bromocriptine was too poor for use as monotherapy, although most of the trials had been performed before domperidone became available to reduce these. The next agonist to be evaluated as monotherapy was lisuride (Rinne 1989). No systematic review is available but it appears that only one randomised controlled trial has been performed in which only 90 patients with early Parkinson's disease were randomised to lisuride or lisuride/levodopa or levodopa and followed for about 4 years. The lisuride/levodopa combination group showed significantly less dyskinesia and motor fluctuations than the pure levodopa group. Insufficient numbers remained on pure monotherapy with lisuride for a conclusion to be drawn. Motor impairments and disability were no different between the groups. This relatively scant evidence with lisuride tends to confirm the trend with bromocriptine for agonist monotherapy/combination therapy causing fewer motor complications than levodopa treatment.

The manufacturers of the 'newer' dopamine agonists cabergoline, pergolide, pramipexole and ropinirole established individual trials with each agent versus levodopa as monotherapy in early disease. All of these studies are now complete but the results have been presented only in abstract form for two of the four trials.

The results that are available are summarised in Table 4.4. Monotherapy with all four agents produces significantly fewer motor complications than with levodopa used on its own. This corroborates the findings with bromocriptine and lisuride. However, this may have been achieved by effectively under-treating the patients with the agonist. In both the ropinirole and pramipexole studies, motor impairments measured with the UPDRS were worse in the agonist arms of the trials (Figure 4.2). However, these differences were small and UPDRS ADL scores were not significantly different in the ropinirole study (Figure 4.2b). Thus, it seems unlikely that under-treatment is the sole explanation for the reduction in complication rates. The tolerability of the agonists has been another contentious issue in monotherapy trials. Hallucinations were significantly worse with ropinirole and somnolence with pramipexole. Withdrawals caused by adverse events were greater with pergolide (18%) than levodopa (10%). Few data on quality of life or health-related quality of life are available from these trials. Data from the pramipexole study showed similar improvements in quality of life measured with the EuroQol and a novel disease-specific scale (PDQUALIF) for those treated with the agonist or levodopa up to the final 2-year assessment when the pramipexole group fared significantly worse (Parkinson Study Group 2000).

Remaining questions in the management of early Parkinson's disease

From the evidence presented above it can be seen that many fundamental questions remain to be answered regarding pharmacotherapy in early Parkinson's disease:

- Is levodopa toxic in vivo?
- Is agonist monotherapy as effective as levodopa in improving health-related quality of life?
- Dopamine agonist monotherapy reduces motor complications but is it cost-effective to change to agonists for all patients?
- Can agonist monotherapy reduce mortality?
- Which age groups should receive agonist monotherapy?
- How effective is selegiline monotherapy in improving quality of life compared with agonists and levodopa?
- Is selegiline cost-effective compared with agonist or levodopa monotherapy?
- Does initial selegiline monotherapy increase or decrease mortality?

Attempts are being made to resolve many of these issues. The UK PD MED Trial, based in the University of Birmingham Clinical Trials Unit, will examine a number of these questions (Figure 4.3). Between 1,500 and 3,000 patients with early Parkinson's disease will be randomised to any levodopa preparation, any dopamine agonist or any MAO B inhibitor. Those clinicians not willing to use an MAO B inhibitor can opt out of this randomisation. Similarly, those who are not willing to use levodopa in young cases can opt out of this randomisation for that individual patient.

Table 4.4 Results of individual trials of 'modern' agonist monotherapy versus levodopa

Agonist	Year	Reference	Design	Duration (years)	Number Ag	LD	Open label levodopa allowed	Incidence of motor complications Dyskinesia Ag	LD	Fluctuations Ag	LD
Cabergoline	U	Rinne (1999)	RCT Parallel groups DB	5	211	208	Yes	Onset of any complication 22% Ag vs 34% LD			
Pergolide	U	Oertel (2000)	RCT Parallel groups DB	3	148	146	No	Onset of any complication 16% Ag vs 33% LD			
Pramipexole	2000	Parkinson Study Group (2000)	RCT Parallel groups DB	2	151	150	Yes	10%	31%	24%	38%
Ropinirole	1999	Rascol (1999)	RCT Parallel groups DB	5	179	89	Yes	20%	46%	NA	NA

Ag, agonist; LD, levodopa; U, unpublished; DB, double-masked; NA, not available; RCT, randomised controlled trial.

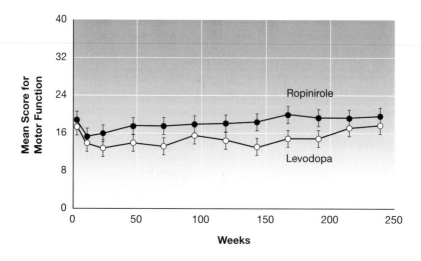

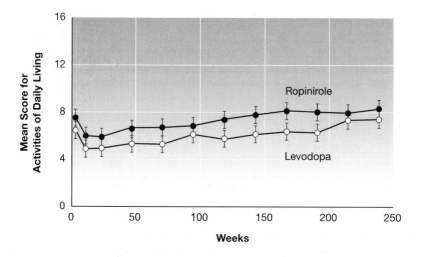

Figure 4.2 (a) UPDRS motor and **(b)** activities of daily living scores in the ropinirole versus levodopa study. (Redrawn from Rascol *et al*. 2000 with permission.)

The primary outcome measures will be quality of life (PDQ 39 and EuroQol) and health economics, but mortality and the incidence of motor complications will also be recorded. PD MED is a pragmatic 'real-life' trial which is likely to randomise older patients than usually enter PD trials, so it should provide information on the use of agonist monotherapy in older patients which is lacking at present.

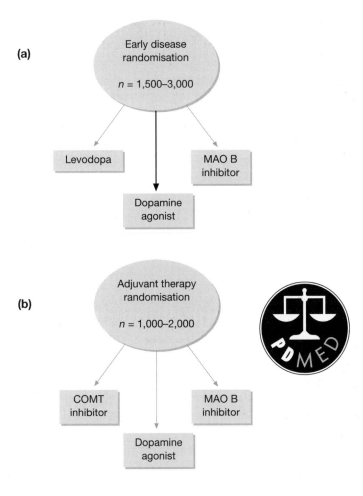

Figure 4.3 Design of the PD MED Trial. **(a)** Early disease randomisation and **(b)** adjuvant therapy randomisation. Stippled arrows indicate optional randomisation.

Later Parkinson's disease

Although the recent trend has been away from the use of levodopa monotherapy, if only in younger patients, a large proportion of patients are still given levodopa as their initial therapy, often only being referred to secondary care when motor complications have already arisen. At this stage, adjunctive therapy with a dopamine agonist, selegiline, or a catechol-O-methyltransferase (COMT) inhibitor is required. When such agents are used in this way the aims of treatment are to:

• reduce the amount of time the patient spends in the off phase

- reduce the dose of levodopa in the hope of reducing motor complications in the future
- improve motor impairments, disability and handicap
- achieve this with an acceptable increase in dyskinesia and other adverse events.

Dopamine agonists

The agonists were first evaluated as adjunctive therapy in later Parkinson's disease. A large number of published and unpublished randomised controlled trials have been performed which have recently been the subject of a number of Cochrane systematic reviews by the current author and others. These are now available on the Cochrane Library.

The review of adjuvant bromocriptine therapy versus placebo reported such heterogeneity in trial design and outcome that no conclusion on efficacy and safety could be reached (van Hilten *et al.* 1999). This finding calls into question the use of this agent in subsequent trials as the 'gold standard' agonist against which the more recent agonists have had to be compared.

Individual Cochrane reviews have compared the 'modern' dopamine agonists cabergoline (Clarke & Deane 2001a), pergolide (Clarke & Speller 1999c), pramipexole (Clarke *et al.* 2000a), and ropinirole (Clarke & Deane 2001c) with placebo in 1,596 patients in 11 randomised controlled trials. No placebo-controlled studies with lisuride were found (Clarke & Speller 1999a). Quantitative synthesis (i.e. meta-analysis) of the results of these trials showed the following:

- Significant improvement in off time with cabergoline, pergolide and pramipexole.
- Dyskinesia reported as an adverse event was significantly worse with all of the 'modern' agonists compared with placebo.
- Significant improvements were noted in the UPDRS motor and ADL scales in most trials with cabergoline and pramipexole, and in the Columbia scale with pergolide in the one randomised controlled trial where this was measured.
- Levodopa dose was significantly reduced with all 'modern' agonists.
- The adverse events of nausea, hallucinations and somnolence were significantly more frequent with the agonists.
- All-cause withdrawal rate was significantly lower with all of the 'modern' agonists.

It is clear from these results that cabergoline, pergolide, pramipexole and ropinirole are effective compared with placebo and measure up well to the demands of adjuvant therapy. Recent concerns about the occurrence of so-called 'sleep attacks' (Frucht *et al.* 1999) have prompted further analysis of somnolence as an adverse effect of these agonists, but more recent data show that daytime somnolence is an issue for around 75% of patients and that this and the sudden onset of sleep can occur with all dopaminergic agents (Ferreira *et al.* 2000).

Although placebo-controlled trials are mandatory for licensing purposes, the clinician is particularly interested in the effects of these 'modern' agonists against their forerunner bromocriptine. Thirteen bromocriptine-controlled trials (six unpublished) in 2,029 patients were located during the Cochrane systematic reviews (Clarke & Speller 1998; Clarke *et al.* 2000b; Clarke & Deane 2001b, 2001d), although the single bromocriptine-controlled study with lisuride was small and contained few relevant data (Clarke & Speller 1999b). Meta-analysis of these studies showed the following:

- A trend for more off time reduction with cabergoline, pramipexole and ropinirole individually, which reached statistical significance on meta-analysis of all of the trials (30 min less off time daily compared with bromocriptine).
- No difference between 'modern' agonists and bromocriptine was seen in dyskinesia, levodopa dose reduction or all-cause withdrawal rate, and no consistent differences in measures of motor impairment and disability were found.

Whether the additional benefit in off time reduction is worth the extra cost of the 'modern' agonists is debatable and cannot be resolved in the absence of further information on quality of life and health economics. To mount a further trial(s) to find such small differences between the agonists conclusively and to provide data on quality of life and health economics would require very large numbers of patients. It is likely that the costs in terms of time and financial outlay would be prohibitive. Therefore, choices regarding which agonist to use as adjuvant therapy must remain based on issues other than efficacy and safety such as dose frequency, ease of titration and affordability.

Selegiline

The author is not aware of any current systematic review of selegiline adjuvant therapy in later Parkinson's disease, although this is under way through the Cochrane Movement Disorders Group. The adjuvant selegiline studies were largely small placebo-controlled trials lasting for up to just 12 weeks and used various rating scales of motor impairments, but not off time. The author's view of this data is that selegiline produces:

- improvement in motor impairments.
- reduction in levodopa dose.

No data on health-related quality of life or health economics are available.

Although many clinicians feel that selegiline is not as effective as the dopamine agonists, there is no trial evidence to support this view.

Over the last few years, a novel type of selegiline has become available. The oral fast-melt Zydis preparation avoids first-pass metabolism in the liver and thus produces fewer amphetamine-like metabolites and possibly fewer side effects. Little trial evidence regarding safety and efficacy is available. In the largest trial to date (Shellenberger *et al.* 2000), 163 patients with severe motor fluctuations (>3 hours off time daily) were randomised to Zydis selegiline 1.25 mg/day, increasing after 6 weeks to 2.5 mg/day for 6 weeks, or placebo. The therapeutic gain (treatment effect minus placebo effect) in off time was significant compared with placebo at 5.4% (about 0.9 h) on 1.25 mg/day and 9.0% (about 1.4 h) on 2.5 mg/day. On and off phase motor UPDRS scores both improved significantly on Zydis selegiline and adverse events were acceptable. Further information on the effects of Zydis selegiline versus active comparitors is awaited.

Entacapone

In spite of combining levodopa with an AADC inhibitor, only 5–10% of the orally administered levodopa crosses the blood–brain barrier, most of the remainder being metabolised to 3O-methyldopa by the enzyme COMT. The COMT inhibitors entacapone and tolcapone act by reducing further peripheral levodopa metabolism, resulting in a 30–50% increase in levodopa half-life and a 25–100% increase in the levodopa concentration versus time curve while leaving the maximum plasma concentration of levodopa unchanged (Bonifati & Meco 1999). In addition, tolcapone has a central effect which may account for what is perceived in practice as its greater clinical efficacy. As a consequence of these actions, a high blood concentration of levodopa is available for longer, so more crosses the blood–brain barrier to produce a more prolonged effect.

Tolcapone was the first of these agents to be introduced into clinical practice. It was withdrawn in November 1998 from European Community countries after a number of cases of fatal hepatic toxicity. This situation continues to be reviewed annually in the light of further experience from North America, where it is still available although carefully monitored. As tolcapone is not currently available in the UK, further results on this agent are not presented.

A Cochrane systematic review of adjuvant therapy with both COMT inhibitors is currently under way. In the meantime, the author thinks that all of the entacapone placebo-controlled trials are detailed in Table 4.5 (Ruottinen & Rinne 1996; Parkinson Study Group 1997; Rinne *et al.* 1998; Deuschl *et al.* 1999; Sagar *et al.* 2000). These studies show that entacapone can:

- improve on time (treatment effect of 1.0–2.1 h/day)
- reduce off time (treatment effect of 1.3–1.5 h/day)
- reduce levodopa dose (treatment effect with 79–140 mg/day).

Insufficient data are available on activities of daily living and motor impairments to reach any firm conclusion. Entacapone generated standard dopaminergic adverse events which were reduced by levodopa dose reduction and both diarrhoea and

Table 4.5 Results of placebo-controlled adjuvant therapy trials with entacapone

Study	No. patients	Motor fluctuations	Design	Duration (weeks)	COMT inhibitor dose (mg/day)	Increase in on time (% treatment effect) (h)	Reduction in off time (% treatment effect) (h)	Reduction in levodopa dose (treatment effect in mg/day)	Improvement in UPDRS motor score in on phase (treatment effect)	Improvement in UPDRS ADL score in on phase (treatment effect)
Ruottinen and Rinne (1996)	26	Present	DB; placebo	4	800–1,200	23% (2.1)*	NA	140*	NA	NA
Parkinson Study Group (1997)	205	Present	DB; placebo	24	800–1,200	5% (1.0)*	NA	100*	2.4	1.1
Rinne et al. (1998)	171	Present	DB; placebo	24	800–2,000	13% (1.2)*	22% (1.3)*	102*	7.2*	1.3*
Deuschl et al. (1999)	301	Mixed	DB; placebo	24	400–2,000	(1.6‡)*	(1.5‡)*	NA	+*	+*
Sagar et al. (2000)	300	Mixed	DB; placebo	24	NA	+*	NA	79*	NA	NA

Treatment effect = outcome of treatment minus placebo outcome.
*Statistically significant compared with placebo or active comparitor.
‡Probably change from baseline rather than treatment effect.
DB, double-masked; NA, not available; ND, not done; +, improvement; =, no improvement compared with placebo or active comparitor.

discoloration of urine. Unlike tolcapone, no changes in liver function tests were found.

These results with entacapone are similar to those recorded with dopamine agonist adjuvant therapy. However, in clinical practice there is an impression that the agonists are more effective. There is no firm evidence to support this view at present.

Apomorphine

Apomorphine is a potent dopamine agonist which is extensively metabolised in the liver and thus has poor oral bioavailability. Its use as either a subcutaneous injection or infusion in late Parkinson's disease was first described in the late 1980s by Andrew Lees and Gerald Stern in London. The author is not aware of any systematic review of the data on apomorphine, which has largely been non-randomised and uncontrolled (Frankel *et al.* 1990). However, recent small placebo-controlled studies have confirmed the benefits of intermittent apomorphine injections (Hutton *et al.* 2000). The significant cost of apomorphine infusion therapy cannot be under-estimated at approximately £10,000 per patient per year, although this may be offset by reductions in other costs such as nursing home placement.

Recently, the use of continuous 'waking day' apomorphine infusions in patients with severe dyskinesia has been shown to reduce dyskinesia by 65% in severity and 85% in frequency and duration, suggesting that apomorphine infusion may be an alternative to surgical intervention for these patients (Colzi *et al.* 1998). Further randomised evidence is required before firm recommendations can be made in this area.

Remaining questions in the management of later Parkinson's disease

The following are the principal questions regarding drug therapy in later Parkinson's disease:

- Which agent is the most cost-effective when used as oral adjuvant therapy in later Parkinson's disease: a dopamine agonist, selegiline or entacapone?
- At what stage of the condition should apomorphine be used?
- Should apomorphine be used before surgical intervention?

The first of these issues will be addressed in the adjuvant therapy part of the PD MED Trial (Figure 4.3b): 1,500–3,000 patients with PD who have motor complications on levodopa therapy will be randomised to any dopamine agonist, any MAO B inhibitor or any COMT inhibitor. For patients already on an MAO B inhibitor, or for clinicians unwilling to use this class of drug, randomisation can be between the other two arms. Similarly, patients already on an agonist can be randomised between MAO B and COMT inhibitor therapy. The primary outcome measures will be quality of life (PDQ 39 and EuroQol) and health economics assessments.

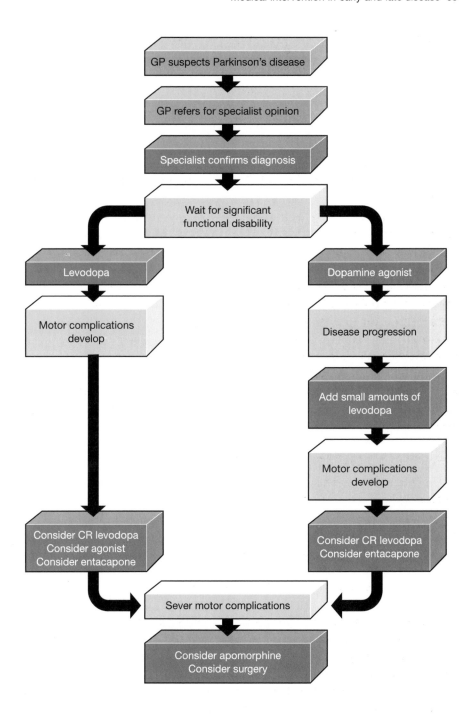

Figure 4.4 Treatment algorithm for Parkinson's disease based on guidelines prepared by a panel of UK-based opinion leaders. (Adapted from Bhatia *et al.* 1998.)

Conclusions

It will be clear from the above that systematic reviews of most drug therapies in Parkinson's disease have either been performed or are under way. So far, such reviews have identified gaps in our evidence base which must be filled by large pragmatic trials in the future.

In the meantime, much of the existing advice about prescribing practice is based on the advice of opinion leaders. Although such guidelines in Parkinson's disease have rarely been produced using rigorous methodology, they can be of some value in providing a rational approach to prescribing (Figure 4.4).

References

Bhatia K, Brooks D, Burn D *et al.* (1998). Guidelines for the management of Parkinson's disease. *Hospital Medicine* **59**, 469–480

Birkmayer W, Knoll J, Riederer P, Youdim MBH, Hars V, Marton J (1985). Increased life expectancy resulting from addition of L-deprenyl to Madopar treatment in Parkinson's disease: a long-term study. *Journal of Neural Transmission* **64**, 113–127

Block G, Liss C, Reines S, Irr J, Nibbelink D, Group TCFS (1997). Comparison of immediate-release and controlled-release carbidopa/levodopa in Parkinson's disease. *European Neurology* **37**, 23–27

Bonifati V & Meco G (1999). New, selective catechol-*O*-methyltransferase inhibitors as therapeutic agents in Parkinson's disease. *Pharmacological Therapeutics* **81**, 1–36

Clarke C, Deane K (2001a). Cabergoline for levodopa-induced complications in Parkinson's disease (Cochrane Review). *The Cochrane Library*, Vol 1. Oxford: Update Software

Clarke C & Deane K (2001b). Cabergoline versus bromocriptine for levodopa-induced complications in Parkinson's disease (Cochrane Review). *The Cochrane Library*, Vol 1. Oxford: Update Software

Clarke C & Deane K (2001c). Ropinirole for levodopa-induced complications in Parkinson's disease (Cochrane Review). *The Cochrane Library*, Vol 1. Oxford: Update Software

Clarke C & Deane K (2001d). Ropinirole versus bromocriptine for levodopa-induced complications in Parkinson's disease (Cochrane Review). The Cochrane Library. Vol 1. Oxford: Update Software

Clarke C & Sampaio C (1997). Movement Disorders Cochrane Collaborative Review Group. *Movement Disorders* **12**, 477–482

Clarke CE & Speller JM (1998). Pergolide versus bromocriptine for levodopa-induced motor complications in Parkinson's disease (Cochrane Review). *The Cochrane Library*, Vol 3. Oxford: Update Software

Clarke C & Speller J (1999a). Lisuride for levodopa-induced complications in Parkinson's disease (Cochrane Review). *The Cochrane Library*, Vol 2. Oxford: Update Software

Clarke C & Speller J (1999b). Lisuride versus bromocriptine for levodopa-induced complications in Parkinson's disease (Cochrane Review). *The Cochrane Library*, Vol 2. Oxford: Update Software

Clarke CE & Speller JM (1999c). Pergolide for levodopa-induced complications in Parkinson's disease (Cochrane Review). *The Cochrane Library*, Vol 2. Oxford: Update Software

Clarke C, Speller J, Clarke J (2000a). Pramipexole for levodopa-induced complications in Parkinson's disease (Cochrane Review). *The Cochrane Library*, Vol 3. Oxford: Update Software

Clarke C, Speller J, Clarke J (2000b). Pramipexole versus bromocriptine for levodopa-induced complications in Parkinson's disease (Cochrane Review). *The Cochrane Library*, Vol 3. Oxford: Update Software

Colzi A, Turner K, Lees AJ (1998). Continuous subcutaneous waking day apomorphine in the long-term treatment of levodopa-induced interdose dyskinesias in Parkinson's disease. *Journal of Neurology, Neurosurgery, and Psychiatry* **64**, 573–576

Deuschl G, Poewe W, Poepping M, The Celomen Study Group (1999). Efficacy and safety of entacapone as an adjunctive to levodopa treatment in Parkinson's disease: experience from the Austrian-German six months study. *Parkinsonism and Related Disorders* **5**(suppl), S75

Dupont E, Anderson A, Boas J *et al.* (1996). Sustained-release Madopar HBS compared with standard Madopar in the long-term treatment of de novo parkinsonian patients. *Acta Neurologica Scandinavica* **93**, 14–20

Fahn S (1998). Welcome news about levodopa, but uncertainty remains. *Annals of Neurology* **43**, 550–553

Fahn S (1999). Parkinson disease, the effect of levodopa, and the ELLDOPA trial. Earlier vs later L-DOPA [see comments]. *Archives of Neurology* **56**, 529–35

Ferreira JJ, Desboeuf K, Galitzky M *et al.* (2000). 'Sleep attacks' and Parkinson's disease: results of a questionnaire survey in a movement disorders outpatient clinic. *Movement Disorders* **15**(suppl 3), 187

Frankel JP, Lees AJ, Kempster PA, Stern GM (1990). Subcutaneous apomorphine in the treatment of Parkinson's disease. *Journal of Neurology, Neurosurgery, and Psychiatry* **53**, 96–101

Frucht S, Rogers JD, Greene PE, Gordon MF, Fahn S (1999). Falling asleep at the wheel: motor vehicle mishaps in persons taking pramipexole and ropinirole. *Neurology* **52**, 1908–1910

Hutton JT, Dewey RB, LeWitt PA, Factor SA (2000). A randomised double-blind placebo-controlled trial of subcutaneously injected apomorphine for parkinsonian off states. *Movement Disorders* 15(suppl 3), 130

Lees AJ, Parkinson's Disease Research Group of the United Kingdom (1995). Comparison of the therapeutic effects and mortality data of levodopa and levodopa combined with selegiline in patients with early, mild Parkinson's disease. *British Medical Journal* **311**, 1602–1607

Oertel WH (2000). Pergolide versus levodopa monotherapy (PELMOPET). *Movement Disorders* **15**(suppl 3), 4

Olanow CW, Hauser RA, Gauger L *et al.* (1995). The effect of deprenyl and levodopa on the progression of Parkinson's disease. *Annals of Neurology* **38**, 771–777

Parkinson Study Group (1989). Effect of deprenyl on the progression of disability in early Parkinson's disease. *New England Journal of Medicine* **321**, 1364–1371

Parkinson Study Group (1996). Impact of deprenyl and tocopherol treatment on Parkinson's disease in DATATOP patients receiving levodopa. *Annals of Neurology* **39**, 37–45

Parkinson Study Group (1997). Entacapone improves motor fluctuations in levodopa-treated Parkinson's disease patients. *Annals of Neurology* **42**, 747–755

Parkinson Study Group (1998). Mortality in DATATOP: a multicentre trial in early Parkinson's disease. *Annals of Neurology* **43**, 318–325

Parkinson Study Group (2000). Pramipexole versus levodopa as initial treatment for Parkinson's disease. *Journal of the American Medical Association* **284**, 1931–1938

Parkinson's Disease Research Group (1993). Comparisons of therapeutic effects of levodopa, levodopa and selegiline, and bromocriptine in patients with early, mild Parkinson's disease: three year interim report. *British Medical Journal* **307**, 469–472

Quinn N, Critchley P, Parkes D, Marsden CD (1986). When should levodopa be started? *Lancet* **ii**: 985–986

Rajput AH, Stern W, Laverty WH (1984). Chronic low-dose levodopa therapy in Parkinson's disease: an argument for delaying levodopa therapy. *Neurology* **34**, 991–996

Ramaker C & van Hilten J (1999a). Bromocriptine versus levodopa in early Parkinson's disease. *Parkinsonism and Related Disorders* **5**(suppl), 83

Ramaker C & van Hilten J (1999b). Bromocriptine/levodopa versus levodopa in early Parkinson's disease. *Parkinsonism and Related Disorders* **5**(suppl), 82

Rascol O (1999). Ropinirole reduces risk of dyskinesia when used in early Parkinson's disease. *Parkinsonism and Related Disorders* **5**(suppl), S83–S84

Rascol O, Brooks D, Korczyn A, De Deyn P, Clarke C, Lang A (2000). A five-year study of the incidence of dyskinesia in patients with early Parkinson's disease who were treated with ropinirole or levodopa. *New England Journal of Medicine* **342**, 1484–1491

Rinne U (1989). Lisuride, a dopamine agonist in the treatment of early Parkinson's disease. *Neurology* **39**, 336–339

Rinne UK (1999). A 5 year double blind study with cabergoline versus levodopa in the treatment of early Parkinson's disease. *Parkinsonism and Related Disorders* **5**(suppl), S84

Rinne U, Larsen JP, Siden A, Worm-Petersen J, The Nomecomt Study Group (1998). Entacapone enhances the response to levodopa in parkinsonian patients with motor fluctuations. *Neurology* **51**, 1309–1314

Ruottinen HM & Rinne UK (1996). Entacapone prolongs levodopa response in a one month double-blind study in parkinsonian patients with levodopa related fluctuations. *Journal of Neurology, Neurosurgery, and Psychiatry* **60**, 36–40

Sagar H, Brooks D, UK–Irish Entacapone Study Group (2000). The UK-Irish double-blind study of entacapone in Parkinson's disease. *Movement Disorders* **15**(suppl 3), 135

Shellenberger MK, Clarke A, Donoghue S (2000). Zydis selegiline reduces 'off' time and improves symptoms in patients with Parkinson's disease. *Movement Disorders* **15**(suppl 3), 116 van Hilten J, Ramaker C, van de Beek W, Finken M (1999). Bromocriptine for levodopa-induced motor complications in Parkinson's disease (Cochrane Review). *The Cochrane Library*, Vol 2. Oxford: Update Software

Verhagen-Metman L, Del Dotto P, van den Munckhof P, Fang J, Mouradian M, Chase T (1998). Amantadine as a treatment for dyskinesias and motor fluctuations in Parkinson's disease. *Neurology* **50**, 1323–1326

Scientific evidence and expert clinical opinion for surgical intervention in Parkinson's disease: criteria governing selection of patients and surgical procedures

Ian R Whittle

Introduction

Many patients with Parkinson's disease (PD) suffer from intractable tremor, drug-induced dyskinesia and severe motor fluctuations that are characterised by 'on' and 'off' periods. As these symptoms are either refractory to medical therapy or partly caused by it, and are disabling, functional neurosurgery is often performed. However, clinical surgical research has been described as 'comic opera . . . with results but no answers'. This is pertinent to neurosurgery for PD because there are only three randomised controlled trials that have examined the role of surgery (de Bie *et al.* 1999; Schuurmann *et al.* 2000; Freed *et al.* 2001) despite a multiplicity of surgical procedures that have evolved over almost 40 years (see Chapter 6). Furthermore, surgical attempts at either altering the course of the disease or ameliorating symptoms have been caught up in the enormous biological and technical advances that characterised the decade of the brain (Melton 2000). We therefore have a large amount of descriptive studies of functional neurosurgical procedures, either ablative or neurostimulatory, to various mesodiencephalic targets, as well as experimental treatments involving neurotransplantation of various neural tissues into varying diencephalic targets. The explosion in publications describing case series is paralleled by numerous reviews of the topic (Bhatia *et al.* 1998; Gross *et al.* 1999; Koller *et al.* 1999; Quinn 1999; Fields & Troster 2000; Follett 2000; Gross & Lozano 2000; Lang 2000) and consensus statements from various august bodies (Hallett *et al.* 2000) that have a direct interest in the management of parkinsonian patients.

As there are excellent recent reviews of this topic this chapter attempts to encapsulate their messages together with additional evidence that has been published in the last 12 months, rather than attempting another exhaustive review of functional surgery for PD. However, it is fair to say that there is no adequately powered, randomised controlled evidence that any particular surgical procedure in Parkinson's disease is superior to another. In the absence of 'evidence' expert opinion from various reviews, statements of august bodies and authoritative descriptive case series have been culled. As neurotransplantation is still undergoing major scientific review and refining, is an extremely complex area and is realistically still in its infancy (Gross *et al.* 1999; Brundin *et al.* 2000), no attempt is made at a thorough overview of all its dimensions, but allusion is made to a relatively recently published clinical trial and its implications (Freed *et al.* 2001; Fischbach & McKhann 2001).

Functional neurosurgery in Parkinson's disease

A conceptual overview

Functional neurosurgical procedures for PD have been done for nearly five decades. The rationale behind functional neurosurgery in PD is to alter neuronal function so that the signs and symptoms attributable to the disease are favourably modulated, resulting in an improved quality of life. The history of early brain surgery for PD has been well reviewed (Quinn 1999; Gross & Lozano 2000; Lang 2000) but over the last decade there has been a dramatic explosion in the knowledge concerning the circuitry underlying the pathophysiology of the disorder, and this has resulted in changes in emphasis from thalamic to current globus pallidum interna (GPi) and subthalamic nucleus (STN) targeting. Improvements in brain imaging software now allow either direct magnetic resonance imaging (MRI) of diencephalic subnuclei or image fusion of MRI and computed tomography (CT) data (Bejjani *et al.* 2000; Houeto *et al.* 2000). The latter obviate worries about geometrical distortion of the brain images by magnetic field inhomogeneity. In addition, fusion of the CT and MRI data can also be assisted by superimposition of stereotactic atlases of the human diencephalon which can be warped to match the geometry of the patients' fusion images. Subsequent displays outline theoretical sites of the diencephalic subnuclei. This enhances the accuracy of surgical targeting.

There is also the option with regard to the surgery being ablative or stimulatory. Although the precise physiological mechanisms of deep brain stimulation (DBS) are not clearly understood, in the last 4 years DBS has become the procedure of choice in many units (Gross & Lozano 2000), more so since a clinical trial has shown lower morbidity with this technique (Schuurman *et al.* 2000). Overall the trend away from brain lesioning to neurostimulation and increasing use of sophisticated neuroimaging has lead to reductions in the morbidity associated with surgery on targets that previously would have been considered too dangerous. Nevertheless the risk of haemorrhage associated with each lesion is estimated to be 3.3% (Rowe *et al.* 1999). Furthermore, many patients with PD may have neurological and systemic problems that continue to render them particularly vulnerable to surgical complications.

Factors in patient selection

Although there are now many options for functional surgery in PD, the most important factor in surgical outcome probably rests with selection of the correct patient (Bhatia *et al.* 1998; Benabid *et al.* 2000a). Ideally patients should be referred from neurologists or geriatricians with an interest in movement disorders. It is essential that parkinsonian-like syndromes have been excluded. The differential diagnosis includes essential tremor, arteriosclerotic pseudo-parkinsonism, progressive supranuclear palsy, Lewy body disease and multisystem atrophy. In the early phase of idiopathic PD many of the symptoms can be controlled by L-dopa, dopamine agonists, dopamine decarboxylase antagonists and other medication (see Chapter 4). However, in many patients symptoms eventually become refractory to conventional medications when pushed to their tolerance limits, or indeed medications may induce additional motor disorders such as levodopa-induced dyskinesias and dystonias. The latter are quite frequently a feature of drug-related motor fluctuations which are characterised by on and off periods. When patients reach this stage in their clinical syndrome, and clearly there will be differences of opinion between physicians about when management becomes 'refractory', as well as the role of subcutaneous apomorphine, they are often referred for a neurosurgical opinion.

Contraindications to surgery include loss of levodopa responsiveness, cognitive decline, hypophonia, anticoagulants and bleeding diathesis, and systemic disorders such as vascular hypertension and ischaemic heart disease. Extensive experience from the Toronto group with pallidotomy and both GPi and STN stimulation showed that patients with borderline cognitive or psychiatric functioning were at risk of postoperative decompensation (Trepanier *et al.* 2000). Most surgical series report better results in younger patients, although precise categorical age exclusion has not been defined (Favre *et al.* 2000; Houeto *et al.* 2000; Kubu *et al.* 2000; Freed *et al.* 2001). Given that the median duration of idiopathic PD is about 16 years this raises the difficult question of timing of referral. Clearly PD patients coming towards the end of the disease process are not going to respond as well as those patients who are relatively better, in the early years of their illness. Conversely, there is the question of whether younger patients should be referred for surgery earlier, because some workers believe that neurostimulation may have a neuroprotective benefit (AL Benabid, personal communication).

Before the advent of pallidal and subthalamic surgery, the predominant symptom for surgical referral was tremor. However, after the introduction of pallidotomy and subthalamic surgery, drug-induced dyskinesias and dystonias, motor fluctuations and freezing are all now also considered appropriate indications for surgery (de Bie *et al.* 1999). Patients with particularly long and difficult off periods, which are characterised by bradykinesia, profound rigidity and freezing, are potentially good candidates. Current evidence suggests that the on period is not likely to be significantly improved, other than the abolition of drug-induced dyskinesias, but that most benefit for the patient is derived by either shortening the off period or ablating some of the distressing symptoms associated with it (de Bie *et al.* 1999; Lang 2000).

Functional neurosurgical options

Thalamic surgery

The evidence that thalamic surgery can decrease the tremor associated with PD is overwhelming (Limousin *et al.* 1999; Lozano, 2000). For patients with tremor-dominant PD either DBS or thalamotomy is an effective operation; however, a recent trial has shown that DBS is safer (Schuurman *et al.* 2000). Thalamotomy should not be performed bilaterally as a result of the high incidence of side effects, particularly on swallowing, voice volume and motor control. Bilateral DBS can be performed but may be associated with not inconsiderable morbidity (Trepanier *et al.* 2000). Either thalamotomy or DBS is a simple operation to perform. However, there is now discussion about whether lesional or even DBS thalamic surgery should be performed because many patients will, later in the course of the disease, develop additional symptoms that may become refractory to medication (Lozano 2000). Pallidal and STN surgery seem to be effective at abolishing tremor but do require greater surgical precision, and seem to be major undertakings in a patient who is has only tremor (Limousin *et al.* 1999).

Pallidal surgery

The evidence that pallidal (GPi) surgery can abolish drug-induced dyskinesia and dystonia by around 50–70%, as well as decreasing tremor, bradykinesia and postural instability, is good (de Bie *et al.* 1999; Eskander *et al.* 2000; see also review by Alkhani & Lozano 2001). There are also subjective improvements in night sleep, muscle pain, freezing reductions and 'off' motor duration, and significant improvements in motor Unified Parkinson's Disease Rating Scale (UPDRS) scores in the off phase (UPDRS 3), extent of disability (UPDRS 2) and activity of daily living scores (de Bie *et al.* 1999; Favre *et al.* 2000). Walking speed is improved as a result of improvement in stride length (Siegel & Metman 2000). A randomised controlled trial (de Bie *et al.* 1999) showed significant benefits from unilateral lesional surgery compared with a control group at 6 months. The major benefit in the on state is a reduction in drug-induced dsykinesias. There are many anecdotal descriptive studies reporting similar findings (Table 5.1). Follow-up on selected groups of patients suggests improvements in off period motor features and on period dyskinesias suggest that benefits can be sustained (Baron *et al.* 2000; Fine *et al.* 2000).

The role of bilateral GPi lesional surgery is controversial. Some reports detail significant morbidity whereas others relate few problems (Scott *et al.* 1998; Favre *et al.* 2000). It would seem that there is a higher risk of postoperative speech deterioration with simultaneous bilateral procedures. Most consensus reports do not recommend bilateral pallidotomy (see below). Some detailed studies do, however, report considerable morbidity and operational mortality after even unilateral pallidotomy (Samuel *et al.* 1998). In addition, in 19 unilateral pallidotomies de Bie *et al.* (1999) described two major and seven minor adverse effects, and four had adverse effects at the 6-month assessment.

Table 5.1 Results of pallidotomy for Parkinson's disease

Series	n	'Off motor' (%)	Akinesia (%)	Dyskinesia (%)	F/U
Giller et al. (1998)	35	35	25	60	6/12
Scott et al. (1998)	18	27 (53% bilateral)	20	65	3/12
Samuel et al. (1998)	26	27	25	67	1 year
de Bie et al. (1999)	37	32	$p < 0.02$	50	6/12
Favre et al. (2000)	44	$p < 0.05$	$p < 0.05$	$p < 0.05$	7/12
Baron et al. (2000)	10	30	NS	64	4 years
Fine et al. (2000)	20	18	43	70	4 years

'Off motor' refers to improvement in function when off medication.
Dyskinesia relates to reduction in 'on' levodopa-induced dyskinesia.
F/U refers to follow-up.

The evidence that pallidal stimulation is equally effective is limited by the relatively small cases series published, but the extant literature reports similar results to those of pallidotomy (Table 5.2). The largest series (Kumar et al. 2000) reports a micro-pallidotomy effect from electrode insertion, and there were no serious adverse neurological events. Longer follow-up is also now being reported for cohorts with beneficial effects.

Table 5.2 Results of studies of pallidal stimulation for Parkinson's disease

Reference	n	H & Y	UPDRS 'off' (%)	Levodopa-induced dyskinesia (%)
Limousin et al. (1997)	6	30	40	Abolished
Volkmann et al. (1998)	9	–	44	Reduced
Tronnier et al. (1997)	6	NS	NS	variable
Krack et al. (1998)	8	–	35	−72
Pahwa et al. (1997)	5	30	28	−75
Burchiel et al. (1999)	5	?	40	$p < 0.05$
Kumar et al. (2000)	22	?	31	−66

Unified Parkinson;' Disease Rating Scale (UPDRS) refers to motor scores in the off phase.
H & Y refers to Hearn and Yahr score; generally these studies note improvements in gait (29%), rigidity (50%), and akinesia (25%).

Subthalamic surgery

One of the most interesting and exciting surgical developments of the last decade has been the evolution of surgery on this small mesodiencephalic nucleus (Benabid et al. 2000b). Experimental work in monkeys given MPTP (1-methyl-4-phenyl-1,2,3, 6-tetrahydropyridine) suggested that lesioning the STN can improve parkinsonian signs. Subsequently pioneering work by Benabid et al. (2000b) in Grenoble has established bilateral STN DBS as a viable option in PD patients with drug-induced dystonias and dyskinesia, bradykinesia, freezing, rigidity and postural problems. The findings from the Grenoble group of reductions in akinesia (42%), rigidity (49%)

and tremor (27%) have been duplicated in other centres (Table 5.3). In most series there is a considerable reduction in the medication requirements after surgery, and this has also contributed to the reduction in drug-induced side effects, especially dyskinesia and dystonia (Fraix *et al.* 2000). Surprisingly, given the strategic locality of the nucleus at the mesodiencephalic junction, reported morbidity has been extraordinarily low (Pinter *et al.* 1999; Houeto *et al.* 2000).

Table 5.3 Results of bilateral subthalamic nuclear stimulation for Parkinson's disease

There are consistent reductions in 'off' state as well as significantly improved motor functions characterised by improvements in gait, reduced tremor, rigidity and bradykinesis as well as decreased drug requirements. The changes in UPDRS 2 refers to reduction in the extent of disability.

	n	UPDRS 2	Bradykinesia (%)	Rigidity (%)	Tremor (%)	Dyskinesia (%)	Drugs (%)
Levesque et al. (1999)	9	$p < 0.05$	50	50 ?	$p < 0.05$	−50	
Pinter et al. (1999)	9	?	50	50	?	75	?
Benabid et al. (2000b)	60	50	42	49	27		
Molinuevo et al. (2000)	15	71	60	66	81	80	−80
Houeto et al. (2000)	23	?	67	67	?	77	−61
Bejjani et al. (2000)	12	?	64	78	?	83	−70

The role of subthalamic nucleotomy in severe motor fluctuation associated with PD is currently being explored by several units. However, series are few, the numbers generally small, follow-up short and publications with respect to motor outcomes are only abstracts. The difficulty with such lesioning is that the subthalamus is relatively small and adjacent to multiple important pathways so that inadvertent lesioning could cause significant and perhaps catastrophic neurological malfunctioning. As a result, lesions are often made that are relatively small but have an initial good effect. As the oedematous component of the lesion resolves and damaged neurons regain function, quite often the symptomatology associated with the motor fluctuations of PD returns. It would appear therefore that the operation is feasible but that there is an extremely fine balance between making a radiofrequency lesion that is large enough to have sustained beneficial effects but not associated with too many complications or side effects (SS Gill, personal communication). Some surgeons have performed repeat surgery. Obviously, this must be associated with some hazard and would be considered a suboptimal option. Nevertheless an initial study has documented few side effects (McCarter *et al.* 2000).

Neurotransplantation

Neurotransplantation for PD has undergone remarkable changes in the last decade. After an initial wave of hysterical publicity and unprecedented adoption of an experimental technique into clinical practice, the morbidity of adrenal medullary autografts was found to be prohibitive and the effects marginal. Subsequently there has been a shift to the use of fetal ventral mesencephalic donor graft transplanted into the putamen and caudate regions (Brudin *et al.* 2000). Variable results have been reported but many current studies are evaluating the optimal neural tissues to graft, the optimal donor site and mechanisms by which donor tissue viability can be extended (Brudin *et al.* 2000; Fischbach & McKhann 2001).

Recently the results of a randomised, double-masked, controlled trial have been published that examined transplants of fetal dopaminergic neurons into PD patients (Freed *et al.* 2001). This study was remarkable because patients were randomised to sham surgery (scalp incision and burrhole but no breech of the dura) or to receive implants of fetal mesencephalic tissue into both putamen. Using the primary outcome measure of subjective improvement, there was no significant benefit at 12 months after surgery. However, there were significant improvements in morning UPDRS and Schwab and England scores, before medication in transplanted patients aged under 60 years. There was, however, no other benefit and 15% of the transplanted patients developed refractory dystonia or dyskinesia. Interestingly 85% of patients showed either *post mortem* or ^{18}F-labelled fluorodopa (on positron emission tomography [PET]) evidence of fibre outgrowth and graft tissue survival, but this did not correlate with clinical outcome. This study should not lead to the discreditation of transplantation in PD patients because so many variables remain to be clarified in this field (Widner 1994). As a result of the many ethical and moral questions, as well as practical problems of provision of adequate fetal material (Fischbach & McKhann 2001), neuroscientists are evaluating cell lines genetically engineered to release dopamine (Melton 2000).

What are areas of current controversy?

At the start of the twenty-first century the place of surgical options in PD evokes several questions, all of which have been raised by previous reviewers, and put most cogently by Lang (2000). These include:

- Which patients are optimally treated by surgery?
- What is the optimal target for functional neurosurgery?
- Is ablative surgery better than neurostimulation?
- Does microelectrode recording make surgery safer and more effective?

- How safe is bilateral surgery?
- What are the side effects of functional surgery?
- What is the role of neurotransplantation in this disease today and in the future?
- How should outcome of neurosurgery for PD be assessed in a manner that creates neurological improvement but also considers impairment disability and handicap?

Unfortunately 'evidence'-based answers to most of these questions are likely to be slow in forthcoming as a result of provincial, personal and institutional biases.

What is the role of microelectrode recording in functional surgery for PD?

A major surgical technical consideration, which is the subject of controversy at present, is the role of microelectrode recordings before performing a surgical lesion or placing a deep brain electrode (Eskander *et al.* 2000; Guridi *et al.* 2000). Much has been learned of the human physiology of the human brain by microelectrode recording techniques of the capsule thalamus, pallidal and subthalamic regions. Using the fine needles required for microelectrode recording, small advances in the deep brain electrode can give rise to a host of electrode and neurophysiological information. However, such procedures are relatively time-consuming and require personnel and capital infrastructure to be optimally and usefully incorporated into the neurosurgical system. Much current functional neurosurgery is done using macroelectrode stimulation by which an electrode is passed into the brain of the awake patient and stimulation of an exposed electrode tip, possibly 1 mm in length and 1.5 mm in diameter, is undertaken and the effects on the patient observed directly. Using such techniques, the electrode can be stimulated at various frequencies and various amplitudes and the effects on hand movement, sensation, tone, speech and eye movement directly recorded. Although there are advocates of microelectrode surgery (Bejjani *et al.* 2000; Houeto *et al.* 2000; Benabid *et al.* 2000a, 2000b) there is by no means through either a consensus (de Bie *et al.* 1999; Eskander *et al.* 2000) or evidence (Carroll *et al.* 1998) that it is obligatory for optimal surgery. The leading centres (Grenoble and Toronto) do, however, use microelectrode guidance and have shown that it facilitates final electrode positioning (Guridi *et al.* 2000).

Lesional versus neurostimulatory surgery?

Before the early 1990s most surgery was ablative in that an electrode was passed into the brain, the stereotactic target identified and that area of the brain thermocoagulated by using a radiofrequency system. Some of the problems associated with such ablative surgery are that the lesion is irreversible, not titratable to the patient's symptomatology and involves destruction of neural tissues. Conversely, placement of a deep brain-stimulating electrode in the same position is not neurodestructive, allows reversible and programmable neurostimulation using variations in pulse width, pulse frequency and pulse amplitude, and perhaps, more importantly, enables bilateral surgery, which is required in many PD patients (Limousin *et al*. 1999; Gross & Lozano 2000).

The pioneer in this area has been Professor Alim Benabid and his talented multidisciplinary group from Grenoble who initially undertook thalamic deep brain stimulation for tremorigenic movement disorders; subsequently they undertook pallidal stimulation and, most recently and dramatically, they have pioneered bilateral subthalamic stimulation in parkinsonian patients (Limousin *et al*. 1999; Limousin-Dowsey *et al*. 1999). The results from this group are outstanding and set a standard that other neurosurgical groups must attempt to obtain. In their multiple publications, the group from Grenoble has shown that deep brain stimulation is effective and relatively safe and that the benefits are long lasting. Bilateral stimulation has also been shown to be effective and even surgery performed in patients who previously have had ablative procedures of the pallidum or thalamus can be undertaken relatively safely, albeit not as safely as in a 'virgin' patient.

The major problems associated with DBS are the cost of the electrodes and pulse generator systems (IPGs) and the requirement for replacement of the batteries at an indeterminable period (between 3 and 5 years) after the initial surgery. Programming of the system to optimise performance is also required. Quite clearly this requires a particular infrastructure and funding commitment. Nevertheless, the results with such surgery have been quite staggering, although not all groups obtain the same beneficial effects published by the Grenoble group. Notwithstanding the considerable financial and personnel implications of DBS the recent study by Schuurman suggesting, at least in the thalamus, that DBS is safer, it is likely that the ascendancy of DBS over lesional surgery will continue (Gross & Lozano 2000). Although several prospective controlled comparative studies of pallidal stimulation versus either GPi or STN stimulation have been performed, they lack any statistical power as a result of their small numbers (Table 5.4). The optimal surgical procedure therefore remains unknown.

Table 5.4 Comparative prospective, controlled trials or studies of one surgical procedure versus another for Parkinson's disease

			n	
Merello *et al*. (1999)	Unilateral	PVP vs PPVstim	13	NS
Burchiel *et al*. (1998)	Bilateral	PVP vs STNstim	10	NS
Levesque *et al*. (1999)	Unilateral	PVP vs STNstim	9	NS

All studies are fundamentally underpowered to detect any difference in beneficial effect.
PVP, posteroventral pallidotomy; STNstim, stimulation of the subthalamic nucleus.

Side effects of functional surgery and impact on cognition

Unilateral posteroventral pallidotomy can cause side effects such as drooling, decreased voice volume, problems with articulation, and impaired concentration with a subjective visual disturbances in 36% (de Bie *et al.* 1999; Favre *et al.* 2000). Word fluency can also be impaired, particularly after left-sided pallidotomy (Kubu *et al.* 2000). The incidence of permanent visual field defects varies between series from 1% to 8% (Eskander *et al.* 2000; Herrera *et al.* 2000). The incidence of documented side effects and complications varies enormously with each series from very low (Eskander *et al.* 2000) to very high (Samuel *et al.* 1998; de Bie *et al.* 1999). A recent meta-analysis of descriptive studies involving 1,959 patients noted an overall mortality rate at 0.4%, persistent side effects in 14% and major adverse side effects (e.g. hemiplegia, visual field defects, intracerebral haemorrhage) in 5.3% (Alkhani & Lozano 2001). Complications are more common with increasing age of PD onset and age at surgery (Kubu *et al.* 2000; Saint-Cyr *et al.* 2000; Trepanier *et al.* 2000).

Bilateral ablative surgery resulted in some catastrophic complications for many patients having thalamic procedures in the 1970s and 1980s. These are marked by incontinence, hypophonia, gait instability and difficulty swallowing. The high frequency of such problems has led to a general consensus that bilateral lesional thalamic should not be performed. There are also some problems with bilateral pallidal surgery. Although such lesions are usually made under MRI guidance, and with either micro- or macroelectrode control, major difficulties with speech volume, swallowing and fine motor function have been described, and subjective visual disturbances occurred in 41% (Favre *et al.* 2000). Given the data from the meta-analysis described above for unilateral pallidotomy, one would assume that morbidity would be greater for bilateral surgery whether performed simultaneously or as staged procedures (Alkhani & Lozano 2001)

There is also now an increasing awareness that the basal ganglia have roles in cognitive function which can be impaired in parkinsonian patients. Such problems are more common in older patients, and may be generally mild (Kubu *et al.* 2000). However, there can be non-lateralising attentional and hemispherical specific impairments of frontostriatal cognitive functions after unilateral pallidotomy, and 'frontal' behavioural dyscontrol may occur in up to 25% (Trepanier *et al.* 2000). Problems with planning, verbal memory and attention were documented after subthalamotomy, with greater deterioration occurring after left-sided surgery (McCarter *et al.* 2000). Transient depression was described in 15% of patients, and deterioration in many aspects of frontal executive functioning in more than 50% of elderly patients undergoing bilateral STN stimulation (Houeto *et al.* 2000; Saint-Cyr *et al.* 2000). A review of cognitive outcomes after DBS for PD suggests that the potential deficits are more than counterbalanced by the motor improvements (Fields & Troster 2000) and there are differences between GPi and STN stimulation (Jahanshahi *et al.* 2000; Trepanier *et al.* 2000). However, these workers noted that many factors remained to be determined such as the long-term effects of DBS, what predisposes to risk, the importance of laterality, effects of stimulation parameters and, perhaps most importantly, whether there could be any improvement in presurgical cognitive dysfunction with DBS.

What are the infrastructural requirements for surgery for PD?

Given that surgical treatment for PD must be performed within a multidisciplinary setting, and that either neurotransplantation or DBS will have important capital costs as well as requiring personnel and resource infrastructure, funding will have to be identified for centres of excellence that are going to undertake this surgery. Given the large number of patients with PD, the amount of surgery currently performed in the UK is relatively small. Whether this situation can be rectified by targeted government and health authority funding remains to be seen.

Another major issue is whether results that are obtained by such units with multidisciplinary support and expertise such as Grenoble and Toronto can be attained in centres beginning such surgery, without the infrastructural and personal expertise available there. Even within the UK, this raises the question of whether outcomes may differ between 'top-grade' and 'second-tier' units that are performing such surgery. How to audit patients having equity of service and excellence needs to be evaluated and addressed. Ideally all units, which must offer a multidisciplinary PD management strategy, would adopt dedicated and comprehensive assessment protocols addressed to answer specific questions about the role of surgery in PD. This approach would also address the inconsistency and bias introduced in non-masked, non-prospective clinical studies, and allow shortcomings or differences in performance between centres to be identified and addressed. In addition, not only patient impairment but also patient handicap and disability should be included in assessments.

Conclusions

From the extant literature on functional neurosurgery for PD, it is possible to conclude that for patients still responsive to levodopa therapy neurostimulation is safer than ablative procedures to the thalamus (for the treatment of tremor). However, whether there is a continued role for thalamic surgery in PD is uncertain. Lesional or DBS surgery in the GPi is effective for drug-induced dyskinesia, and off period bradykinesis, rigidity and tremor; bilateral ablative surgery to the GPi can be hazardous. Bilateral stimulation of the STN is a promising treatment for many motor features as well as enabling reduction of medication dosage. Subthalamic nucleotomy is currently being evaluated but there are no publications about motor outcomes. Although one randomised prospective clinical trial has shown no benefit from neurotransplantation with fetal cells, there remain many scientific and clinical issues that need to be overcome before successful use of neurotransplantation. Relative contraindications to surgery are advanced age, cognitive dysfunction, voice dysfunction and parkinsonian 'plus' syndromes. The major surgical unknowns at this stage, given that categories of surgical responses have now been identified, are when surgery should be performed, which target (pallidal or STN) is best and safest to stimulate, how long the beneficial effects of surgery last and whether results from centres of excellence, with their multidisciplinary well-resourced facilities, can be reproduced at the average UK neuroscience unit. Answering these questions requires prospective, randomised, multicentre, controlled trials, and a national minimal database about outcome for parkinsonian patients treated at the various centres performing functional neurosurgery. Without adequate planning and investment, to provide the necessary infrastructure, the UK will not make significant contributions to solving these questions.

References

Alkhani A, Lozano AM (2001). Pallidotomy for Parkinson disease: a review of contemporary literature. *Journal of Neurosurgery* **94**, 43–49

Baron MS, Vitek JL, Bakay RA *et al.* (2000). Treatment of advanced Parkinson's disease by unilateral posterior GPi pallidotomy: 4-year results of a pilot study. *Movement Disorders* **15**, 230–237

Bejjani BP, Dormont D, Pidoux B *et al.* (2000). Bilateral subthalamic stimulation for Parkinson's disease by using three-dimensional stereotactic magnetic resonance imaging and electrophysiological guidance. *Journal of Neurosurgery* **92**, 615–625

Benabid AL, Krack PP, Benazzouz A, Limousin P, Koudsie A, Pollak P (2000a). Deep brain stimulation of the subthalamic nucleus for Parkinson's disease: methodologic aspects and clinical criteria. *Neurology* **55**: S40–4

Benabid AL, Koudsie A, Benazzouz A *et al.* (2000b). Subthalamic stimulation for Parkinson's disease. *Archives for Medical Research* **31**, 282–289

Bhatia K, Brooks DJ, Burn DJ *et al.* (1998). Guidelines for the management of Parkinson's disease. *Hospital Medicine* **59**, 469–480

Brudin P, Pogarell O, Hagell P *et al.* (2000). Bilateral caudate and putamen grafts of embryonic mesencephalic tissue treated with lazaroids in Parkinson's disease. *Brain* **123**, 1380–1390

Burchiel KJ, Anderson VC, Favre J, Hammerstad JP (1999). Comparison of pallidal and subthalamic nucleus deep brain stimulation for advanced Parkinson's disease: results of a randomized, blinded pilot study. *Neurosurgery* **45**, 1375–1382; discussion 1382–1384.

Carroll CB, Scott R, Davies LE, Aziz T (1998). The pallidotomy debate. *British Journal of Neurosurgery* **12**, 146–150

de Bie RM, de Haan RJ, Nijssen *et al.* (1999). Unilateral pallidotomy in Parkinson's disease: a randomised, single-blind, multicentre trial. *Lancet* **354**, 1665–1669

Eskander EN, Shinobu LA, Penney JB Jr, Cosgrove GR, Counihan TJ (2000). Stereotactic pallidotomy performed without using microelectrode guidance in patients with Parkinson's disease: surgical technique and 2-year results. *Journal of Neurosurgery* **92**, 375–383

Favre J, Burchiel KJ, Taha JM, Hammerstad J (2000). Outcome of unilateral and bilateral pallidotomy for Parkinson's disease: patient assessment. *Neurosurgery* **46**, 344–353

Fields JA & Troster AI (2000). Cognitive outcomes after deep brain stimulation for Parkinson's disease: a review of initial studies and recommendations for future research. *Brain Cognition* **42**, 268–293

Fine J, Duff J, Chen R *et al.* (2000). Long-term follow-up of unilateral pallidotomy in advanced Parkinson's disease. *New England Journal of Medicine* **342**, 1708–1714

Fischbach GD & McKhann GM (2001). Cell therapy for Parkinson's disease. *New England Journal of Medicine* **344**, 763–765

Follett KA (2000). The surgical treatment of Parkinson's disease. *Annual Review of Medicine* **51**, 135–147

Fraix V, Pollak P, Van Blercom N, Xie J, Krack P, Koudsie A, Benabid AL (2000). Effect of subthalamic nucleus stimulation of levodopa-induced dyskinesia in Parkinson's disease. *Neurology* **55**, 192–193

Freed CR, Green PE, Breeze RE *et al.* (2001). Transplantation of embryonic dopamine neurons for severe Parkinson's disease. *New England Journal of Medicine* **344**, 710–719

Giller CA, Dewey RB, Ginsburg MI, Mendelsohn DB, Berk AM (1998). Stereotactic pallidotomy and thalamotomy using individual variations of anatomic landmarks for localization. *Neurosurgery* **42**, 56–62

Gross RE, Boraud T, Guehl D, Bioulac B, Bezard E (1999). From experimentation to the surgical treatment of Parkinson's disease: prelude or suite in basal ganglia research? *Progress in Neurobiology* **59**, 509–532

Gross RE & Lozano AM (2000). Advances in neurostimulation for movement disorders. *Neurological Research* **22**, 247–258

Guridi J, Rodriguez-Oroz MC, Lozano AM *et al.* (2000). Targeting the basal ganglia for deep brain stimulation in Parkinson's disease. *Neurology* **55**(suppl 6), S21–S28

Hallett M, Litvan I & Members of Task Force for Surgery for Parkinson's Disease of the American Academy of Neurology Therapeutic and Technology. Assessment Committee (2000). Scientific position paper of the Movement Disorder Society Evaluation of Surgery for Parkinson's Disease. *Movement Disorders* **15**, 436–438

Herrera EJ, Viano JC, Caceres M, Costello G, Suarez M, Suarez JC (2000). Posteroventral pallidotomy in Parkinson's disease. *Acta Neurochirurgica (Wien)* **142**, 169–175

Houeto JL, Damier P, Bejjani BP *et al.* (2000). Subthalamic stimulation in Parkinson disease: a multidisciplinary approach. *Archives of Neurology* **57**, 461–465

Jahanshahi M Ardouin CM, Brown RG *et al.* (2000). The impact of deep brain stimulation on executive function in Parkinson's disease. *Brain* **123**, 1142–1154

Koller WC, Pahwa R, Lyons KE, Albanese A (1999). Surgical treatment of Parkinson's disease. *Journal of Neurological Science* **167**, 1–10

Krack P, Pollak P, Limousin P, Hoffmann D, Xie J, Benazzouz A, Benabid AL (1998). Subthalamic nucleus or internal pallidal stimulation in young onset Parkinson's disease. *Brain* **121**, 451–457

Kubu CS, Grace GM, Parrent AG (2000). Cognitive outcome following pallidotomy: the influence of side of surgery and age of patient at disease onset. *Journal of Neurosurgery* **92**, 384–9

Kumar R, Lang AE, Rodriguez-Oroz MC *et al.* (2000). Deep brain stimulation of the globus pallidus pars interna in advanced Parkinson's disease. *Neurology* **55**(suppl 6), S34–S39.

Lang AE (2000). Surgery for Parkinson disease. A critical evaluate of the state of the art. *Acta Neurologica* **57**, 1118–1125

Lang AE, Duff J, Saint-Cyr *et al.* (1999). Posteroventral medial pallidotomy in Parkinson's disease. *Journal of Neurology* **246**(suppl 2), 1128–1141

Levesque MF, Taylor S, Rogers R, Le MT, Swope D (1999). Subthalamic stimulation in Parkinson's disease. Preliminary result. *Stereotactic and Functional Neurosurgery* **72**, 170–173

Limousin P, Greene J, Pollak P, Rothwell J, Benabid AL, Frackowiak R (1997). Changes in cerebral activity pattern due to subthalamic nucleus or internal pallidum stimulation in Parkinson's disease. *Annals of Neurology* **42**, 283–291

Limousin P, Speelman JD, Gielin F, Janssens M (1999). Multicentre European study of thalamic stimulation in Parkinsonian and essential tremor. *Journal of Neurology, Neurosurgery and Psychiatry* **66**, 289–296

Limousin-Dowsey P, Pollak P, Van Blercom N, Krack P, Benazzouz A, Benabid A (1999). Thalamic, subthalamic nucleus and internal pallidum stimulation in Parkinson's disease. *Journal of Neurology* **246**(suppl 2), 1142–1145

Lozano AM (2000).Vim thalamic stimulation for tremor. *Archives of Medical Research* **31**, 266–269

McCarter RJ, Walton NH, Rowan AF, Gill SS, Palomo M (2000). Cognitive functioning after subthalamic nucleotomy for refractory Parkinson's disease. *Journal of Neurology, Neurosurgery, and Psychiatry* **69**, 60–66

Melton L (2000).Neural transplantation: new cells for old brains. *The Lancet* **355**, 2142

Merello M, Nouzeilles MI, Kuzis G *et al.* (1999). Unilateral radiofrequency lesion versus electrostimulation of posteroventral pallidum: a prospective randomized comparison. *Movement Disorders* **1**, 50–56

Molinuevo JL, Valldeoriola F, Tolosa E *et al.* (2000). Levodopa withdrawal after bilateral subthalamic nucleus stimulation in advanced Parkinson disease. *Archives of Neurology* **57**, 983–8

Pahwa R, Wilkinson S, Smith D, Lyons K *et al.* (1997). High-frequency stimulation of the globus pallidus for the treatment of Parkinson's disease. *Neurology* **49**, 249–253

Pinter MM, Alesch F, Murg M, Seiwald M, Helscher RJ, Binder H (1999). Deep brain stimulation of the subthalamic nucleus for control of extrapyramidal features in advanced idiopathic Parkinson's disease: one year follow-up. *Journal of Brain Transmission* **106**, 693–709

Quinn N (1999). Progress in functional neurosurgery for Parkinson's disease. *The Lancet* **354**, 1658–1659

Rowe JG, Davies LE, Scott R, Gregory R, Aziz TZ (1999). Surgical complications of functional neurosurgery treating movement disorders: results with anatomical localisation. *Journal of Clinical Neuroscience* **6**, 36–37

Saint-Cyr JA, Trepanier LL, Kumar R, Lozano AM, Lang AE (2000). Neuropsychological consequences of chronic bilateral stimulation of the subthalamic nucleus in Parkinson's disease. *Brain* **123**, 2091–2108

Samuel M, Caputo E, Brooks DJ, Schrag A, Scaravilli T (1998). A study of medial pallidotomy for Parkinson's disease: clinical outcome, MRI location and complications. *Brain* **121**, 59–75

Schmand B, de Bie RM, Koning-Haanstra M, de Smet JS, Speelman JD, van Zomeren AH (2000). Unilateral pallidotomy in PD: a controlled study of cognitive and behavioural effects. The Netherlands Pallidotomy Study (NEPAS) group. *Neurology* **54**, 1058–1064

Schuurman PR, Bosch DA, Bossyt PM, Bonsel GJ *et al.* (2000). A comparison of thalamic stimulation and thalamotomy for suppression of severe tremor. *New England Journal of Medicine* **342**, 461–468

Scott R, Gregory R, Hines N *et al.* (1998). Neuropsychological, neurological and functional outcome following pallidotomy for Parkinson's disease. A consecutive series of eight simultaneous bilateral and twelve unilateral procedures. *Brain* **121**, 659–675

Siegel KL & Metman LV (2000). Effects of bilateral posteroventral pallidotomy on gait of subjects with Parkinson disease. *Archives of Neurology* **57**, 198–204

Trepanier LL, Kumar R, Lozano AM, Lang AE, Saint-Cyr JA (2000). Neuropsychological outcome of GPi pallidotomy and GPi on STN deep brain stimulation in Parkinson's disease. *Brain and Cognition* **42**, 324–347

Tronnier VM, Fogel W, Kronenbuerger M, Krause M, Steinvorth S (1997). Is the medial globus pallidus a site for stimulation or lesioning in the treatment of Parkinson's disease? *Stereotactic and Functional Neurosurgery* **69**(2), 62–68

Volkmann J, Sturm V, Weiss P, Kappler J, Voges J, Koulousakis A, Lehrke R, Hefter H, Freund HJ (1998). Bilateral high-frequency stimulation of the internal globus pallidus in advanced Parkinson's disease. *Annals of Neurology* **44**, 953–961

Widner H (1994). NIH neural transplantation funding. *Science* **263**, 737

A systematic review of surgical trials of lesioning and deep brain stimulation for Parkinson's disease

Rebecca Stowe

Introduction

The past decade has witnessed a resurgence of functional stereotactic neurosurgery for the management of Parkinson's disease (PD). This renaissance follows the successful introduction of surgical procedures for PD in the 1950s and their subsequent large-scale abandonment with the advent of levodopa and other dopaminergic agents in the 1960s. In the mid-1980s, renewed interest was prompted by increasing recognition of the limitations of drug therapy, increased understanding of the pathophysiology of the basal ganglia, coupled with major advances in neuroimaging and enhanced surgical techniques.

Currently, stereotactic neurosurgical operations for PD are performed at three sites: the thalamus, globus pallidus (GP) and subthalamic nucleus (STN); they involve either lesioning or deep brain 'stimulation' (DBS). Both methods are stereotactic neurosurgical procedures, which involve fixing a frame to the patient's skull under local anaesthesia and mild sedation. The brain is then imaged using computed tomography (CT), magnetic resonance imaging (MRI) or intraoperative ventriculography, in which contrast medium is injected into the ventricles. All of these imaging methods allow the precise localisation of target structures in the brain. A small hole is then drilled in the skull and a cannula inserted. The procedures differ in which part of the brain is targeted and what is done to them. The aim of ablative procedures and DBS is to reduce or eliminate the abnormal output discharges from the basal ganglia to the cortex and brain stem, although the underlying neurodegenerative process remains unmodified; these are therefore treatments of symptoms.

Lesioning involves destruction of the appropriate target brain structure using a high-frequency electric current. This lesion should be large enough to provide long-term benefit but small enough to avoid irreversible neurological deficits. DBS is essentially identical to lesioning except for the final part when the stimulating electrode is placed in the target instead of making a lesion. As DBS mimics the effects of a lesion, it is probable that the high-frequency stimulation used results in inhibition of neurons surrounding the electrode tip. Lesions have the advantage that the effects are permanent, but morbidity might be higher than with DBS. Stimulation is reversible but is much more costly and requires multiple postoperative visits to tune the stimulator and, in due course, indefinitely for periodic battery replacement.

Fetal nigral cell grafting offers an alternative surgical option, attempting to replace the dopaminergic deficit in PD by placing dopaminergic cells in the striatum. The intention is to compensate for degeneration of lost nigral neurons, thereby arresting progression of the disease. However, the use of human fetal tissue transplantation has been limited by ethical and logistical (shortage of tissue) issues. For more detail on the surgical options available for PD and factors in patient selection, the reader is referred to Chapter 5.

This chapter does not aim to provide another review of the results of surgery for PD nor does it attempt to provide guidelines for the recommended management of PD; indeed there are already many excellent reviews available (Goetz *et al.* 1993; Koller *et al.* 1998, 1999; Starr *et al.* 1998; Gross *et al.* 1999; Quinn 1999; Follett 2000; Lang 2000; Utti 2000) as well as a number of guideline documents and consensus statements produced from various working groups for the management of PD (Clough 1991; Koller 1994; Bhatia *et al.* 1998; Hallett & Litvan 1999, 2000).

This chapter aims to provide an evidence-based 'overview' of the studies involving stereotactic neurosurgery that have been conducted in this field over the past decade and the new directions in which this area is going. In particular it aims to look at the quality of the evidence that currently exists and demonstrate that current evidence is based on a huge number of publications, describing mostly uncontrolled case series, and that there is no adequate evidence from the few randomised controlled trials (RCTs) that have been undertaken.

Methods for identifying studies of surgery for Parkinson's disease

The data in this chapter are based on a systematic search of the literature for publications between 1990 and March 2002; this time period covers the recent renewed interest in surgical procedures for the management of PD. For systematic reviews, the Cochrane Library, NHS Centre for Reviews and Dissemination and Health Technology Assessment databases were searched. For primary research a number of databases were searched including Medline (Ovid version), Embase (Ovid version), PubMed and the Web of Science. Major journals in the field were hand searched for relevant material. These included *Movement Disorders*, *Parkinsonism and Related Disorders*, *Neurology* and *Journal of Neurology, Neurosurgery, and Psychiatry*. This hand searching also involved searching conference proceedings to identify presentations made at meetings. Experts in the field were contacted in an attempt to identify studies not identified by electronic and hand searching (including material presented at conferences and seminars), and trials in process that have not been formally published. Research registers including the National Research Register (NRR), Controlled Clinical trials, PD Clinical Studies, ClinicalTrials.gov, Computer Retrieval of Information on Scientific Projects (CRISP) and HSRProj were searched to identify ongoing research. Additional information was sought from scanning reference lists of already retrieved papers, in particular review papers and websites relating to PD.

Studies were included if they assessed one or more neurosurgical procedures for the treatment of PD, included patients with advanced idiopathic Parkinson's disease and measured clinical outcomes rather than scientific observations. No restrictions were made on study design because the aim was to produce a very broad picture of the quantity and quality of evidence that exists.

The search terms that were used to retrieve studies included (Parkinson or Parkinson's and disease or Parkinson*), lesion*, (stimulat* or neurostimulat* or deep brain stimula* or DBS), (Stereotax* or Stereotac*), (Globus pallid* or Pallidotomy or Pallid*), (Thalamotomy or Thalam*), (Subthalam* or Sub-thalam* or Subthalamotomy or Sub-thalamotomy). RCTs were identified by combining these last search terms with the Cochrane search strategy specifically developed for the identification of RCTs (Dickersin & Larson 1996). All papers on potential RCTs were obtained, but only abstracts were used to evaluate the non-randomised studies because of the large number of studies. For all non-randomised studies, information on patient numbers and length of follow-up where possible were abstracted from abstracts only; otherwise the full paper was obtained.

Published trials of surgery for Parkinson's disease

The systematic literature search conducted in this study demonstrated that the great majority of studies looking at surgery for PD have been small, non-randomised, evaluation studies, most of which are case series. This observation is supported by a number of systematic reviews, which provide summaries of the existing evidence and make recommendations based on the quality of the available evidence (Robert 1996; Harstall & Hailey 1997; Kottler & Hayes 1998; Gregory & Bowen 1999; Nicholson & Milne 1999).

The majority (87%) of the studies identified in the present review involve reports of a single surgical intervention such as pallidotomy. Studies of more than one intervention included those containing two or more series of patients undergoing different surgical procedures that were not necessarily compared, and also comparative studies comparing different techniques in the same brain area or the same technique in different brain areas or both.

Table 6.1 demonstrates that almost 11,000 patients have been included in more than 500 reported studies, with an average of approximately 22 patients per study. Only 2.4% of the studies involve 100 or more patients and only 9% involve 50 or more. Therefore, the great majority (91%) of studies involve fewer than 50 patients and almost half of these studies (47%) involve 10 or fewer patients. There have also been many isolated case reports. Of the relatively few studies that have included large patient numbers (more than 100), 60% of these are studies of pallidotomy (Iacono *et al.* 1995a, 1995b; Laitinen 1995; Hariz & De Salles 1997; Shinobu *et al.* 1998). The remaining 40% of studies include one study of thalamic stimulation (Limousin *et al.* 1999) and studies of more than one intervention (Benabid *et al.* 1994, 1998; Laitinen 1994). Importantly, these statistics are based on reported findings; the actual number of PD patients who have been included in studies worldwide will be much higher. Making a conservative estimate that only one in ten such patients are reported, the total figure is likely to be tenfold higher – representing a very large number of patients.

Table 6.1 Summary data for non-randomised surgical studies for Parkinson's disease

Technique and site	Total no. of studies	Total no. of patients	Average no. of patients per study	Average duration of follow-up per patient (months)
Single procedure studies				
Lesioning				
Globus pallidus	153	4,358	28	12.9
Thalamus	19	562	30	32.0
Subthalamic nucleus	15	162	11	18.0
Subtotal	187	5,082	27	15.2
Deep brain stimulation				
Globus pallidus	46	417	9	10.5
Thalamus	61	1,044	7	16.7
Subthalamic nucleus	136	1,868	14	12.6
Subtotal	243	3,329	14	13.9
Total	430	8,411	20	14.7
Studies of more than one intervention/comparative studies				
Total	71	1,736	35	13.9
Overall total	501	8,989	22	14.3

These studies are also characterised by relatively short-term follow-up. Overall there is considerable variation in the duration of patient follow-up, ranging from hours to years. The present review found that average follow-up was 14 months per patient, with only 23% of studies evaluating patients for more than 12 months. Very few studies have followed patients up for 5 or more years (e.g. Diederich *et al.* 1992; Benabid *et al.* 1993; Taha *et al.* 1997; Moriyama *et al.* 1999; Hariz & Bergenheim 2001). Furthermore the average length of follow-up reported in the present study is likely to be slightly overestimated, because many studies report a range for the follow-up period, e.g. 6–24 months, in which case the upper limit was recorded for this study. By reporting the results at a follow-up duration where the benefits are likely to be maximal, an over-optimistic impression of the true benefit of surgery might be obtained.

There are obviously exceptions to the general statement that these studies are characterised by small patient numbers and short-term follow-up. There have been studies with large patient numbers and long-term follow-up but, interestingly, the data show that large patient numbers are not necessarily associated with longer follow-up. Only 2% of studies have included more than 50 patients and have followed them up for more than 12 months (e.g. Benabid *et al.* 1993; Young *et al.* 1998; Moriyama *et al.* 1999; Lai *et al.* 2000). It thus appears that very few studies have both large numbers and long patient follow-up.

Although these studies demonstrate that surgery is clearly beneficial for some patients in the short term, it is impossible to assess reliably the long-term role of surgery from such small non-randomised studies. The studies offer a relatively weak study design that does not provide strong evidence of effectiveness. Although such series can suggest relationships between interventions and outcomes, they are inappropriate for generating unbiased evidence about size of benefits and adverse effects. This is caused, for example, by the potential for substantial selection bias among the patients included, the lack of comparative control groups and because small series, which look promising, are more likely to be reported than those that look unpromising ('publication bias'). Indeed there is a statistically significant association between significant results and publication (e.g. Dickersin *et al.* 1992). The validity of conclusions regarding the safety and efficacy of scientific interventions is threatened by knowledge that fails to be disseminated. If this failure to publish research findings were a random event, the pool of information would be unbiased, albeit somewhat limited. However, this does not appear to be the case and failure to publish results is not a random event. Several studies have shown that publication is dramatically influenced by the direction and strength of research findings (Dickersin *et al.* 1992; Dickersin 1997). Furthermore, an even stronger relationship between significant results and publication has been observed for clinical trials (Dickersin 1997). It is interesting that publication bias originates primarily with investigators and not journal editors (Dickersin *et al.* 1992). Development of registration systems for clinical trials would be one way of minimising this bias.

Generally, the overall quality of studies is poor as is the level of reporting. A number of the systematic reviews identified in this study highlight the severe methodological problems associated with most studies evaluating surgery for PD (e.g. Kottler & Hayes 1998; Nicholson & Milne 1999). Thus, many studies poorly define patient selection criteria, inadequately describe patient characteristics and do not use masked assessment. Only a few studies have used masked assessments of the effects of surgery on PD (e.g. Lozano *et al.* 1995; Koller *et al.* 1997; Galvez-Jimenez *et al.* 1998; Kumar *et al.* 1998; Ondo *et al.* 1998). For many studies it is also difficult to determine the completeness of follow-up, which makes it hard to determine the level and duration of benefit. Furthermore, outcome measures are often inadequately described in the methods section and results inconsistently reported compared with the methods section. Further difficulties in interpreting these studies arise from the wide variation in the methods of performing the interventions and the choice of target even within broad intervention categories.

Evaluation of PD patients is typically carried out by means of clinician-based rating assessments of neurological signs and disability, which fail to assess the impact of the disease on health-related quality of life. It is particularly difficult to translate outcomes from individual subscales into changes that are meaningful to patients. PD, in its advanced stages, is complicated by additional problems such as depression, dementia and sleep disturbances (Lees *et al*. 1988; Cummings 1992; Arsland *et al*. 1996), which may have much greater impact on the patient's quality of life than the cardinal features of PD. Although many trials report relief of symptoms of PD, reliable, validated quality-of-life measures have rarely been used in trials to date.

At present, surgery for PD is based on a strong consensus of class III evidence, which is evidence, provided by expert opinion, non-randomised historical controls or case reports of one or more patients (Table 6.2) (Hallett & Litvan 1999, 2000). The second study is a report of the Therapeutics and Technology Assessment Subcommittee of the American Academy of Neurology. This report summarises that, in selected cases, thalamotomy and DBS of the thalamus can safely and effectively control tremor although they are not effective in treating bradykinesia, which is considered the major disability in most PD patients. Unilateral pallidotomy is effective for severe dyskinesias and motor fluctuations, but the use of bilateral pallidotomy is limited by its substantial risk. Pallidal DBS is still under investigation, although results seem favourable in PD patients with severe fluctuations and dyskinesias. It may offer an alternative, especially as it appears to be safer if done bilaterally. STN stimulation typically performed bilaterally appears very promising for the control of most PD symptoms, although a number of complications have occurred and it too is still considered to be investigational.

Table 6.2 Classes of evidence (as described by Hallett & Litvan 1999)

Classes of evidence	Description
I	Evidence provided by one or more well-designed randomised controlled clinical trials
II	Evidence provided by one or more well-designed clinical studies such as prospective open, case–control studies, etc.
III	Evidence provided by expert opinion, non-randomised historical controls, or case reports of one or more patients

Surgical procedures for PD have also been reviewed for the Safety and Efficacy Register of New Interventional Procedures of the Medical Royal Colleges (SERNIP). This involves a simple system of grading the safety and efficacy of new procedures.

Table 6.3 summarises the recent SERNIP classification (March 2001) of the different surgical procedures. Despite the availability of guideline documents on the safety and efficacy of the individual surgical techniques for PD, it should be appreciated that we now need evidence on comparative efficacy. This involves assessing not only efficacy between surgical procedures but also efficacy of procedures compared with medical treatments, and weighing up all the advantages and disadvantages to demonstrate which is best overall. The only reliable way of assessing this is to undertake RCTs.

Table 6.3 SERNIP classification of surgical procedures for PD (March 2001)

Classification	Description	Procedure(s)
A	Safety and efficacy established: procedure may be used Pallidotomy	Thalamotomy Pallidal stimulation Thalamic stimulation
B	Efficacy established but further evaluation required to confirm safety: procedure can be used as part of a surveillance programme registered with SERNIP	Subthalamic stimulation
C	Safety and efficacy not proven: procedure should be used only as part of a primary research programme, using appropriate methodology and registered with SERNIP	Subthalamotomy

Randomised controlled trials of surgery for Parkinson's disease

There are a number of problems inherent to conducting RCTs of surgical treatments for PD, which may help to explain the limited number that have been undertaken to date. These issues were discussed in depth by Lang (2000) and include randomising patients unmasked to surgical and non-surgical arms, conducting masked assessment of outcomes, and the ethical issues surrounding sham surgery. Furthermore, there is substantial variation in the methods of surgery that can be used, including the exact choice of target, imaging methods, recording techniques, type of electrode used, and method of electrode placement. Hariz (2001) discussed that it is very difficult to assess the long-term efficacy of surgery in a progressive disorder such as PD, which affects elderly individuals who are most probably in the advanced stages of disease and may also suffer from additional concurrent illnesses or indeed undergo subsequent surgical procedures. However, despite these considerations, it should be appreciated that, in trials of surgery versus no surgery, variations in precise target of brain, for example, are not important. Similarly, when patients suffer from concurrent illnesses, for example, the process of randomisation within RCTs balances out these factors.

To date, seven RCTs of surgery in PD have been identified that address a variety of different questions, including the effectiveness of pallidotomy compared with medical treatment (Vitek *et al.* 1998a, 1998b, 2000) or versus delayed pallidotomy (De Bie *et al.* 1999a, 1999b; Schmand *et al.* 2000). Pallidotomy has also been compared with pallidal stimulation (Merello *et al.* 1998, 1999, 2000, 2001) and thalamotomy has been compared with thalamic stimulation. (Speelman *et al.* 1998; Schuurman *et al.* 1999, 2000). Two trials have addressed the question of pallidal stimulation versus subthalamic stimulation (Hammerstad *et al.* 1997, 1999, 2000; Burchiel *et al.* 1999; Clay *et al.* 2000; Marks *et al.* 2000; Walker *et al.* 2000). The main features of these randomised trials are summarised in Table 6.4, but, in general, they are mainly single-centre trials and contain small numbers of patients (196 patients in total and an average of 30 patients per trial). As with the non-randomised studies, these RCTs are characterized by relatively short-term follow-up ranging from 3 to 30 months, but averaging only 6 months of follow-up per patient. In addition, patients within the RCTs have mainly been assessed using clinician-based rating scales, although a few trials have also evaluated patients' assessment of their functioning through quality-of-life measurement (de Bie *et al.* 1999a, 1999b; Clay *et al.* 2000).

The need for large simple trials of surgery for Parkinson's disease

Unfortunately the many reported benefits of surgery for PD are weakened by the overall limited quality of the available evidence; this is unsatisfactory when so many patients have participated in these studies. Strength of evidence is based on how well bias and confounding factors are controlled in the design and conduct of a study. Characteristics that strengthen the validity of findings include presence of randomisation, contemporaneous control subjects and masking, a prospective design, sufficient power and a multicentre design. Although the existing RCTs have achieved some of these standards, they have been too small to evaluate reliably the relatively moderate differences that can realistically be expected between the various treatment modalities. To detect such differences requires large trials with hundreds (rather than tens) of patients randomised (Collins *et al.* 1996). Furthermore, although there is reasonably sound evidence that surgery can be effective in the short term, there are few data on the long-term effects. As discussed earlier, it is essential in a disease with a long time course such as PD to evaluate the long-term effectiveness and safety of surgery, based on clinically and socially important outcomes, and to assess the patients' perceptions of benefit (using appropriate quality-of-life measures) as well as that of clinicians. In addition, it would be beneficial to distinguish between symptomatic benefit and true cellular neuroprotection to the patient. However, this may be impossible with measurements of clinical data only and may require long-term positron emission tomography (PET) studies.

Today, there remain substantial uncertainties about fundamental aspects of surgery for PD, including the optimal site, technique and timing of surgery. Consequently there are many important questions still to be answered in future trials of surgical therapies for PD (Lang 2000). There is an urgent need for collaborative work to be undertaken involving large, multicentre randomised trials with long-term follow-up.

Table 6.4 Randomised controlled trials of surgery in Parkinson's disease

References	Intervention	Subjects	Outcome measures	Length of follow-up	Authors' conclusion(s)
Vitek et al. (1998a, 1998b, 2000)	Pallidotomy vs medical treatment	27 with advanced idiopathic PD 14 pallidotomy 13 medical treatment	Unified Parkinson's Disease Rating Scale (UPDRS) Timed tests of motor function Schwab & England Scale Neuropsychological battery Psychiatric evaluation)	6 months (27 patients 36 months (14 patients)	Pallidotomy patients show significant improvement in all motor features of PD and reduced medication complications. Patients in the medical arm show continued decline
De Bie et al. (1999a, 1999b)	Pallidotomy vs delayed pallidotomy	37 with advanced idiopathic PD	Primary outcome: UPDRS-III	6 months	Pallidotomy improves patients' disability in off phase and is safe with respect to cognition and behaviour but may lead to minor deterioration in verbal fluency
Schmand (2000)		19 pallidotomy 18 delayed pallidotomy	Secondary outcomes: Clinical rating scales: UPDRS-III (on phase), Dyskinesia rating scale, Pain visual analogue scale (VAS), UPDRS 2 (Activities of Daily Living), Schwab & England Scale, Parkinson's disease Quality of Life questionnaire (PDQL) Timed tests Patients' diaries Recording of pharmacological treatment Neuropsychological examinations Mood and behavioural rating scales		

... contd

Table 6.4 cont'd

References	Intervention	Subjects	Outcome measures	Length of follow-up	Authors' conclusion(s)
Merello et al. (1998, 1999)	Pallidotomy (PVP) vs globus pallidus stimulation (PVS)	13 with advanced idiopathic PD 7 PVP 6 PVS	Primary outcomes: UPDRS-III ADL Secondary outcomes: Bradykinesia, tremor, rigidity, gait and postural instability score (PIGD), dyskinesia	3 months	The short-term effect and safety of both procedures is comparable
Merello et al. (2000, 2001)	Bilateral pallidotomy vs unilateral pallidotomy + GP stimulation	6 with advanced idiopathic PD	Core assessment programme for intracerebral transplantation (CAPIT) UPDRS ADL Dyskinesia score Psychiatric and neuropsychological evaluations	3 months	Bilateral simultaneous GP lesions may produce severe motor and psychiatric problems. Pallidotomy combined with GP stimulation improves Parkinson symptoms not associated with the side effects induced by bilateral lesions
Hammerstad et al. (1997, 1999, 2000) Burchiel et al. (1999)	Globus pallidus (GP) stimulation vs subthalamic nucleus (STN) stimulation	10 with advanced idiopathic PD 4 GP stimulation 6 STN stimulation	Primary outcomes: UPDRS (items 18–31) Secondary outcomes: UPDRS subscores of: rigidity, tremor, bradykinesia, postural stability, gait Dyskinesia (dyskinesia rating scale)	12 months (9 patients) 30 months (6 patients)	Both procedures appear safe and efficacious but a larger study is need to establish whether there is a difference in efficacy between GP and STN stimulation and to determine whether some symptoms respond better to simulation of one target or another ... contd

Table 6.4 cont'd

References	Intervention	Subjects	Outcome measures	Length of follow-up	Authors' conclusion(s)
Speelman et al. (1998) Schuurman et al. (1999, 2000)	Thalamotomy vs thalamic stimulation	45 with advanced idiopathic PD 23 thalamotomy 22 thalamic stimulation	Primary outcome: Frenchay Activities Index Secondary outcomes: Severity of tremor Patients' assessment of outcome Number of adverse effects	6 months (40–45 PD patients depending on outcome measure)	Thalamotomy and thalamic stimulation are equally effective for the suppression of drug-resistant tremor, but thalamic stimulation has fewer adverse effects and results in greater improvement in function
Clay et al. (2000) Marks et al. (2000) Walker et al. (2000)	Globus pallidus (stimulation vs subthalamic nucleus stimulation	49 with advanced idiopathic PD 39 unilateral procedures 13 bilateral DBS implants	UPDRS-III score Neuropsychological tests Sickness Impact Profile (SIP) to measure quality of life	Clay et al. (2000) 3 months (11 patients) Marks et al. (2000) 6 months (15 patients) Walker et al. (2000) 3 months (18 patients)	Stimulation of both sites improves motor function to a similar extent. No consistent pattern of improvement observed for neuropsychological tests and no clear differences between target site Preliminary results suggest parallel improvements in both quality of life and motor function, but there were exceptions

Ongoing surgical trials for Parkinson's disease

Various research registers were searched in attempt to identify RCTs in progress or recently completed trials not yet published. A number of records of interest were found which, after contact with the reported investigator, were either not in progress or were not randomised trials.

A randomised trial of early versus deferred pallidotomy for PD conducted at Oxford and at Charing Cross Hospital, London is about to be published. This trial has looked at quality-of-life measurements, including SF36, PDQ-39 and a functional limitations profile, together with video-taped assessments for masked evaluation (Nicholson & Milne 1999).

After a randomised trial of pallidotomy versus medical management for PD, Vitek's group at Emory University in Atlanta, USA are conducting a trial supported by the National Institutes of Health (NIH) evaluating the short- and long-term effects of DBS in the GP and STN on motor function, neuropsychology and quality of life in patients with PD.

A multicentre randomised controlled trial is currently underway in the UK. PD SURG is coordinated at the University of Birmingham Clinical Trials Unit and was set up to answer some of the key unanswered questions in this area and to provide evidence on the cost-effectiveness of surgery for PD to the NHS and government. The true costs of these procedures to society might be expected to be high, but the reverse may be true if, as a result of surgery, patients have reduced medication requirements, are able to continue to work and do not have to be taken into residential care. PD SURG is a large, simple "real-life" trial that will determine reliably whether early surgery is more effective than medical therapy (with surgery deferred) for advanced PD. It will evaluate the role of subthalamic (STN) and pallidal (GPi) surgery, by either stimulation or lesioning, compared to medical therapy (with surgical intervention delayed as long as possible) in patients with advanced PD that is not adequately controlled by their current medical treatment. Patients allocated to medical therapy will receive whatever drug treatment is considered appropriate (this may include continuous apomorphine infusion).

In view of the fact that there is no consensus as to the optimal timing of surgery for PD, the PD SURG trial adopts a pragmatic approach. Some clinicians may consider that surgery should be performed at a relatively earlier stage of the disease than others, while factors such as the level of disability of a patient are also potential determinants of the appropriateness of different treatments. In order to obtain the large number of patients needed to provide reliable answers, and to maximise the clinical relevance of the findings, the trial is designed to fit in with routine practice as far as possible and to impose minimal additional workload by keeping extra clinic-based tests and evaluations to a minimum. The primary endpoint will be the patient's self-evaluation of their functional status using the PDQ-39 questionnaire. Secondary endpoints will evaluate other aspects of functioning, as well as safety including quality of life (EuroQol), Dementia Rating Scale-2, clinical assessment of functioning (UPDRS, Hoehn & Yahr stage), neuropsychological evaluation, burden on carers, toxicity and side effects, including mortality rates. An economic evaluation will also be undertaken as part of the trial. The intention is to estimate the incremental cost of STN surgery compared to medical therapy, the incremental effectiveness measured in life years and quality adjusted life years, and the incremental cost-effectiveness. Progression of PD may lead to increased requirements for formal domiciliary or residential care as care within the home becomes untenable. Transitions to more intensive forms of care can be viewed both as outcome and as costs. The economic evaluation will include both direct and indirect costs. Indirect costs will include loss of earnings.

Within the PD SURG trial randomisations, there will be subgroup analyses by years since initial diagnosis of PD (<5 years, 5–9 years, 10–14 years, 15+ years), age at entry (<60, 61–69, 70+ years), disease stage (Hoehn & Yahr stage ≤3.0, ≥4.0), reason for considering surgical intervention (tremor, dyskinesia, severe "off" periods, other reason), type of surgery (stimulation, lesion) and site (STN, GPi) to be performed if allocated surgery and type of medical therapy to be given if allocated medical therapy (continuous apomorphine, other). A subgroup analysis by time period, to investigate "learning curve" effects, will also be performed. Because of the serious dangers of misinterpretation, all subgroup analyses would be interpreted cautiously. An independent Data Monitoring Committee (DMC) will monitor the progress of the trial and provide advice to the trial's Steering Committee. For example, if surgery for PD really is substantially better or worse than medical therapy with respect to the main endpoints, or survival, then this may become apparent before the target recruitment has been reached. Alternatively, new evidence might emerge from other sources that surgery is definitely more, or less, effective than medical therapy.

The results of the PD SURG trial will allow decisions on how to treat PD patients to be evidence-based (i.e. the trial will determine whether surgery is a beneficial and cost-effective intervention and, if so, the optimal timing, compared to medical therapy), leading to more patients receiving the most appropriate therapy and to more cost-effective use of the available clinical resources. Furthermore, it will establish a collaborative group of clinicians (neurosurgeons and neurologists), experts in trial methodology and patients (represented by the PDS), both in the UK and abroad, with an interest in surgery for PD that will go on to undertake further trials (e.g. cell transplantation and gene therapy are two emerging areas of research with the potential to be semi-curative). The trial hopes to emulate the success of other trial series, such as the MRC leukaemia trials and the ISIS (International Study of Infarct Survival) trials.

Conclusions

Previous studies of surgery for PD have methodological flaws that make systematic and random errors likely and prevent reliable interpretation. There remains considerable uncertainty as to the true role of surgery in PD. To provide reliable evidence on the optimum timing, site and technique of surgery for PD, and to determine which types of patient benefit, much larger trials with long-term follow-up and endpoints of more relevance to the patient are needed. A few well-designed trials are currently under way that hope to answer some of these important questions.

Acknowledgements

I would like to thank the following people who have provided comments on this chapter or information for inclusion: Professor Richard Gray, Dr Keith Wheatley, Professor Adrian Williams, Dr Carl Clarke, Professor Ian Whittle, Dr Ralph Gregory, Professor Niall Quinn, Professor Jerrold Vitek and Dr Daniel Corcos.

References

Arsland D, Tandberg E, Larsen JP, Cummings JL (1996). Frequency of dementia in PD. *Archives of Neurology* **53**, 538–542

Benabid AL, Pollak P, Seigneuret E, Hoffmann D, Gay E, Perret J (1993). Chronic VIM thalamic stimulation in Parkinson's disease, essential tremor and extra-pyramidal dyskinesias, *Acta Neurochirurgica Supplementum* **58**, 39–44

Benabid AL, Pollack P, Benazzouz D, Hoffmann D, Limousin P (1994). Vim and STN stimulation in Parkinson's disease. *Movement Disorders* **9**(suppl 1), M39

Benabid AL, Benazzouz A, Hoffmann D, Limousin P, Krack P, Pollak P (1998). Long-term electrical inhibition of deep brain targets in movement disorders. *Movement Disorders* **13**(suppl 3), 119–125

Bhatia K, Brooks DJ, Burn DJ *et al.* (1998). Guidelines for the management of Parkinson's Disease. *Hospital Medicine* **59**, 469–480

Burchiel KJ, Andersen VC, Favre J, Hammerstad JP (1999). Comparison of pallidal and subthalamic nucleus deep brain stimulation for advanced PD: results of a randomised, blinded pilot study. *Neurosurgery* **45**, 1375–1382

Clay H, Christine C, Starr P, Marks W Jr (2000). Quality of life in patients with PD undergoing chronic pallidal or subthalamic deep brain stimulation. *Movement Disorders* **15**(suppl 3), P414

Clough CG (1991). Parkinson's disease: management. *The Lancet* **337**, 1324–1327

Collins R, Peto R, Gray R, Parish S (1996). Large scale randomised evidence: trials and overviews. In Weatherall D, Ledingham JGG, DA Warrell, eds, *Oxford Textbook of Medicine*. Oxford: Oxford University Press, pp 21–36

Cummings JL (1992). Depression and PD: a review. *American Journal of Psychiatry* **149**, 443–454

de Bie RMA, de Haan RJ, Nijssen PCG *et al.* (1999a). Unilateral pallidotomy in PD: a randomised, single blind, multicentre trial. *The Lancet* **354**, 1665–1669

de Bie RMA, Schuurman PR, Bosch DA, Speelman JD (1999b). Unilateral pallidotomy in PD: a randomised, single blind, multicentre trial, *Parkinsonism and Related Disorders* **5**(suppl), P-WE-010

Dickersin K (1997). How important is publication bias? A synthesis of available data. *AIDS Education and Prevention* **9**(suppl 1), 15–21

Dickersin K & Larson K (1996). Establishing and maintaining an international register of RCTs. In *The Cochrane Library*. Oxford: Update Software.

Dickersin K, Min YI, Meinert CL (1992). Factors influencing publication of research results. Follow-up of applications submitted to two institutional review boards. *Journal of the American Medical Association* **267**, 374–378

Diederich N, Goetz CG, Stebbins GT *et al.* (1992). Blinded evaluation confirms long-term asymmetric effect of unilateral thalamotomy or subthalamotomy on tremor in Parkinson's disease. *Neurology* **42**, 1311–1314

Follett KA (2000). The surgical treatment of Parkinson's disease. *Annual Review of Medicine* **51**, 135–147

Galvez-Jimenez N, Lozano A, Tasker R, Duff J, Hutchison W, Lang AE (1998). Pallidal stimulation in Parkinson's disease patients with a prior unilateral pallidotomy. *Canadian Journal of Neurological Science* **25**, 300–305

Goetz CG, De Long MR, Penn RD, Bakay RA (1993). Neurosurgical horizons in Parkinson's disease. *Neurology* **43**, 1–7

Gregory R & Bowen J (1999). Posteroventral pallidotomy for advanced PD: a systematic review. *Neurology Reviews International* **3**(1): 8–12

Gross CE, Boraud T, Guehl D, Bioulac B, Bezard E (1999). From experimentation to the surgical treatment of Parkinson's disease: prelude or suite in basal ganglia research? *Progress in Neurobiology* **59**, 509–532

Hallett M & Litvan I (1999). Evaluation of surgery for Parkinson's disease: a report of the Therapeutics and Technology Assessment Subcommittee of the American Academy of Neurology. The Task Force on Surgery for Parkinson's Disease. *Neurology* **53**, 1910–1921.

Hallett M & Litvan I (2000). Scientific position paper of the Movement Disorder Society evaluation of surgery for Parkinson's disease. Task Force on Surgery for Parkinson's Disease of the American Academy of Neurology Therapeutic and Technology Assessment Committee. *Movement Disorders* **15**, 436–438

Hammerstad JP, Burchiel KJ, Favre J, Burchiel KJ (1997). Bilateral deep-brain stimulation for PD: Comparison of pallidal versus subthalamic nucleus targets, *Neurology* **48** A137

Hammerstad J, Andersen V, Favre J (1999). Comparison of pallidal versus subthalamic nucleus deep brain stimulation. *Neurology* **52**(suppl 2), A271

Hammerstad J, Andersen V, Burchiel K (2000). Pallidal vs. subthalamic nucleus stimulation for advanced PD: 30-month follow-up. *Movement Disorders* **15**(suppl 3), P370

Hariz MI (2001). Surgery for Parkinson's disease. A critical evaluation of the state of the art: should we use the same criteria as for drug trials? *Archives of Neurology* **57**, 315–317

Hariz MI & Bergenheim AT (2001). A 10-year follow-up review of patients who underwent Leksell's posteroventral pallidotomy for Parkinson disease. *Journal of Neurosurgery* **94**, 552–558

Hariz MI & De Salles AA (1997). The side-effects and complications of posteroventral pallidotomy. *Acta Neurochirurgica Supplementum* **68**, 42–8

Harstall C & Hailey D (1997). *Posteroventral pallidotomy in Parkinson's disease*. Alberta Heritage Foundation for Medical Research.

Iacono RP, Lonser RR, Oh A, Yamada S (1995a). New pathophysiology of Parkinson's disease revealed by posteroventral pallidotomy. *Neurological Research* **17**, 178–80

Iacono RP, Shima F, Lonser RR, Kuniyoshi S, Maeda G, Yamada S (1995b). The results, indications, and physiology of posteroventral pallidotomy for patients with Parkinson's disease. *Neurosurgery* **36**, 1118–1127

Koller WC (1994). An algorithm for the management of Parkinson's disease. *Neurology* **12**(suppl 10), S1–S52

Koller WC, Pahwa R, Busenbark K *et al.* (1997). High-frequency unilateral thalamic stimulation in the treatment of essential and parkinsonian tremor. *Annals of Neurology* **42**, 292–29

Koller WC, Wilkinson S, Pahwa R, Miyawaki EK (1998). Surgical treatment options in Parkinson's disease. *Neurosurgical Clinics of North America* **9**, 295–306

Koller WC, Pahwa R, Lyons KE, Albanese A (1999). Surgical treatment of Parkinson's disease. *Journal of Neurological Science* **167**(1), 1–10

Kottler A & Hayes D (1998*). Stereotactic Pallidotomy for Treatment of PD. Technology Assessment Program Report No. 8.* US Department of Veterans Affairs (VATAP), p 17

Kumar R, Lozano AM, Kim YJ *et al.* (1998). Double-blind evaluation of subthalamic nucleus deep brain stimulation in advanced Parkinson's disease. *Neurology* **51**, 850–855

Lai EC, Jankovic J, Krauss JK, Ondo WG, Grossman RG (2000). Long-term efficacy of posteroventral pallidotomy in the treatment of Parkinson's disease. *Neurology* **55**, 1218–1222

Laitinen LV (1994). Ventroposterolateral pallidotomy. *Stereotactic Functional Neurosurgery* **62**, 41–52

Laitinen LV (1995). Pallidotomy for Parkinson's disease. *Neurosurgical Clinics of North America* **6**, 105–112

Lang AE (2000). Surgery for Parkinson's Disease. A critical evaluation of the state of the art. *Archives of Neurology* **57**, 1118–1125

Lees AJ, Blackburn NA, Campell VL (1988). The nightmare problems of PD. *Clinical Neuropharmacology* **11**, 512–519

Limousin P, Speelman JD, Gielen F, Janssens M (1999). Multicentre European study of thalamic stimulation in parkinsonian and essential tremor. *Journal of Neurology, Neurosurgery, and Psychiatry* **66**, 289–296

Lozano AM, Lang AE, Galvez-Jimenez N *et al.* (1995). Effect of GPi pallidotomy on motor function in Parkinson's disease. *The Lancet* **346**, 1383–1387

Marks W, Christine C, Clay H, Heath S, Aminoff M, Starr P (2000). Unilateral and bilateral deep brain stimulation of the Globus pallidus or subthalamic nucleus in patients with medically refractory PD: short term results from a randomized trial. *Movement Disorders* **15**(suppl 3), P366

Merello M, Nouzeilles MI, Cammarota A, Betti O, Leiguarda R (1998). Randomized prospective comparison between unilateral Posteroventral pallidotomy vs. unilateral Postero ventral stimulation. *Movement Disorders* **13**(suppl 2), P1.198

Merello M, Nouzeilles MI, Kuzis G *et al.* (1999). Unilateral radiofrequency lesion versus electrostimulation of posteroventral pallidum: a prospective randomised comparison. *Movement Disorders* **14**, 50–56

Merello M, Cammarota A, Starkstein S, Leiguarda R (2000). Simultaneous bilateral GPi lesion versus bilateral GPi lesion plus contralateral GPi stimulation for PD. *Neurology* **54**(suppl 3), A187

Merello M, Starkstein S, Nouzeilles MI, Kuzis G (2001). Bilateral pallidotomy for treatment of Parkinson's disease induced corticobulbar syndrome and psychic akinesia avoidable by globus pallidus lesion combined with contralateral stimulation. *Journal of Neurology, Neurosurgery and Psychiatry* **71**, 611–614

Moriyama E, Beck H, Miyamoto T (1999). Long-term results of ventrolateral thalamotomy for patients with Parkinson's disease. *Neurologica Meico-Chirurgica (Tokyo)* **39**, 350–356

Nicholson T & Milne R (1999). *Pallidotomy, Thalamotomy and Deep Brain Stimulation for Severe PD*. Southampton: Wessex Institute for Health Research and Development. Development and Evaluation Committee Report No. 105

Ondo W, Jankovic J, Schwartz K, Almaguer M, Simpson RK (1998). Unilateral thalamic deep brain stimulation for refractory essential tremor and Parkinson's disease tremor. *Neurology* **51**, 1063–1069

Quinn N (1999). Progress in functional neurosurgery for Parkinson's disease. *The Lancet* **354**, 1658–1659

Robert G (1996). *Pallidotomy for PD*. Southampton: Wessex Institute for Health Research and Development. Development and Evaluation Committee Report No. 51

Schmand B, de Bie RMA, Koning-Haanstra M (2000). Unilateral pallidotomy in PD: a controlled study of cognitive and behavioural effects. *Neurology* **54**, 1058–1064

Schuurman PR, Bosch DA, Speelman JD (1999). Thalamic stimulation versus thalamotomy in a prospective randomised trial. *Parkinsonism and Related Disorders* **5**(suppl), P-WE-048

Schuurman PR, Bosch DA, Bossuyt PM *et al.* (2000). A comparison of continuous thalamic stimulation and thalamotomy for suppression of severe tremor. *New England Journal of Medicine* **342**, 505–507

Shinobu LA, Counihan TJ, Eskandar EN, Cosgrove GR Penney JB (1998). Sensorimotor and Neuropsychiatric phenomena in a pallidotomy population. *Movement Disorders* **13**(suppl 2), P4.201

Speelman JD, Schuurman PR, Bosch DA (1998). Thalamic stimulation versus thalamotomy in a prospective randomised trial. *Movement Disorders* **13**(suppl 2), P3.202

Starr PA, Vitek JL, Bakay RA (1998). Ablative surgery and deep brain stimulation for Parkinson's disease. *Neurosurgery* **43**, 989–1013

Taha JM, Favre J, Baumann TK, Burchiel KJ (1997). Tremor control after pallidotomy in patients with Parkinson's disease: correlation with microrecording findings. *Journal of Neurosurgery* **86**, 642–647

Uitti RJ (2000). Surgical treatments for Parkinson's disease. *Canadian Family Physician* **46**, 368–373

Vitek JL, Bakay RAE, Freeman A *et al.* (1998a) Randomized clinical trial of pallidotomy versus medical therapy for PD. *Movement Disorders* **13**(suppl 2), P4.203

Vitek JL, Bakay RAE, Freeman A *et al.* MR (1998b) Randomized trial of pallidotomy for PD. *Neurology* **50**(suppl 4), A80

Vitek JL, Bakay RAE, Freeman A *et al.* (2000). Three year follow-up of pallidotomy for Parkinson's disease. *Neurology* **54**(suppl 3), A477.

Walker J, Rothlind J, Christine C, Starr P, Marks W Jr (2000). Pre-operative and post-operative neuropsychological testing following unilateral deep brain stimulation of the Globus pallidus or subthalamic nucleus in patients with medically refractory PD: short term results from a randomized trial. *Movement Disorders* **15**(suppl 3), P407

Young RF, Shumway-Cook A, Vermeulen SS *et al.* (1998). Gamma knife radiosurgery as a lesioning technique in movement disorder surgery. *Journal of Neurosurgery* **89**, 183–193

PART 3

Neuropsychiatry

Scientific evidence and expert clinical opinion for the management of depression

Max J Henderson and Brian K Toone

Introduction

Changes in mood and behaviour are commonplace in all neurodegenerative diseases and Parkinson's disease (PD) is no exception. These symptoms cause distress to both patients and their carers, while posing diagnostic dilemmas and management difficulties to professionals managing their care. Despite a substantial body of literature, we remain some way off complete understanding of the links between depression and PD. This chapter aims to summarise the current state of our knowledge while highlighting the areas of confusion that still exist. This includes discussion of the exact prevalence of depressive illness in PD, the risk factors for its development, some of the differential diagnoses and options for management.

Prevalence

That mood disturbance is associated with PD has been increasingly noted since early in the twentieth century. A number of studies have looked at the prevalence of depression and found widely differing rates of 5–90% (Hoehn & Yahr 1967; Mindham 1970; Tandberg *et al.* 1996). Many of these studies are now more than 25 years old and have limited validity for several reasons. First, our concept of PD has been refined with idiopathic PD seen as distinct from post-encephalitic PD (much more prevalent 25 years ago), vascular pseudo-Parkinson's disease and the Parkinson's plus syndromes. Early studies will have been contaminated with all these additional groups, whereas modern studies try very hard to avoid this. What we mean by depression has also changed, with diagnostic criteria being standardised to include a certain minimum of symptoms for a certain length of time. It is impossible to tell what proportion of patients interviewed for studies in the early 1970s would meet 'caseness' for either the *International Classification of Diseases* tenth revision (ICD-10: WHO 1992) or the *Diagnostic and Statistical Manual of Mental Disorders*, 4th edn (DSM-IV: American Psychiatric Association 1994) category 'Major Depressive Episode'. These studies used only a clinical interview to assess depression. Starkstein's is perhaps the closest to a 'gold-standard' study: 105 patients were assessed using the Present State Examination to produce DSM-III diagnoses. This found that 21 had 'Major Depression' and 20 had 'Minor Depression'.

Liu *et al.* (1997) produced similar findings: 18% and 25% respectively. The total is consistent with the consensus figure of 40% suggested by Cummings (1992), but highlights that what a number of assessment tools call depression may in fact only be 'minor' and might not in itself require treatment. These studies were conducted in secondary or tertiary care settings and historically these have produced high prevalence (Mindham 1970). Tandberg *et al.* (1996) looked at a large community sample of PD patients using the Montgomery–Asberg Depression rating scale. Eight per cent were found to have 'Major Depression' and 45% milder depressive symptoms. A smaller but more recent study in London found 10% with 'moderate' depression and a further 9% with 'severe' depression (Schrag *et al.* 2001). In conclusion, it appears that depressive symptomatology is common in PD although frank depressive illness is less so, at about 10% in community studies and 20–25% in hospital-based studies.

Risk factors

The difficulties of interpreting the data for prevalence of depression in PD are identical to those for the risk factors. If anything the literature is more contradictory. Certain factors do, however, appear to be consistently highlighted as associated with mood disturbance. These include cognitive impairment, atypical parkinsonian signs (such as prominent autonomic signs with falls, pyramidal signs and rapid downhill course) (Quinn & Marsden 1986), motor fluctuations, early onset of the disease and a positive family history (Tandberg *et al.* 1997). Of course these are not in themselves independent variables and Starkstein *et al.* (1989) have suggested that they may cluster as a subtype of PD.

A second group of risk factors includes psychosis (Tandberg *et al.* 1997) and being placed in nursing home accommodation. These are also not independent. Goetz and Stebbins (1993) have shown that the single greatest risk factor for nursing home placement is itself psychosis. Those factors that *a priori* might seem good candidates as risk factors, such as age, sex, length of illness or duration or dose of L-dopa treatment, have been confirmed as such in some studies. The results are, however, contradictory and they have not been consistently found to be associated with depression (Cummings 1992).

The key question and one that continues to divide many in the field is that of the possible relationship between disease severity and depression. The earliest explanatory models for depression in PD claimed that it was the result of the psychological trauma that the illness caused, and as such it would be expected that a positive correlation between depression and PD severity could be demonstrated. No such correlation has been found (Brown & Jahanshahi 1995). The most widely quoted work is that of Starkstein *et al.* (1990b) who found a U-shaped curve with depression being more common in the early and late stages of the disease, but less so in the middle. The most common explanation given for this is that the early depressives are reacting to the 'shock' of the diagnosis, whereas the later depressives are reacting to increasing dependence and progressive deterioration. This appears to be rather simplistic, ignoring the coarse nature of the Hoehn and Yahr (1967) staging and the limitations of the concept of 'disease severity'. It has however been replicated by Schrag et al. (2001).

A model that distinguishes disease severity, disability and handicap appears to be more pertinent. Such an approach was used by Brown and McCarthy (1990) who found a significant correlation between depression and disability but not disease severity. Schrag has taken this a stage further and studied a group of PD patients with the WHO model of impairment, disability and handicap (WHO 1980) in mind. Simply put, 'impairment' is the objective disease severity, 'disability' the functional impact of such impairment, and 'handicap' refers to the disadvantages experienced by the individual, particularly in fulfilling their social roles, which derive from the disability. This model highlights that similar levels of impairment can produce different levels of disability in different people depending, for example, on the impact of a co-morbid diagnosis. More importantly still, similar levels of disability produce different levels of handicap, depending on the age, social and personal circumstances of the patient, and are related at least in part to the patient's *own perceptions* of their difficulties. Schrag and colleagues (2001) found that, although objective measures of impairment accounted for only 28% in the variance of depression, handicap predicted more than 50%. They suggest that the high levels of depression seen in recently diagnosed PD decline over time as the process of adaptation to the disease, combined with effective treatment, reduce the perceived handicap. In time, however, disease progression and treatment complications combine to worsen handicap and levels of depression rise.

If depression is simply a function of the disability or handicap caused, then perhaps there is nothing particular about the relationship between PD and depression – rates of depression should be similar in other diagnoses causing similar disability. Several groups have indeed looked at this issue although the results remain conflicting. PD patients have been found to be more depressed than medically ill (Warburton 1967; Singer 1974) or paraplegic (Horn 1974) patients. Gotham et al. (1986) compared PD patients with those suffering from rheumatoid arthritis and normal controls. They found equally elevated levels of depression in both patient groups. Ehmann et al. (1990), however, have found significantly more depression in a PD group compared with controls matched for disability.

That underlying pathophysiological disposition to depression in patients with PD is supported by the finding of several authors of high rates of depression either before or at diagnosis (Fukunishi et al. 1991; Santamaria et al. 2001). Several other strands of evidence suggest a biological basis to the depression of PD. A number of authors have noted that the dopaminergic system is not the only one affected in PD. Serotoninergic and adrenergic projections also degenerate and it has been suggested that depression is associated with this much wider monoaminergic disturbance (Fibiger 1984; Mayeux et al. 1984). On a broader note dysfunction in certain brain areas and damage to certain neurological circuits have received much attention (Cummings 1993; Lafer *et al.* 1997). Depressed PD patients show greater frontal lobe impairment than non-depressed ones and Taylor *et al.* (1986) have hypothesised that depression is associated with dysfunction of frontal links to the caudate, whereas Starkstein (1999) suggests the lesion lies with the frontal dopaminergic innervation from the ventral tegmental area.

Mayberg *et al.* (1990) found that depressed PD patients had reduced glucose metabolism in the orbital and inferior frontal lobes compared with their non-depressed controls. More recently, Ring *et al.* (1994) demonstrated reduced regional cerebral blood flow in the anteromedial part of the medial frontal cortex, an area previously associated with depression in non-PD patients (Baxter *et al.* 1989; Bench *et al.* 1992). A further piece of evidence comes from clinical observation of fluctuations in mood and motor behaviour. Nissenbaum *et al.* (1987), in a small study, found that, in patients with motor fluctuations secondary to long-term levodopa therapy, two-thirds experienced on–off mood swings. In 10 of her 31 patients' mood swung between 'elated' when 'on' and 'depressed' or 'anxious' when 'off'.

Depression in PD is multifactorial as it is in all other settings. The 'biological' nature of the identified risk factors highlights the possibility that cerebral pathology in PD contributes directly to the risk of depression, opening up the way for possible targeted pharmacological treatments when this relationship is fully elucidated. The close relationship between depression and disability and/or handicap reminds us that PD affects each of our patients differently and that only by understanding this aspect of the illness will we identify and manage the psychological consequences correctly.

Making the diagnosis

Knowing the risk factors helps identify a population who need particular monitoring, but it is in the assessment of the individual patient that the difficult relationship between depression and PD is most clearly shown. The symptom overlap between depression and PD is such that making the diagnosis in all but extreme cases is very challenging. How much of the loss of facial expression or slowness or sleep disturbance is the result of PD and how much of depression? The first step may be the use of objective assessment tools, such as the Beck Depression Inventory (BDI) (Beck *et al.* 1961), but these have been challenged as continuing to muddle somatic elements of depression with symptoms more correctly attributable to PD. Levin *et al.* (1988) examined this issue using cluster analysis. They were able to demonstrate that the somatic items that may have been endorsed by non-depressed PD patients actually clustered with depressive rather than motor scores. This would suggest that these somatic items score 'true'. However, the limitations of the BDI in PD have been demonstrated by Leentjens *et al.* (2000b) who assessed its performance in terms of sensitivity and specificity. They showed that it could be used as a screening tool if a score of 8/9 was the cut-off. This produced high sensitivity but low specificity, i.e. too many false positives. For it to be an effective diagnostic tool, the cut-off needed to be raised to 16/17 at which point the sensitivity was too low, i.e. too many false negatives. Thus scores in the (broad) range of 9–16 were very difficult to interpret.

A number of alternatives to the BDI have been studied. Meara *et al.* (1999) assessed a community sample using the shortened version of the Geriatric Depression Scale: the GDS-15. This has been validated in medical inpatients although not specifically in PD. Using the cut-off of 5, they found that 64% had significant depressive symptoms. This figure is somewhat high compared with other studies and suggests that this tool over-scores the somatic elements. In a further study, Leentjens *et al.* (2000a) compared the Montgomery–Asberg Depression Rating Scale (MADRS) (Montgomery & Asberg 1979) and the Hamilton Rating Scale for depression (HAMD-17) (Hamilton 1967) to a gold standard DSM-IV diagnosis produced by use of the Schedule for Assessment in Neuropsychiatry. Various cut-offs were then examined to see which produced the best sensitivity and specificity. Both tests performed well – the HAMD slightly better than the MADRS. The optimum cut-off was 13/14 for the HAMD, giving a sensitivity of 88% and a specificity of 89%. The positive predictive value at this level was 0.74, i.e. 74% of those who score 'positive' will in fact be 'true positives' and be depressed on the gold standard.

Standardised tools may thus be useful although they are not always practical in the clinic setting. Which symptoms carry the greatest weight in making a diagnosis of depression in this group? The worst discriminators appear to be sleep disturbance, low energy and 'slowness'. In an elegant study, Hoogendijk *et al.* (1998) examined a group by using a normal 'inclusive' method of looking at depressive symptoms. They then removed any items that were felt either to fluctuate with the motor PD symptoms or to be relieved by dopaminergic medication. The most commonly removed items were 'loss of energy' and 'psychomotor agitation'. 'Loss of interest' was also removed in a proportion of patients and this posed a problem in terms of diagnosis, because it was a mandatory feature in DSM-IIIR depression. Although helping to refine the way in which symptoms are interpreted, the assumption that all that fluctuates with PD motor symptoms can be ignored must be viewed with caution in light, for example, of the work of Nissenbaum *et al.* (1987), as described above, and the potential for dopaminergic agents to have at least a transient beneficial effect on mood. Brown and MacCarthy (1990) have highlighted the relative absence of cognitive features in the presentation of depression in PD. These include guilt and the negative triad of hopelessness, helplessness and worthlessness.

The diagnosis of a depressive illness in PD remains a challenging clinical problem. Although not designed specifically for the purpose, the use of objective rating scales can be justified, so long as they form part of a wider assessment and the results are not adhered to rigidly. The Hamilton Depression Rating Scale appears to perform best in this patient group with a cut-off of 13/14. In terms of symptoms, a diagnosis should not be based on the presence of sleep disturbance, loss of energy or slowness. Physicians should not be fooled by an absence of guilt or other depressive cognitions. Harder evidence comes from low mood or loss of interest that does not fluctuate with motor symptoms. Suicidal ideas and plans are fortunately rare but should always be enquired about.

Differential diagnoses and associated syndromes

In this section several grey areas around depression in PD are discussed. These are syndromes that overlap with depression but are also to some extent distinct. Their existence certainly makes the diagnosis of depression yet more complicated, but it is only by recognising them that their proper place can be established. Some of them deserve treatment in their own right whereas others remain as yet untreatable.

Apathy

This is defined as a reduction in goal-directed behaviour, goal-directed cognitions and in the emotional concomitants of goal-directed behaviour. As such it refers not only to a lack of effort and initiative but to a lack of interest in making such an effort and an overall emotional indifference (Marin 1991). Apathy can form part of the clinical picture in dementia and delirium, or can be a primary syndrome. There is some evidence to suggest an association between apathy and cognitive impairment in PD. Apathy correlates with depression but is by no means fully explained by it (Shulman 2000). Apathy and depression are both common across the spectrum of neurodegenerative disorders. In a fascinating study Levy et al. (1998) compared their degree of association in a number of conditions including PD, Huntington's disease, progressive supranuclear palsy (PSP), Alzheimer's disease and frontotemporal dementia. He showed that, although both depression and apathy were present in each condition, the degree to which they were associated varied widely. In PD, 5% had apathy alone but 28% had apathy and depression, whereas in PSP 77% had apathy alone and 14% apathy plus depression. Starkstein et al. (1992) has also looked at the correlation between apathy and depression in PD. In his study he found that 12% of patients had apathy alone, 30% had both depression plus apathy and 26% had depression without apathy. Hence, apathy can be a symptom of a wider depressive illness or exist as a discrete neuropsychiatric entity.

New work is emerging on the biological basis of apathy. In the work of Liddle et al. (1989) on subtypes of schizophrenia, apathy was a feature of the psychomotor poverty syndrome which was associated with hypoperfusion of the left dorsolateral prefrontal cortex. In addition, Davidson et al. (1999) has demonstrated an association between positive goal attainment and activity in this area whereas primate studies have shown that participants become apathetic if lesioned in the prefrontal cortex. That activity or lack of it in the prefrontal cortex is of interest in depressed PD patients has been supported by the work of Ring et al. (1994). They showed that regional cerebral blood flow was reduced in the prefrontal cortex in depressed PD patients compared with non-depressed PD patients.

The presence of apathy has a great effect on the quality of life both for the patient and his or her carers. Without a high index of suspicion, apathy may be difficult to pick up in a routine outpatient appointment. Partners and carers may, however, produce good descriptions if prompted. Apathy on its own tends to respond poorly to antidepressants and there is no specific treatment as yet available. There is some suggestion that cholinesterase inhibitors, currently used to treat cognitive impairment in Alzheimer's disease, may reduce apathy and behavioural disturbance in PD (Kaufer *et al.* 1996). In addition a trial of pramiprexole, a selective D_3-receptor agonist, is under way and the new physical treatments such as transcranial magnetic stimulation and deep brain stimulation offer possibilities in the future (Szegedi *et al.* 1997; Shulman 2000).

Anxiety

That anxiety and depression are well correlated in non-PD patients has been established. Henderson *et al.* (1992) demonstrated that large numbers of depressed PD patients also had anxiety. In a survey of more than 300 patients and age-matched controls, 61% had depressive symptoms, of whom almost two-thirds also had anxiety. Anxiety alone was present in only 7%. That each had similar associations with PD itself further underscored the close relationship between the two affective disturbances: 22% of those with depressive symptoms and 21% of those with anxiety noted their onset before a diagnosis of PD; the frequency of symptoms (daily vs weekly, etc.) was very similar and the subjective impression of a link with motor symptoms was almost identical. The authors suggest that the particular neurodegenerative changes seen in PD may predispose to a depressive syndrome in which anxiety features are common, the high levels of affective disturbance before diagnosis providing evidence of an organic basis to mood symptoms. These findings were supported by Menza *et al.* (1993) who found that 67% of depressed PD patients also had anxiety whereas 97% of anxious PD patients had depression. They too suggested that this was evidence of underlying neurochemical disturbance.

Fatigue

'Loss of energy' is one of the core features of any depressive episode, and as such is alluded to in studies that use tools including such a symptom. However, in recent years, the close study of fatigue as a symptom and also of chronic fatigue syndrome has enabled fatigue to be seen as a distinct entity from depression (Wessely *et al.* 1999). There are but a few studies examining fatigue in PD, although they make interesting reading. Friedman and Friedman (1993) examined a group of non-demented PD patients and compared their scores on scales of fatigue, depression and disease severity with a control group. Depression, as expected, was common but so was fatigue. Fatigue was significantly more common in the PD group and almost a third rated fatigue as their most disabling symptom. Although fatigue was significantly correlated with depression, there were many non-depressed patients with significant complaints of fatigue. It is of note that fatigue did not correlate with disease severity. In an elegant study, Karslen *et al.* (1999) in Norway studied 233 PD patients and 100 healthy controls. Fatigue was reported in 44% of patients and 18% of controls.

The only factor that was associated with fatigue was depression. Following this the authors excluded all patients with depression (BDI > 18) and cognitive impairment (Mini Mental State Examination or MMSE < 24 – Folstein *et al.* 1975) and reanalysed the data. Remarkably the proportion of PD patients reporting fatigue remained almost identical – 43.5% compared with 4.5% of controls. This is therefore further evidence that, in PD, fatigue cannot wholly be explained by depression. Nor in this study could it be explained by more advanced disease or greater physical disability. The study of Hoogendijk *et al.* (1998) of symptom overlap in depression in PD found that, in more than half of the patients who complained of fatigue, it fluctuated with motor symptoms or was relieved by dopaminergic medication. The authors used these criteria as evidence of the 'intrinsic' nature of a symptom rather than being caused by depression. Thus, fatigue appears to be an independent feature of PD. Its exact pathophysiology awaits further elucidation.

Pain

This is included here not so much for the confusion it may cause in diagnosis but rather to highlight a common symptom that might increase the burden of depressive symptomatology in a PD population. The links between pain and depression are well documented (Dworkin *et al.* 1995, 1999) but less is known about pain in PD. Sandyk and Snider (1985) drew attention to the presence of sensory symptoms in PD and Goetz *et al.* (1986) have classified the pain syndromes in PD. That pain in PD is most intense when in the off state suggests that L-dopa may have a role in central analgesic control. The presence of depression in PD should prompt an assessment of pain and vice versa.

Treatment

Drug treatments

For a clinical problem that has been so extensively described and researched, it is somewhat disappointing that so little work has been done on the treatment of depression in PD, particularly when set against the explosion of new antidepressants drugs available in the last 20 years. Klassen *et al.* (1995) attempted a meta-analysis of studies involving the drug treatment of depression in PD and found only 12 studies. At this point there had been no trials of serotonin specific re-uptake inhibitors (SSRIs) in PD. Sadly the methodology used in the studies found was so universally poor that Klassen concluded that there was in fact no evidence base for the treatment of depression in PD.

Since then several studies using SSRIs have been published, but large controlled studies comparing the efficacy and tolerability of different antidepressants in PD are still awaited.

It is beyond dispute that much depressive illness in PD goes either unrecognised or untreated (Cummings 1992). The diagnostic difficulties discussed above contribute significantly to this but so must the doubts about suitable treatments. In the study by Meara *et al.* (1999) in Wales, 60% of patients scored above the cut-off of 5 on the GDS-15 but only 7% were on antidepressants. This contrasts with the survey of neurologists in the Parkinson's Study Group in the USA, which found that 26% of patients were on antidepressants (Richard & Kurlan 1997), although some would argue that even this is too low.

The role of L-dopa in depression has aroused much interest. It has been argued that L-dopa can either cause (Damasio *et al.* 1970) or treat (Yahr *et al.* 1969) depression in PD. Choi *et al.* (2000) prospectively examined 34 patients who commenced L-dopa. As expected, the Unified Parkinson's Disease Rating Scale (UPDRS) motor score improved significantly. Although two initially depressed patients became euthymic and five non-depressed patients became depressed over the course of the study (up to 28 months), there was no overall change in the population BDI score. The authors concluded that long-term dopamine replacement did not alter parkinsonian depression.

The best studied group of antidepressants is the tricyclics (TCAs), being in 5 of the 12 studies analysed by Klassen *et al.* (1995). Although of undoubted efficacy in the general population, their tolerability in an often elderly parkinsonian population has been questioned. TCAs act on a number of different neurotransmitters and hence have a wide range of side effects. An elderly population with a high burden of co-morbid illnesses, including cardiovascular problems, is less able to tolerate the cardiac side effects. The PD population are at increased risk of orthostatic hypotension and are more susceptible to confusion caused by the anticholinergic effects. Less common problems include impaired L-dopa absorption and rarely the development of extrapyramidal side effects. Their danger in overdose, although less of an issue in this particular population, needs always to be borne in mind. Lofepramine with fewer cholinergic and serotoninergic side effects, and relative safety in overdose, would appear to be the best option, although data supporting this are lacking.

With much less anticholinergic and antiadrenergic activity, SSRIs appear to be much better tolerated in this group. Since Klassen's review, studies have been done on the three most commonly used SSRIs, namely fluoxetine, paroxetine and sertraline (Hauser & Zesiewicz 1997; Ceravolo *et al.* 2000; Tesei *et al.* 2000). These have been small, generally open label and not controlled, and as such the results need to be interpreted with similar caution to the earlier TCA studies. These drugs would, however, appear to be at least as effective in a PD population as in the general population. They also appear to be as well tolerated as they would be in an age-matched population. This does not mean, however, that they are side effect free. The most commonly reported adverse effects are gastrointestinal symptoms including nausea, diarrhoea and vomiting. The significance of these in an elderly population should not be underestimated. In addition there has been some debate about the propensity of SSRIs to worsen the motor symptoms of PD. There have been case reports of fluoxetine causing parkinsonian signs in a non-PD population (Meltzer *et al.* 1979; Bouchard *et al.* 1989) and as such SSRIs should be used with caution in PD. Although there have been case reports of worsening PD with all SSRIs, this is both rare and generally reversible on cessation. Caley and Friedman (2001) examined a group of 23 patients, 3 of whom suffered mild worsening of symptoms with fluoxetine. They were unable to link these subtle changes directly to the fluoxetine and indeed two of the other patients noted motor improvements on the drug! The important lesson from this is that patients started on SSRIs should be reviewed soon after commencing the drug and at regular intervals thereafter. There is potential for SSRIs to interact with selegiline to produce a neuroleptic malignant-like syndrome and this combination is ideally avoided.

Selegiline was the drug used in a further five of the studies examined by Klassen *et al.* (1995). The outcome was rather mixed and selegiline would appear to have some antidepressant effects. However, there would seem little indication to use it when so many other more effective agents are available. Another group of older antidepressants, the monoamine oxidase inhibitors (MAOIs), are rarely used. They interact with L-dopa causing hypertensive crises. There are theoretical reasons for thinking that some of the newer antidepressants such as venlafaxine, nefazadone and mirtazapine may all be effective and well tolerated in parkinsonian depression, although to date no published data are available. Pramiprexole is licensed as treatment for the motor symptoms of PD, but there have been successful open trials of its use as an antidepressant in non-PD depression (Szegedi *et al.* 1997) and as such it may find a use in the depression of PD in the future.

Electroconvulsive therapy (ECT) is a highly effective treatment for depression that is perhaps underused in the general population. It can be unpopular with patients who may view it as old fashioned or barbaric. In fact it is so safe that its major risk is that of the anaesthetic rather than the ECT. Its most problematic side effect is a mild, generally short-lived impairment in short-term memory. Although often reserved for the most severe cases of depression where its swift action is most needed, Tom and Cummings (1998) have reported that its efficacy and tolerability exceeded that of TCAs. An additional benefit is that the motor symptoms of PD can also improve. All motor symptoms have been observed to respond and such changes often antedate the mood changes. Motor improvements are normally short-lived but have been reported to be more sustained (Douyon *et al.* 1989). Transcranial magnetic stimulation is a much more recent physical treatment. There is early evidence that it can be both effective and well tolerated in depression in the general population. Functional imaging studies suggest that it increases regional cerebral blood flow in the left prefrontal cortex. It has also been studied as treatment for the motor symptoms of PD and as such in due course may prove to be a useful additional treatment for the depression of PD patients (Balldin *et al.* 1980; Andersen *et al.* 1987). Again well-designed trials are awaited.

Non-drug treatment

The evidence base for the pharmacological treatment of depression may be limited, but that for the psychological care of such patients is entirely lacking. The possible causes for this are outside the scope of this chapter, but presumably involve some combination of limited awareness of the different modalities of treatment among neurologists, together with access problems caused by the separation of physical and psychiatric services. There are good theoretical reasons for thinking that both cognitive behavioural therapy and family therapy may have much to offer the depressed PD patient and this was highlighted by MacCarthy and Brown (1989) a decade ago. Much work remains to be done in this crucial area.

Implications of depression

Depression is an unpleasant illness when it occurs in the general population, and its presence in a patient already troubled by PD is worse still. In any case of depression there is an imperative to treat assertively, but are there additional reasons for such an approach in the PD patient?

Parkinson's disease and the patients who suffer from it rarely exist in isolation; the symptoms and disabilities impact on couples, families and other groups. If anything depression is yet more toxic. Meara *et al.* (1999) studied a group of PD patients and their carers for depressive symptoms. They found that 60% of patients and 35% of carers scored above the cut-off on the GDS-15. The single best predictor of depression in the carer was depression in the patient; the burden of caring for a PD patient can be great enough but to add depression to the equation can make the situation intolerable. It requires not a great deal of imagination to see how such a situation can spiral. Holistic care of the PD patient must involve not only the non-motor symptoms of the illness but also the wider context of the patient's illness.

The presence of PD itself predisposes to depression, but what effect if any can depression have on PD? Starkstein *et al.* (1990b) prospectively studied a group of PD patients over a year looking at the impact of depression on a number of domains. The group was divided into major depression, minor depression and no depression. Activities of daily living were assessed using the Northwest Disability Scale. Depressed patients showed a faster decline in scores even when the length of illness was taken into account. Even more persuasively, a dose–response curve was demonstrated for the effect of depression on disease progression: 67% of those with major depression moved on at least one stage in the Hoehn and Yahr scale compared with 41% with minor depression and 20% with no depression. There was a similar finding with changes on the MMSE where 83% of patients with major depression dropped their score: 63% of those with minor depression did likewise, but only 53% of those without depression. Intriguingly, in a separate paper Starkstein *et al.* (1990a) showed that the cognitive decline, as measured by the MMSE on a group of PD patients treated for depression, was half that of the untreated controls when followed up 3–4 years later. Treatment of depression could have wider implications than lifting mood. More work is needed in this area.

Increasing importance is being attached to the impact of both disease and treatment on the patients' quality of life (QoL) and this is discussed in much more detail in Chapter 18. In PD the impact of depression on QoL is becoming clear. Kuopio *et al.* (2000) examined a group of PD patients in the community using the SF36, and looked at a number of domains when assessing QoL:

- physical function
- role limitation – physical
- role limitation – emotional
- social function
- bodily pain
- mental health
- vitality
- health perceptions.

They found that, in the 'Physical Function' domain, the patient's Hoehn and Yahr stage accounted for 48% of the variance. Depression was the second most important factor. In *all* other domains, the presence of depression was the single factor accounting for the greatest variance in QoL. The impact of depression on the quality of a PD patient's life cannot be underestimated.

References

American Psychiatric Association (1994). *Diagnostic and Statistical Manual of Mental Disorders*, 4th edn. Washington DC: APA

Andersen K, Balldin J, Gottfries CG *et al.* (1987). A double-blind evaluation of electroconvulsive therapy in Parkinson's disease with 'on-off' phenomena. *Acta Neurologica Scandinavica* **76**, 191–199

Balldin J, Eden S, Granerus AK *et al.* (1980). Electroconvulsive therapy in Parkinson's syndrome with 'on-off' phenomenon. *Journal of Neural Transmission* **47**, 11–21

Baxter LR Jr, Schwartz JM, Phelps ME *et al.* (1989). Reduction of prefrontal cortex glucose metabolism common to three types of depression. *Archives of General Psychiatry* **46**, 243–250

Beck AT, Ward CH, Mendelson M, Mock J, Erbaugh J (1961). An inventory for measuring depression. *Archives of General Psychiatry* **4**, 53–63

Bench CJ, Friston KJ, Brown RG, Scott LC, Frackowiak RS, Dolan RJ (1992). The anatomy of melancholia—focal abnormalities of cerebral blood flow in major depression. *Psychological Medicine* **22**, 607–615

Bouchard R, Pourcher E, Vincent P (1989). Fluoxetine and extrapyramidal side effects (letter). *American Journal of Psychiatry* **146**, 1352–1353

Brown R & Jahanshahi M (1995). Depression in Parkinson's disease: a psychosocial viewpoint. *Advances in Neurology* **65**, 61–84

Brown RG & MacCarthy B (1990). Psychiatric morbidity in patients with Parkinson's disease. *Psychological Medicine* **20**, 77–87

Caley C & Friedman J (2001). Does Fluoxetine exacerbate Parkinson's disease. *Journal of Clinical Psychiatry* **53**, 278–282

Ceravolo R, Nuti A, Piccinni A *et al.* (2000). Paroxetine in Parkinson's disease: effects on motor and depressive symptoms. *Neurology* **55**, 1216–1218

Choi C, Sohn Y, Lee J, Kim J-S (2000). The effect of long-term levodopa therapy on depression level in de novo patients with Parkinson's disease. *Journal of Neurological Sciences* **172**, 12–16

Cummings JL (1992). Depression and Parkinson's disease: a review. *American Journal of Psychiatry* **149**, 443–454

Cummings JL (1993). The neuroanatomy of depression. *Journal of Clinical Psychiatry* **54**(suppl), 14–20

Damasio AR, Antunes JL, Macedo C (1970). L-dopa, parkinsonism, and depression. *The Lancet* **ii**, 611–612

Davidson RJ, Abercrombie H, Nitschke JB, Putnam K (1999). Regional brain function, emotion and disorders of emotion. *Current Opinion in Neurobiology* **9**, 228–234

Douyon R, Serby M, Klutchko B, Rotrosen J (1989). ECT and Parkinson's disease revisited: a 'naturalistic' study. *American Journal of Psychiatry* **146**, 1451–1455

Dworkin RH, Clark W, Lipsitz JD (1995). Pain responsivity in major depression and bipolar disorder. *Psychiatry Research* **56**, 173–181

Dworkin RH, Hetzel RD, Banks SM (1999). Toward a model of the pathogenesis of chronic pain. *Seminars in Clinical Neuropsychiatry* **4**, 176–185

Ehmann TS, Beninger RJ, Gawel MJ, Riopelle RJ (1990). Coping, social support, and depressive symptoms in Parkinson's disease. *Journal of Geriatric Psychiatry and Neurology* **3**, 85–90

Fibiger HC (1984). The neurobiological substrates of depression in Parkinson's disease: a hypothesis. *Canadian Journal of Neurological Sciences* **11**(suppl), 105–107

Folstein MF, Folstein SE, McHugh PR (1975). 'Mini-mental state'. A practical method for grading the cognitive state of patients for the clinician. *Journal of Psychiatric Research* **12**, 189–198

Friedman J & Friedman H (1993). Fatigue in Parkinson's disease. *Neurology* **43**, 2016–2018

Fukunishi I, Hosokawa K, Ozaki S (1991). Depression antedating the onset of Parkinson's disease. *Japanese Journal of Psychiatry and Neurology* **45**, 7–11

Goetz CG & Stebbins GT (1993). Risk factors for nursing home placement in advanced Parkinson's disease. *Neurology* **43**, 2227–2229

Goetz CG, Tanner CM, Levy M, Wilson RS, Garron DC (1986). Pain in Parkinson's disease. *Movement Disorders* **1**, 45–49

Gotham AM, Brown RG, Marsden CD (1986). Depression in Parkinson's disease: a quantitative and qualitative analysis. *Journal of Neurology, Neurosurgery, and Psychiatry* **49**, 381–389

Hamilton M (1967). Development of a rating scale for primary depressive illness. *British Journal of Social and Clinical Psychology* **6**, 278–296

Hauser RA & Zesiewicz TA (1997). Sertraline for the treatment of depression in Parkinson's disease. *Movement Disorders* **12**, 756–759

Henderson R, Kurlan R, Kersun JM, Como P (1992). Preliminary examination of the comorbidity of anxiety and depression in Parkinson's disease. *Journal of Neuropsychiatry and Clinical Neurosciences* **4**, 257–264

Hoehn MM & Yahr MD (1967). Parkinsonism: onset, progression and mortality. *Neurology* **17**, 427–442

Hoogendijk WJ, Sommer IE, Tissingh G, Deeg DJ, Wolters EC (1998). Depression in Parkinson's disease. The impact of symptom overlap on prevalence. *Psychosomatics* **39**, 416–421

Horn S (1974). Some psychological factors in Parkinsonism. *Journal of Neurology, Neurosurgery & Psychiatry* **37**, 27–31

Karlsen K, Larsen JP, Tandberg E, Jorgensen K (1999). Fatigue in patients with Parkinson's disease. *Movement Disorders* **14**, 237–241

Kaufer DI, Cummings JL, Christine D (1996). Effect of tacrine on behavioral symptoms in Alzheimer's disease: an open-label study. *Journal of Geriatric Psychiatry and Neurology* **9**, 1–6

Klaassen T, Verhey FR, Sneijders GH, Rozendaal N, de Vet HC, van Praag HM (1995). Treatment of depression in Parkinson's disease: a meta-analysis. *Journal of Neuropsychiatry and Clinical Neurosciences* **7**, 281–286

Kuopio AM, Marttila RJ, Helenius H, Toivonen M, Rinne UK (2000). The quality of life in Parkinson's disease. *Movement Disorders* **15**, 216–223

Lafer B, Renshaw PF, Sachs GS (1997). Major depression and the basal ganglia. *Psychiatric Clinics of North America* **20**, 885–896

Leentjens AF, Verhey FR, Lousberg R, Spitsbergen H, Wilmink FW (2000a). The validity of the Hamilton and Montgomery-Asberg depression rating scales as screening and diagnostic tools for depression in Parkinson's disease. *International Journal of Geriatric Psychiatry* **15**, 644–649

Leentjens AF, Verhey FR, Luijckx GJ, Troost J (2000b). The validity of the Beck Depression Inventory as a screening and diagnostic instrument for depression in patients with Parkinson's disease. *Movement Disorders* **15**, 1221–1224

Levin BE, Llabre MM, Weiner WJ (1988). Parkinson's disease and depression: psychometric properties of the Beck Depression Inventory. *Journal of Neurology, Neurosurgery, and Psychiatry* **51**, 1401–1404

Levy ML, Cummings JL, Fairbanks LA *et al.* (1998). Apathy is not depression. *Journal of Neuropsychiatry and Clinical Neurosciences* **10**, 314–319

Liddle PF, Barnes TR, Morris D, Haque S (1989). Three syndromes in chronic schizophrenia. *British Journal of Psychiatry* Suppl 7, 119–122

Liu CY, Wang SJ, Fuh JL, Lin CH, Yang YY, Liu HC (1997). The correlation of depression with functional activity in Parkinson's disease. *Journal of Neurology* **244**, 493–498

MacCarthy B & Brown R (1989). Psychosocial factors in Parkinson's disease. *British Journal of Clinical Psychology* **28**(Pt 1), 41–52

Marin RS (1991). Apathy: a neuropsychiatric syndrome. *Journal of Neuropsychiatry and Clinical Neurosciences* **3**, 243–254

Mayberg HS, Starkstein SE, Sadzot B *et al.* (1990). Selective hypometabolism in the inferior frontal lobe in depressed patients with Parkinson's disease. *Annals of Neurology* **28**, 57–64

Mayeux R, Stern Y, Cote L, Williams JB (1984). Altered serotonin metabolism in depressed patients with Parkinson's disease. *Neurology* **34**, 642–646

Meara J, Mitchelmore E, Hobson P (1999). Use of the GDS-15 geriatric depression scale as a screening instrument for depressive symptomatology in patients with Parkinson's disease and their carers in the community. [see comments]. *Age & Ageing* **28**, 35–38

Meltzer H, Young M, Metz J (1979). Extrapyramidal side effects and increased serum prolactin following fluoxetine, a new antidepressant. *Journal of Neural Transmission* **45**, 165–175

Menza MA, Robertson-Hoffman DE, Bonapace AS (1993). Parkinson's disease and anxiety: comorbidity with depression. *Biological Psychiatry* **34**, 465–470

Mindham RH (1970). Psychiatric symptoms in Parkinsonism. *Journal of Neurology, Neurosurgery, and Psychiatry* **33**, 188–191

Montgomery SA, Asberg M (1979). A new depression scale designed to be sensitive to change. *British Journal of Psychiatry* **134**, 382–389

Nissenbaum H, Quinn NP, Brown RG, Toone B, Gotham AM, Marsden CD (1987). Mood swings associated with the 'on-off' phenomenon in Parkinson's disease. *Psychological Medicine* **17**, 899–904

Quinn N & Marsden CD (1986). Lithium for painful dystonia in Parkinson's disease. *The Lancet* **i**, 1377

Richard IH. & Kurlan R (1997). A survey of antidepressant drug use in Parkinson's disease. Parkinson Study Group. *Neurology* **49**, 1168–1170

Ring, HA, Bench CJ, Trimble MR, Brooks DJ, Frackowiak RS, Dolan RJ (1994). Depression in Parkinson's disease. A positron emission study. *British Journal of Psychiatry* **165**, 333–339

Sandyk R & Snider SR (1985). Sensory symptoms: Parkinson's disease. *Neurology* **35**, 619–620

Santamaria J, Tolosa E, Valles A (2001). Mental depression in untreated Parkinson's disease of recent onset. *Advances in Neurology* **45**, 443–446

Schrag A, Jahanshahi M, Quinn NP (2001). What contributes to depression in Parkinson's disease? *Psychological Medicine* **31**, 65–73

Shulman L (2000). Apathy in patients with Parkinson's disease. *International Review of Psychiatry* **12**, 298–306

Singer E (1974). The effect of treatment with levodopa on Parkinson patients' social functioning and outlook on life. *Journal of Chronic Diseases.* **27**, 581–594

Starkstein SE (1999). Neurological models of depression. *Advances in Biological Psychiatry* **19**, 123–135

Starkstein SE, Berthier ML, Bolduc PL, Preziosi TJ, Robinson RG (1989). Depression in patients with early versus late onset of Parkinson's disease. [see comments]. *Neurology* **39**, 1441–1445

Starkstein SE, Bolduc PL, Mayberg HS, Preziosi TJ, Robinson RG (1990a). Cognitive impairments and depression in Parkinson's disease: a follow up study. *Journal of Neurology, Neurosurgery and Psychiatry* **53**, 597–602

Starkstein SE, Preziosi TJ, Bolduc PL, Robinson RG (1990b). Depression in Parkinson's disease. *Journal of Nervous and Mental Disease.* **178**, 27–31

Starkstein SE, Mayberg HS, Preziosi TJ, Andrezejewski P, Leiguarda R, Robinson RG (1992). Reliability, validity, and clinical correlates of apathy in Parkinson's disease. *Journal of Neuropsychiatry and Clinical Neurosciences* **4**, 134–139

Szegedi A, Hilbert A, Wetzel H, Klieser E, Gaebel W, Benkert O (1997). Pramiprexole, a dopaminergic agonist in major depression: antidepressant tolerability in an open label study with multiple doses. *Clinical Neuropharmacology* **20**, S36–S45

Tandberg E, Larsen JP, Aarsland D, Cummings JL (1996). The occurrence of depression in Parkinson's disease. A community-based study. *Archives of Neurology* **53**, 175–179

Tandberg E, Larsen JP, Aarsland D, Laake K, Cummings JL (1997). Risk factors for depression in Parkinson disease. *Archives of Neurology* **54**, 625–630

Taylor AE, Saint-Cyr JA, Lang AE, Kenny FT (1986). Parkinson's disease and depression. A critical re-evaluation. *Brain* **109**(Pt 2), 279–292

Tesei S, Antonini A, Canesi M, Zecchinelli A, Mariani CB, Pezzoli G (2000). Tolerability of paroxetine in Parkinson's disease: a prospective study. *Movement Disorders* **15**, 986–989

Tom T & Cummings JL (1998). Drug treatment for Alzheimer's disease. *Western Journal of Medicine* **168**, 264

Warburton JW (1967). Depressive symptoms in Parkinson patients referred for thalamotomy. *Journal of Neurology, Neurosurgery, and Psychiatry* **30**, 368–370

Wesely S, Hotopf M, Sharpe M (1999). *Chronic Fatigue and its Syndromes.* Oxford: Oxford University Press

World Health Organization (1980). *International Classification of Impairments, Disabilities and Handicaps: A Manual of Classification Relating to Consequences of Disease.* Geneva: WHO

World Health Organization (1992). *International Classification of Diseases*, 10th revision. Geneva: WHO

Yahr MD, Duvoisin RC, Schear MJ, Barrett RE, Hoehn MM (1969). Treatment of parkinsonism with levodopa. *Archives of Neurology* **21**, 343–354

Chapter 8

Scientific evidence and expert clinical opinion for the management of psychosis

Max J Henderson and Brian K Toone

Introduction

Authors have commented on mental changes in Parkinson's disease (PD) since the end of the nineteenth century (Ball 1882; Mallie 1908), but it is since the advent of L-dopa that there has been a marked increase in the recognition of psychosis occurring within PD. Initial descriptive studies have been followed by various hypotheses about causation. In the process our understanding of the pathological basis of both psychosis and PD has been enhanced. For all but the last couple of years, such basic and clinical research has had disappointingly little impact on the treatment of the problem. However, much excitement has accompanied the publication of two randomised controlled trials demonstrating the effectiveness and tolerability of the atypical antipsychotic drug clozapine.

Prevalence

Levodopa was first used in the 1960s. Although it brought significant improvement in motor symptoms, it was soon noted that more PD patients were becoming psychotic (Barbeau 1969; Calne *et al.* 1969; Celesia & Barr 1970). These studies tended to report quite high rates for several reasons. The methodology of most studies was substantially less rigorous than would be expected today. Non-random samples were studied and different definitions of psychosis were used. Some authors included confusion and delirium whereas others did not. Diagnosis was almost always on the basis of clinical examination alone, without the use of structured interviews or predetermined diagnostic criteria. This also has implications for the validity of the diagnosis of PD. Patient groups would undoubtedly have included participants with postencephalitic parkinsonism and vascular pseudo-parkinsonism, both of which appear to have higher levels of psychosis than true idiopathic PD. Lewy body disease (LBD) had not been described and a proportion of patients would not have had PD but LBD instead. Mindham's (1970) study used more stringent criteria and found visual hallucinations in 10% and delusions in 29%. He acutely observed the low (2 of 89) prevalence of schizophrenic illness.

A modern consensus would suggest that between 20% and 30% of PD patients suffer from psychosis at some point. Psychosis here would be defined as hallucinations and/or delusions occurring in clear consciousness. Perhaps the best epidemiological work has been done in Norway. Aarsland *et al.* (1999c) studied a community sample of 139 patients with PD diagnosed by a neurologist. Using the Neuropsychiatric Inventory, a validated tool that looks at symptoms during the last month, 27% had hallucinations and 16% delusions. Studies in specialist settings tend to show higher levels, e.g. Fenelon *et al.* (2000) looked at patients in two French PD clinics: 39.8% had hallucinations.

Phenomenology

Visual hallucinations remain the classic and most commonly reported psychotic symptom in PD. Their content varies hugely and examples are plentiful in the literature – they are often vividly and eloquently described. Animate objects including people (both real and fictional) and animals are particularly common. One patient had daily hallucinations of her sister even though she lived on the other side of Paris (Fenelon *et al.* 2000). Another saw a miniature 'Uncle Sam' who jumped about on the furniture (Henderson & Mellers 2000). Typically these hallucinations are not threatening and although frequent are not stereotyped. They are most common towards the end of the day, although they may occur at any time. They can last from seconds to hours. Interestingly such hallucinations occur most often in isolation from other psychotic symptoms.

Visual hallucinations in a clear sensorium should be distinguished from abnormal perceptual experiences that occur in delirium. Clouding of consciousness and disorientation will often be present in delirium. As such, the description given by the patient will generally be poor; hallucinations may be difficult to separate from illusions. An informant history is essential in these cases. Such a careful history will often reveal episodes of confusion and allow the correct diagnosis to be made. This has important management implications. Such a delirium is most often caused by medications such as those with anticholinergic effects. The patient will also need a thorough physical assessment to exclude intercurrent infections.

Fenelon *et al.* (2000) have drawn attention to the phenomenon of 'minor hallucinations' that occurred in 25% of his sample. The most common of these was the 'presence hallucination' in which the patient complained of the vivid sensation of someone either directly behind them or somewhere else in the room. The person was commonly unidentified. On one occasion it was a rat. The second perceptual abnormality was the 'passage hallucination'. Here the complaint was of a person or animal passing sideways. The animal was most commonly a cat or a dog; on two occasions it was of an animal previously owned by the patient. These experiences do not form part of any standard assessment tool and are rarely volunteered spontaneously by the patient. It is possible that the under-reporting of such experiences has led to a slight underestimation of the burden of psychotic experience in PD.

Hallucinations can occur in other modalities. Auditory hallucinations have been noted but occur much less often than visual hallucinations. It is quite unusual for auditory hallucinations to be the sole psychotic phenomenon. Moskovitz *et al.* (1978) found that 9.7% of their patients had only auditory hallucinations but 25.8% had both auditory and visual. Graham *et al.* (1997) found only 6% had pure auditory hallucinations and Fenelon *et al.* (2000) only 2.3%. Inzelberg *et al.* (1998) found no patients at all who had only auditory hallucinations. The voices heard in such experiences are typically less threatening than those described in schizophrenia, being non-imperative and non-paranoid. They tend to be in the first or second person. In concurrent auditory and visual hallucinations, it is rare for the visual hallucinations to be the source of the voices, but it can happen (Fenelon *et al.* 2000). Tactile (Moskovitz *et al.* 1978) and olfactory (Asaad & Shapiro 1986) hallucinations have been described, as have synaesthetic hallucinations where a perception in one sensory modality leads to an hallucination in another (Jimenez-Jimenez *et al.* 1997).

A significant proportion of psychotic experiences in PD are neither threatening nor distressing. Importantly the patients often retain insight into the nature of their experiences. This is most true of the mildest and most common forms of psychosis. In Fenelon's study 96% of patients with isolated 'minor' hallucinations such as the passage hallucinations had retained insight whereas only 77% of those with frank visual hallucinations had insight. This is comparable with Graham's study which reported intact insight in 70%. Aarsland and Karlsen (1999) drew a distinction between 'organic psychosis', meaning hallucinations with insight, and 'psychosis', which included both hallucination without insight and delusions. The 1-week prevalence of the former was 10% compared with 6% for psychosis. Delusions are seen in 3–10% of PD patients. Certain themes predominate in the literature. These include various conspiracy theories and concerns about spousal infidelity. Capgras' syndrome, in which the patient believes that people close to him or her have been replaced by doubles, has been reported (Lippen 1976). Rarely, the psychosis can be manic in its presentation (Menza & Chastlea 1989; Alcantara Lapaz *et al.* 1997). Formal thought disorder is most uncommon. This underscores the observation of Mindham (2001) that, despite a sometimes florid presentation, a schizophreniform psychosis is most unusual.

Sleep disturbance is common in PD (Kales *et al.* 1971) for a number of reasons, but sleep disorders are most commonly seen after treatment. This is particularly true of abnormal dream phenomena. Aarsland *et al.* (1999c) reported that 25.5% of patients in a community sample had noted abnormal dreams within the last week and 26.8% at some point in time. Moskovitz *et al.* (1978) described a similar prevalence of 30.7%. Pappert *et al.* (1999) studied patients in a specialist setting and reported even higher rates: 48% of his patients had experienced abnormal dream phenomena in the preceding 30 days. Such dreams are reported by the patients as being different from their normal dreams, but they are not necessarily nightmares because they are often affectively neutral (Nausieda *et al.* 1982). A close link between abnormal dream phenomena and psychosis in PD has been described by several authors. Up to 90% of those reporting hallucinations also report altered dreams (Moskovitz *et al.* 1978; Nausieda *et al.* 1982; Pappert *et al.* 1999). It has been proposed that sleep disorders herald the onset of psychosis, although longitudinal studies have yet to confirm this. More recently Arnulf *et al.* (2000), in a small case–control study, found that hallucinators had reduced mean sleep latency, and several had bursts of muscle tone during rapid eye movement (REM) sleep, when typically they should be hypotonic. Five hallucinating patients had two or more episodes of REM sleep during the day *after which they complained of hallucinations.* No patients fulfilled criteria for narcolepsy. They concluded that psychosis in PD patients may be related to a narcolepsy-like REM sleep disorder. Further studies are needed.

It can thus be seen that a number of different entities can be described under the term 'psychosis'. The breadth of the concept, although useful for discussing aetiologies and treatments in broad terms, limits its value as a diagnostic label. There are of course a number of diagnoses of which some form of psychosis forms a part, such as paranoid schizophrenia (ICD F20.0) and manic psychosis (ICD F30.2). Inasmuch as it is too narrow to describe either of these conditions simply as 'psychosis', it seems to these authors that it is too broad to use the term 'psychosis' as a diagnosis when there is such a wide range of potential clinical meanings. The use of standardised terms from the *International Classification of Diseases*, 10th revision (WHO 1992) with more precise meanings, such as 'Organic Hallucinosis' (ICD F06.0) and 'Organic Delusional Disorder' (ICD F06.2), would not only increase the accuracy of communications between clinicians and researchers in the field, but also perhaps serve as a starting point in examining possible differences between patients in a very heterogeneous group.

Risk factors

There is a substantial body of work describing the possible risk factors for psychosis in PD. Much of this is, however, of questionable value given the methodological limitations of many of the studies. The factors that appear most commonly in such studies are cognitive impairment, greater duration of illness and increased age (Celesia & Barr 1970; Sacks *et al.* 1970; Glantz *et al.* 1987). Using multivariate analysis on a population drawn from a specialist clinic setting French investigators found that the three factors that independently predicted hallucinations were cognitive impairment, a disease duration greater than 8 years and the presence of daytime somnolence (Fenelon *et al.* 2000). There have, however, been negative findings. Although the study of Aarsland *et al.* (1999a) did find an association with cognitive impairment, neither duration of disease nor duration of treatment was associated. Others (Fischer *et al.* 1990; Meco *et al.* 1990; Danielcyzk 1992) also failed to confirm a link with cognitive impairment.

A number of investigators have identified a link between psychosis and levodopa-induced dyskinesias, although, here too, opinion is divided. Hence although Friedman and Sienkiewicz (1991) found that 90% of patients with complex psychiatric complications had dyskinesias compared with 55% of those with simple complications, Tanner *et al.* (1983) found no such link in a study involving 775 patients. One study (Fernandez *et al.* 2001) found that hallucinations were more likely in the on period, although others have found that they are more common in the off period (Sage & Duvoisin 1986; Nissenbaum *et al.* 1987; Steiger *et al.* 1991). No particular disease characteristic (rigidity, tremor or bradykinesia) appears to be associated with hallucinations. One study (Shergill *et al.* 1998) found a trend towards more psychosis in patients with right-sided disease whereas another found a trend towards predominantly left-sided disease (Aarsland *et al.* 1999c).

The timing of the onset of psychotic symptoms has important implications both for our understanding of the biology of hallucinations in PD and for their management. Graham *et al.* (1997) distinguished between early hallucinators (within 5 years of treatment) and late hallucinators (> 5 years treatment). Early hallucinators had a shorter time to L-dopa-related motor fluctuations and were prescribed more dopaminergic medications. The late hallucinators were more cognitively impaired. Goetz *et al.* (1998a) defined 'early' as within 3 months and 'late' as after 12 months of treatment. Early hallucinators were more troubled by their experiences, and were more likely to have auditory as well as visual hallucinations and to have symptoms during the day as well as the night. They had a reduced 5-year survival. Significantly, at follow-up after 5 years, two-thirds had had their diagnosis changed, either to Alzheimer's disease or LBD. Hence psychotic symptoms soon after commencing dopaminergic medication should highlight the possibility of a misdiagnosis.

More sophisticated possible risk factors have been examined recently. Makoff *et al.* (2000) studied polymorphisms in both the dopamine D_2- and D_3-receptors. The results were equivocal with no association between any of the polymorphisms and the whole group of hallucinators. They did, however, find an association between late-onset hallucinators and one of the polymorphisms that they hypothesise may be in linkage disequilibrium with another mutation on the D_2-receptor. De la Fuente-Fernandez *et al.* (1999) examined the prevalence of the apolipoprotein ε4 allele. This has previously been studied in relation to Alzheimer's disease. Even after adjustment for other known risk factors, as discussed above, an association between the occurrence of visual hallucinations and the presence of the ε4 allele was found. Further work is needed both on the link with apolipoprotein E and with dopaminergic receptors and transporters.

The dramatic increase in reports of psychosis after the introduction of levodopa has been viewed as evidence that hallucinations and delusions are simply a side effect of parkinsonian medication. It has also been used to study the relationship between movement disorders and psychosis in terms of symptoms, medication and underlying pathophysiological mechanism (Crow *et al.* 1976). That levodopa can directly produce psychosis was demonstrated by Tobias and Merlin (197) when it produced a worsening of the mental state of their schizophrenic patients. L-Dopa exacerbated the original psychosis of schizophrenic patients whose neuroleptic treatment had caused parkinsonian side effects. There is, however, good evidence to suggest the relationship is not so straightforward. Goetz *et al.* (1988a) gave intravenous levodopa to PD patients who were already hallucinating and it did not provoke any worsening in their condition. Despite initial claims of a dose–response relationship between L-dopa and psychosis, several studies have produced no support for this.

Anticholinergic drugs were associated with psychiatric side effects in PD patients even before the advent of L-dopa (Porteous & Ross 1956). The mental changes produced by this group of drugs tend to be slightly different, inasmuch as the hallucinosis often forms part of a delirium. The hallucinations are characteristically more threatening and less well formed than those supposedly secondary to dopaminergic drugs. Some patients are particularly sensitive. Minagar *et al.* (1999) report a case of a PD patient who became psychotic after the administration of a single hyoscine patch.

Psychiatric side effects are the most common reason for withdrawal of dopamine agonists. Saint-Cyr *et al.* (1993) suggest that psychosis is two to three times more likely to follow treatment with dopamine agonists than with L-dopa. It would be wrong, however, to conclude from this that such drugs are more psychotogenic than L-dopa. Dopamine agonists are normally a second-line treatment for PD and added when treatment with levodopa alone is causing intolerable side effects such as wearing-off effects and dyskinesias. Almost by definition, therefore, such patients are older, and have had PD for longer and may be more cognitively impaired. Thus, patients on dopamine agonists are often also on a combination antiparkinsonian medication. It is difficult to be certain in such circumstances about the exact origin of psychiatric side effects.

There are reports of psychosis complicating treatment with all dopaminergic drugs. This includes pergolide (Jankovic 1985; Lieberman *et al.* 1985), lisuride (Vaamonde *et al.* 1991), apomorphine (Frankel *et al.* 1990) and cabergoline (Lera *et al.* 1993), as well as older drugs such as bromocriptine. Several authors (Jankovic 1985; Vaamonde *et al.* 1991) suggest that the psychosis associated with these drugs is more florid and persistent than that with levodopa alone. Others have found better evidence of a dose–response relationship. One important negative finding was that of Turner *et al.* (1984) who found very low levels of psychosis in patients treated with dopamine agonists for other, often endocrine, reasons. Although the evidence is only anecdotal, some authors (Kempster *et al.* 1990; Pollack *et al.* 1990) claim that apomorphine of all the dopamine agonists has the lowest risk of precipitating psychosis.

Amantadine is used much less now than 20 years ago. It has been associated with delirium and hallucinatory states by many investigators (Schwab *et al.* 1969; Bauer & McHenry 1974; Postma & Van Tilburg 1975). There are reports of selegiline precipitating psychosis in patients already on levodopa (Kurlan & Dimitsopulos

1992). Used alone, however, it would appear to be relatively free of psychiatric side effects. Rather, its psychotogenic effects derive from potentiation of levodopa. There is one report of fluoxetine producing hallucinations when added to stable antiparkinsonian medication (Lauterbach 1993).

Although the infrequency of psychosis in untreated PD suggests that antiparkinsonian medication is largely necessary for the development of psychotic symptoms, it is not sufficient. Wide variations in reported rates and lack of clear dose–response curves point instead to an interaction with as-yet-unspecified (neurodegenerative) processes. These probably involve more than one neurotransmitter system, are related in some way to cognitive impairment and proceed to a greater or lesser degree independently of deterioration in motor function.

Differential diagnosis

The study by Goetz *et al.* (1998b), in which a diagnosis of PD was subsequently revised, highlights the importance of not assuming that psychosis in PD is simply related in some way to the antiparkinsonian medication. A number of conditions can either exist co-morbidly with PD or masquerade as PD and produce a psychotic picture. A full discussion of these conditions is outside the scope of this chapter but Table 10.1 lists the key differential diagnoses and the features that are important to consider.

Table 8.1 Key differential diagnoses and important features of co-morbid conditions

Diagnosis	Features
Parkinson's disease PLUS schizophrenia	Predominance of auditory hallucinations Thought disorder Loss of insight more prominent More paranoid flavour to symptoms
Lewy body dementia	Fluctuations in consciousness Prominence of falls Greater cognitive impairment
Frontotemporal dementia	Personality change Progressive aphasia
Alzheimer's disease with hallucinations and prominent extrapyramidal signs	Greater cognitive impairment Pyramidal signs Loss of insight more prominent

Treatment

The clear link with dopaminergic treatments led to medication adjustments being the initial mainstay of treatment for psychosis in Parkinson's disease. A 'drug holiday' was often advocated. This involved the abrupt temporary withdrawal of antiparkinsonian medication (Klawans *et al.* 1983; Friedman 1985). Although there are occasional reports of success (Goetz *et al.* 1982), this treatment has largely been discredited as lacking convincing evidence, being uncomfortable for the patients and even dangerous (Marsden & Fahn 1981). Several reports of a condition similar to neuroleptic malignant syndrome have appeared (Guze & Baxter 1985; Addonzio *et al.* 1987) and this treatment is no longer recommended.

A more gradual reduction and withdrawal of antiparkinsonian medication appears much safer. At the point where psychosis normally arises, patients are often on more than one drug. If a new medication has recently been added, it would seem sensible to withdraw it. However, if the psychosis arises in the context of a stable drug regimen, medication should be withdrawn in the following order:

1. Anticholinergics
2. Selegiline
3. Amantadine
4. Dopamine agonists
5. catechol *O*-methyltransferase (COMT) inhibitors
6. L-Dopa.

The literature appears quite consistent about these recommendations (Quinn 1995; Duncan & Taylor 1996; Fernandez & Friedman 1999; Juncos 1999), although they are empirical; the studies have not been done. Withdrawal should be slowly over weeks; the positive effects sadly often lag behind the negative motor effects. Patients will need close monitoring because there have been several reports of a withdrawal psychosis after removal of dopaminergic medication (Jenkins & Groh 1970; Mayeauz *et al.* 1985). If the changes are well tolerated, it is possible that antiparkinsonian medication might be reintroduced cautiously at a later stage without exacerbation of psychotic symptoms. This would ideally be a drug with a low propensity for producing hallucinations; Ray-Chaudhuri *et al.* (1991) and Ellis and Lemmens Parker (1995) suggest that apomorphine is the drug of choice. There may be occasions, such as poorly controlled PD, when it would seem more prudent to add an antipsychotic straight away rather than delaying their introduction while medications are adjusted. However, antipsychotic medications are not without side effects and may be difficult to withdraw. In addition, the fact that the PD is poorly controlled should prompt a review of the diagnosis. Nevertheless, the withdrawal of antiparkinsonian medication is not a hard-and-fast prerequisite for commencement of antipsychotic drugs.

When the psychotic symptoms do not respond to alterations in the antiparkinsonian drug regimen, for a long period conventional antipsychotics were all physicians could offer. In most patients this led to an unacceptable worsening in motor symptoms (Scholz & Dichgans 1985; Wolk & Douglas 1992; Greene *et al.* 1993), even if low-potency drugs (Crow *et al.* 1976; Hale & Bellizzi 1980) or low doses (Shaw *et al.* 1980) are used. In addition, the risks of neuroleptics in patients with LBD (Ballard *et al.* 1995) have been highlighted recently, risks that were not known about 30 years ago.

The advent of the atypical antipsychotics appeared at first to be the answer to the difficulties of treating psychosis in PD. These drugs had a much lower incidence of extrapyramidal side effects and would presumably be well tolerated in a parkinsonian population. Early work with risperidone appeared promising (Meco *et al.* 1994; Ballard *et al.* 1995), but it became clear that even at low doses this drug could still cause intolerable side effects (Ford *et al.* 1994; Rich *et al.* 1995; Friedman 1998).

Olanzapine too seemed very effective (Wolters *et al.* 1996; Graham *et al.* 1998), but again evidence of poor tolerability soon emerged with olanzapine causing both extrapyramidal side effects and sedation. A recent study (Aarsland *et al.* 1999d) planned to compare olanzapine with clozapine in over 30 patients. However, it had to be stopped after only 15 patients as there was a marked exacerbation of parkinsonian symptoms in the olanzapine group compared with the clozapine group. A multicentre placebo-controlled, double-masked trial of olanzapine is currently under way. Quetiapine is a more recently licensed atypical antipsychotic drug. Early results were most promising, with the drug being both effective and well tolerated (Parsa & Bastani 1998). Rosenfeld *et al.* (1998) reported 24 patients of whom 20 improved without worsening of motor symptoms, whereas Targum and Abbott (2000) described positive results in 10 of 11 patients. Fernandez (2000) recently highlighted a case where olanzapine was ineffective but the patient improved without adverse motor effects on quetiapine.

Clozapine is different from other atypical antipsychotics in many ways. These include its indication as a treatment for treatment-resistant schizophrenia, but also frustratingly its need for weekly haematological monitoring. It was first described as a treatment for psychosis in PD in 1985 (Scholz & Dichgans 1985) and, as with other atypical drugs, initial results were favourable. It was thus disappointing that the first randomised controlled trial of clozapine did not confirm the results of the case series (Wolter *et al.* 1990). The drug appeared poorly tolerated; 50% of patients dropped out. This may have been the result of the dose being too high (75–250 mg) and the initial titration too rapid. Since then, there have been further case reports of successful use at lower doses. Importantly, there has been only one case of agranulocytosis in this patient group and this was reversed on cessation of the clozapine (Greene *et al.* 1993).

In 1999 two elegant randomised controlled trials (French Clozapine Parkinson Study Group 1999; Parkinson Study Group 1999) confirmed both the efficacy and tolerability of low dose clozapine. The Parkinson Study Group looked at 60 patients, giving them a mean dose of only 35 mg. Only three patients from each of the groups dropped out and in fact in many patients the tremor actually improved rather than worsening. Overall, clozapine appears to produce significant improvement in a much greater proportion of psychotic PD patients than it does in schizophrenia, and at a substantially lower dose.

A number of alternative treatments have been used in parkinsonian psychosis with varying degrees of success. Ondansetron is perhaps the most exciting. This is a serotonin

5HT$_3$ antagonist normally used in the treatment of nausea associated with cytotoxic chemotherapy. Zoldan *et al.* (1993, 1995, 1996) have described improvement in patients without a worsening of motor symptoms and a randomised controlled trial is under way. Electroconvulsive therapy (ECT) remains a treatment option that, although often reserved for the most difficult refractory cases, should perhaps be used more often. The bulk of the literature refers to ECT in the treatment of depression in PD, but there are also reports of its successful use in psychosis (Hurwitz *et al.* 1988; Abrams 1989; Factor *et al.* 1995). Results may be short-lived or last many months (Friedman & Sienkiewicz 1991). Of note is the positive effect that ECT can have on the motor symptoms of PD. In a novel approach, Factor *et al.* (1995) treated two patients with ECT initially, but subsequently maintained them successfully on low-dose clozapine.

Impact of psychosis

Although hallucinations with preserved insight may not be particularly troublesome to a proportion of patients, this is not universally true. The additional burden of intrusive mental symptoms on top of a motor disorder that profoundly affects many aspects of daily living is most unwelcome. PD patients often have carers and they in particular find the psychiatric aspects difficult to deal with. Indeed carers report that psychotic symptoms are associated with greater distress than the motor symptoms (Carter *et al.* 1998). Aarsland *et al.* (1999b) found that caregiver distress was predicted by a higher score on the Neuropsychiatric Inventory, in addition to depression and cognitive impairment. Perhaps the most significant sequel of psychosis is reported by Goetz and Stebbins (1993, 1995), who found that it was the single most important factor leading to placement in a nursing home. Once in such care facilities, patients rarely leave and the mortality rate is much higher than outside in the community.

References

Aarsland D & Karlsen K (1999). Neuropsychiatric aspects of Parkinson's disease. *Current Psychiatry Report* 1(1), 61–68

Aarsland D, Larsen JP, Cummins JL, Laake K (1999a). Prevalence and clinical correlates of psychotic symptoms in Parkinson disease: a community-based study. *Archives of Neurology* 56, 595–601

Aarsland D, Larsen JP, Karlsen K, Lim NG, Tandberg E (1999b). Mental symptoms in Parkinson's disease are important contributors to caregivers distress. *International Journal of Geriatric Psychiatry* 14, 866–874

Aarsland D, Larsen JP, Lim NG *et al.* (1999c). Range of neuropsychiatric disturbances in patients with Parkinson's disease. *Journal of Neurology, Neurosurgery, and Psychiatry* 67, 492–496

Aarsland D, Larsen JP, Lim NG, Tandberg E (1999d). Olanzapine for psychosis in patients with Parkinson's disease with and without dementia. *Journal of Neuropsychiatry and Clinical Neurosciences.* 11, 392–394

Abrams R (1989). ECT for Parkinson's disease. *American Journal of Psychiatry* **146**, 1391–1393

Addonizio G, Susman VL, Roth SD (1987). Neuroleptic malignant syndrome: review and analysis of 115 cases. *Biology and Psychiatry* **22**, 1004–1020

Alcantara Lapaz A, Ortega R, Morcillo L, Barcia D (1997). Concomitant bipolar disorder and Parkinson's disease treated with clozapine. *Psiquis* **18**(3), 41–43

Arnulf I, Bonnet AM, Damier P *et al.* (2000). Hallucinations, REM sleep, and Parkinson's disease: a medical hypothesis. *Neurology* **55**, 281–288

Asaad G & Shapiro B (1986). Hallucinations: theoretical and clinical overview. *American Journal of Psychiatry* **143**, 1088–1097

Ball B (1882). De l'insanite dans la paralysie agitante. *Encephale* **2**, 22–52

Ballard C, Bannister C, Graham C, Oyebode F, Wilcock G (1995). Associations of psychotic symptoms in dementia sufferers. *British Journal of Psychiatry* **167**, 537–540

Barbeau A (1969). L-dopa therapy in Parkinson's disease. A critical review of nine years experience. *Canadian Medical Association Journal* **101**, 791–800

Bauer RB. & McHenry JT (1974). Comparison of amantadine, placebo, and levodopa in Parkinson's disease. *Neurology* **24**, 715–720

Calne DB, Spiers A, Stern GM, Laurence DR, Armitage P (1969). L-dopa in idiopathic parkinsonism. *The Lancet* **ii**, 973–976

Carter J, Stewart B, Archbold P (1998). Living with a person who has Parkinson's disease: the spouse's perspective by stage of disease. *Movement Disorders* **13**, 20–28

Celesia GG & Barr AN (1970). Psychosis and other psychiatric manifestations of levodopa therapy. *Archives of Neurology* **23**, 193–200

Crow TJ, Johnstone EC, McClelland HA (1976). The coincidence of schizophrenia and Parkinsonism: some neurochemical implications. *Psychological Medicine* **6**, 227–233

Danielczyk W (1992). Mental disorders in Parkinson's disease. *Journal of Neural Transmission* **38**(suppl), 115–127

de la Fuente-Fernandez R, Nunez MA, Lopez E (1999). The apolipoprotein E epsilon 4 allele increases the risk of drug-induced hallucinations in Parkinson's disease. *Clinical Neuropharmacology* **22**, 226–230

Duncan D & Taylor D (1996). Treatment of psychosis in Parkinson's disease. *Psychiatric Bulletin* **20**, 157–159

Ellis C & Lemmens Parker J (1995). Use of apomorphine in Parkinsonism patients with neuropsychiatric complications to oral treatment. *Neurology* **45**(suppl 4), A251

Factor SA, Molho ES, Brown DL (1995). Combined clozapine and electroconvulsive therapy for the treatment of drug-induced psychosis in Parkinson's disease. *Journal of Neuropsychiatry and Clinical Neurosciences* **7**, 304–307

Fenelon G, Mahieux F, Huon R, Ziegler M (2000). Hallucinations in Parkinson's disease: prevalence, phenomenology and risk factors. *Brain* **123**(Pt 4), 733–745

Fernandez HH (2000). Quetiapine for L-dopa-induced psychosis in PD. *Neurology* **55**, 899

Fernandez HH & Friedman J (1999). The role of atypical antipsychotic in the treatment of movement disorders. *CNS Drugs* **11**, 467–483

Fernandez W, Stern GM, Lees AJ (2001). Hallucinations and Parkinsonian motor fluctuations. *Behavioural Neurology* **5**, 83–86

Fischer P, Danielczyk W, Simanyi M, Streifler MB (1990). Dopaminergic psychosis in advanced Parkinson's disease. *Advances in Neurology* **53**, 391–397

Ford B, Lynch T, Greene P (1994). Risperidone in Parkinson's disease. [letter; comment]. *The Lancet* **344**, 681

Frankel JP, Lees AJ, Kempster PA, Stern GM (1990). Subcutaneous apomorphine in the treatment of Parkinson's disease. *Journal of Neurology, Neurosurgery, and Psychiatry* **53**, 96–101

French Clozapine Parkinson Study Group (1999). Clozapine in drug-induced psychosis in Parkinson's disease. *The Lancet* **353**, 2041–2042

Friedman A & Sienkiewicz J (1991). Psychotic complications of long-term levodopa treatment of Parkinson's disease. *Acta Neurologica Scandinavica.* **84**, 111–113

Friedman J (1998). Risperidone induced tardive dyskinesia ('fly-catcher tongue') in a neuroleptic naive patient. *Medical Health Review* **81**, 271–272

Friedman JH (1985). 'Drug holidays' in the treatment of Parkinson's disease. A brief review. *Archives of Internal Medicine* **145**, 913–915

Glantz RH, Bieliauskas L, Paleologos N (1987). Behavioral indicators of hallucinosis in levodopa-treated Parkinson's disease. *Advances in Neurology* **45**, 417–420

Goetz CG & Stebbins GT (1993). Risk factors for nursing home placement in advanced Parkinson's disease. *Neurology* **43**, 2227–2229

Goetz CG & Stebbins GT (1995). Mortality and hallucinations in nursing home patients with advanced Parkinson's disease. *Neurology* **45**, 669–671

Goetz CG, Tanner CM, Klawans HL (1982). Drug holiday in the management of Parkinson disease. *Clinical Pharmacology* **5**, 351–364

Goetz CG, Pappert EJ, Blasucci LM *et al.* (1998a). Intravenous levodopa in hallucinating Parkinson's disease patients: high-dose challenge does not precipitate hallucinations. [see comments]. *Neurology* **50**, 515–517

Goetz CG, Vogel C, Tanner CM, Stebbins GT (1998b). Early dopaminergic drug-induced hallucinations in parkinsonian patients. *Neurology* **51**, 811–814

Graham JM, Grunewald RA, Sagar HJ (1997). Hallucinosis in idiopathic Parkinson's disease. *Journal of Neurology, Neurosurgery, and Psychiatry* **63**, 434–440

Graham JM, Sussman JD, Ford KS, Sagar HJ (1998). Olanzapine in the treatment of hallucinosis in idiopathic Parkinson's disease: a cautionary note. *Journal of Neurology, Neurosurgery, and Psychiatry* **65**, 774–777

Greene P, Cote L, Fahn S (1993). Treatment of drug-induced psychosis in Parkinson's disease with clozapine. *Advances in Neurology* **60**, 703–706

Guze BH & Baxter LR Jr (1985). Current concepts. Neuroleptic malignant syndrome. *New England Journal of Medicine* **313**, 163–166

Hale MS & Bellizzi J (1980). Low dose perphenazine and levodopa/carbidopa therapy in a patient with Parkinsonism and a psychotic illness. *Journal of Nervous and Mental Disease* **168**, 312–314

Henderson MJ & Mellers JD (2000). Psychosis in Parkinson's disease: 'between a rock and a hard place'. *International Review of Psychiatry* **12**, 319–334

Hurwitz TA, Calne DB, Waterman K (1988). Treatment of dopaminomimetic psychosis in Parkinson's disease with electroconvulsive therapy. *Canadian Journal of Neurological Science* **15**, 32–34

Inzelberg R, Kipervasser S, Korczyn AD (1998). Auditory hallucinations in Parkinson's disease. *Journal of Neurology, Neurosurgery, and Psychiatry* **64**, 533–535

Jankovic J (1985). Long-term study of pergolide in Parkinson's disease. *Neurology* **35**, 296–299

Jenkins RB & Groh RH (1970). Mental symptoms in Parkinsonian patients treated with L-dopa. *The Lancet* **ii**, 177–179

Jimenez-Jimenez FJ, Orti-Pareja M, Gasall T, Tallon-Barranco A, Cabrera-Valdivia F, Fernandez-Lliria A (1997). Cenesthetic hallucinations in a patient with Parkinson's disease. *Journal of Neurology, Neurosurgery, and Psychiatry* **63**, 120

Juncos JL (1999). Management of psychotic aspects of Parkinson's disease. [Review] [161 refs] *Journal of Clinical Psychiatry* **60**(suppl 8), 42–53

Kales A, Ansel RD, Markham CH, Scharf MB, Tan TL (1971). Sleep in patients with Parkinson's disease and normal subjects prior to and following levodopa administration. *Clinical Pharmacology and Therapeutics* **12**, 397–406

Klawans HL, Goetz CG, Tanner CM, Nausieda PA, Weiner WJ (1983). Levodopa-free periods ('drug holidays') in the management of parkinsonism. *Advances in Neurology* **37**, 33–43

Kurlan R & Dimitsopulos T (1992). Selegiline and manic behavior in Parkinson's disease. *Archives of Neurology* **49**, 1231

Lauterbach EC (1993). Dopaminergic hallucinosis with fluoxetine in Parkinson's disease. *American Journal of Psychiatry* **150**, 1750

Lera G, Vaamonde J, Rodriguez M, Obeso JA (1993). Cabergoline in Parkinson's disease: long-term follow-up. *Neurology* **43**, 2587–2590

Lieberman AN, Leibowitz M, Gopinathan G et al. (1985). The use of pergolide and lisuride, two experimental dopamine agonists, in patients with advanced Parkinson disease. *American Journal of Medical Science* **290**, 102–106

Lipper S (1976). Letter: Psychosis in patient on bromocriptine and levodopa with carbidopa. *The Lancet* **ii**, 571–572

Makoff AJ, Graham JM, Arranz MJ et al. (2000). Association study of dopamine receptor gene polymorphisms with drug-induced hallucinations in patients with idiopathic Parkinson's disease. *Pharmacogenetics* **10**, 43–48

Mallie A (1908). Les troubles psychiques chez parkinsoniens. Bordeaux. Thesis.

Marsden CD. & Fahn S eds (1981). *Movement Disorders.* London: Butterworth Scientific

Mayeux R, Stern Y, Mulvey K, Cote L (1985). Reappraisal of temporary levodopa withdrawal ('drug holiday') in Parkinson's disease. *New England Journal of Medicine* **313**, 724–728

Meco G, Bonifati V, Cusimano G, Fabrizio E, Vanacore N (1990). Hallucinations in Parkinson disease: neuropsychological study. *Italian Journal of Neurological Science.* **11**, 373–379

Meco G, Alessandria A, Bonifati V, Giustini P (1994). Risperidone for hallucinations in levodopa-treated Parkinson's disease patients [see comments]. *The Lancet* **343**, 1370–1371

Menza M & Chastka E (1989). Idiopathic Parkinson's disease and mania: the effect of mania on the movement disorder. *Neuropsychiatry, Neuropsychology and Behavioural Neurology* **2**, 301–305

Minagar A, Shulman LM, Weiner WJ (1999). Transderm-induced psychosis in Parkinson's disease [see comments]. *Neurology* **53**, 433–434

Mindham RH (1970). Psychiatric symptoms in Parkinson's disease. *Journal of Neurology, Neurosurgery, and Psychiatry* **33**, 188–191

Mindham RH (2001). Visual hallucinations in Parkinson's disease: their nature, frequency, and origins. *Journal of Neurology, Neurosurgery, and Psychiatry* **70**, 719–720

Moskovitz C, Moses H III, Klawans HL (1978). Levodopa-induced psychosis: a kindling phenomenon. *American Journal of Psychiatry* **135**, 669–675

Nausieda PA, Weiner WJ, Kaplan LR, Weber S, Klawans HL (1982). Sleep disruption in the course of chronic levodopa therapy: an early feature of the levodopa psychosis. *Clinical Neuropharmacology* **5**, 183–194

Nissenbaum H, Quinn NP, Brown RG, Toone B, Gotham AM, Marsden CD (1987). Mood swings associated with the 'on-off' phenomenon in Parkinson's disease. *Psychological Medicine* **17**, 899–904

Pappert EJ, Goetz CG, Niederman FG, Raman R, Leurgans S (1999). Hallucinations, sleep fragmentation, and altered dream phenomena in Parkinson's disease. *Movement Disorders* **14**, 117–121

Parkinson Study Group (1999). Low-dose clozapine for the treatment of drug-induced psychosis in Parkinson's disease. *New England Journal of Medicine* **340**, 757–763

Parsa MA & Bastani B (1998). Quetiapine (Seroquel) in the treatment of psychosis in patients with Parkinson's disease. *Journal of Neuropsychiatry and Clinical Neurosciences* **10**, 216–219

Pollack P, Champay A, Gaio J *et al.* (1990). Administration sous-cutanee d'apomorphine dans les fluctuations motrices de la maladie de Parkinson. *Revue Neurologique (Paris)* **146**, 116–122

Porteous H & Ross D (1956). Mental symptoms in parkinsonism following benzhexol hydrochloride therapy. *British Medical Journal* **ii**, 138–140

Postma JU & Van Tilburg W (1975). Visual hallucinations and delirium during treatment with amantadine (Symmetrel). *Journal of the American Geriatric Society* **23**, 212–215

Quinn, N (1995). Drug treatment of Parkinson's disease. *British Medical Journal* **310**, 575–579

Ray-Chaudhuri K, Abbott RJ, Millac PA (1991). Subcutaneous apomorphine for parkinsonian patients with psychiatric side effects on oral treatment. *Journal of Neurology, Neurosurgery, and Psychiatry* **54**, 372–373

Rich SS, Friedman JH, Ott BR (1995). Risperidone versus clozapine in the treatment of psychosis in six patients with Parkinson's disease and other akinetic-rigid syndromes. *Journal of Clinical Psychiatry* 56, no. 12, 556–559

Rosenfeld M, Friedman J, Jacques C (1998). Quetiapine pilot trial in dopaminomimetic psychosis (DP) in Parkinson's disease (PD). Presented at the International Congress on Parkinson's Disease and Movement Disorders, October 10–14, New York

Sacks OW, Messeloff CR, Schwartz WF (1970). Long-term effects of levodopa in the severely disabled patient. *Journal of the American Medical Association* **213**, 2270

Sage JI & Duvoisin RC (1986). Sudden onset of confusion with severe exacerbation of parkinsonism during levodopa therapy. *Movement Disorders* **1**, 267–270

Saint-Cyr JA, Taylor AE, Lang AE (1993). Neuropsychological and psychiatric side effects in the treatment of Parkinson's disease. *Neurology* **43**(suppl 6), S47–S52

Scholz E & Dichgans J (1985). Treatment of drug-induced exogenous psychosis in parkinsonism with clozapine and fluperlapine. *European Archives of Psychiatry and Neurological Sciences* **235**, 60–64

Schwab RS, England AC Jr, Poskanzer DC, Young RR (1969). Amantadine in the treatment of Parkinson's disease. *Journal of the American Medical Association* **208**, 1168–1170

Shaw KM, Lee, AJ, Stern GM (1980). The impact of treatment with levodopa on Parkinson's disease. *Quarterly Journal of Medicine* **49**, 283–293

Shergill SS, Walker Z, Le Katona C (1998). A preliminary investigation of laterality in Parkinson's disease and susceptibility to psychosis. *Journal of Neurology, Neurosurgery, and Psychiatry* **65**, 610–611

Steiger MJ, Quinn NP, Toone B, Marsden CD (1991). Off-period screaming accompanying motor fluctuations in Parkinson's disease. *Movement Disorders* **6**, 89–90

Tanner CM, Vogel C, Goetz CC, Klawans H (1983). Hallucinations in Parkinson's disease: a population based study. *Annals of Neurology* **14**, 136

Targum SD & Abbott JL (2000). Efficacy of quetiapine in Parkinson's patients with psychosis. *Journal of Clinical Psychopharmacology* **20**, 54–60

Tobias JA & Merlis S (1970). Levodopa and schizophrenia. *Journal of the American Medical Association* **211**, 1857

Turner TH, Cookson JC, Wass JA, Drury PL, Price PA, Besser GM (1984). Psychotic reactions during treatment of pituitary tumours with dopamine agonists. *British Medical Journal (Clinical Research Edition)* **289**, 1101–1103

Vaamonde J, Luquin MR, Obeso JA (1991). Subcutaneous lisuride infusion in Parkinson's disease. Response to chronic administration in 34 patients. *Brain* **114** (Pt 1B), 601–617

Wolk SI & Douglas CJ (1992). Clozapine treatment of psychosis in Parkinson's disease: a report of five consecutive cases [see comments]. *Journal of Clinical Psychiatry* **53**, 373–376

Wolters EC, Hurwitz TA, Mak E *et al.* (1990). Clozapine in the treatment of parkinsonian patients with dopaminomimetic psychosis. *Neurology* **40**, 832–834

Wolters EC, Jansen EN, Tuynman-Qua HG, Bergmans PL (1996). Olanzapine in the treatment of dopaminomimetic psychosis in patients with Parkinson's disease [see comments]. *Neurology* **47**, 1085–1087

World Health Organization (1992). *International Classification of Diseases*, 10th revision. Geneva: WHO

World Health Organisation (1992). *International Statistical Classification of Diseases and Related Health Problems*. Geneva: WHO

Zoldan J, Friedberg G, Goldberg-Stern H, Melamed E (1993). Ondansetron for hallucinosis in advanced Parkinson's disease. *The Lancet* **341**, 562–563

Zoldan J, Friedberg G, Livneh M, Melamed E (1995). Psychosis in advanced Parkinson's disease: treatment with ondansetron, a 5-HT3 receptor antagonist [see comments]. *Neurology* **45**, 1305–1308

Zoldan J, Friedberg G, Weizman A, Melamed E (1996). Ondansetron, a 5-HT3 antagonist for visual hallucinations and paranoid delusional disorder associated with chronic L-DOPA therapy in advanced Parkinson's disease. *Advances in Neurology* **69**, 541–544

Scientific evidence and expert clinical opinion for the management of cognitive dysfunction and dementia

Richard G Brown

Introduction

Dementia in Parkinson's disease

There is no longer any controversy surrounding the existence of non-motor features in idiopathic Parkinson's disease (PD) and other parkinsonian (Parkinson plus) syndromes. (Note that the abbreviation PD will be used to include all parkinsonian syndromes unless specified in the text.) Although the motor symptoms may be the first, most obvious and most readily treatable symptoms of PD, a wide range of other cognitive, behavioural and psychiatric symptoms can also be observed in a significant proportion of patients. Although the focus of this chapter is the cognitive impairment associated with the disease, it is inaccurate and unhelpful to consider these problems in isolation from either the major motor symptoms or the wide range of neuropsychiatric features (see below).

Cognitive change is common in PD, and it is likely that all patients will show a degree of cognitive impairment at some stage in their disease. In some, it may be mild and clinically insignificant, perhaps detectable only on the basis of detailed neuropsychological investigation. Such cognitive impairments are unlikely to be a major consideration in the overall clinical management, or a significant source of complaint to the patient or his or her family. In contrast some patients will show a more marked and clinically significant decline, perhaps earlier in the course of the disease, which may even dominate the clinical profile when combined with some of the associated neuropsychiatric complications. It is these latter patients that are the focus of this chapter.

The exact prevalence of such dementia in PD is still unclear, but is generally quoted in the range of 20–40% depending on the study. Estimates vary according to the instruments and diagnostic criteria used, and the extent to which the study excludes 'atypical' PD (e.g. progressive supranuclear palsy [PSP], dementia with Lewy bodies [DLB] or multiple system atrophy [MSA]). Although differential diagnosis may be difficult (see Chapter 3), it has major implications for the management of associated cognitive and neuropsychiatric change, as well as the motor symptoms.

It is still unclear whether 'pure' Lewy body Parkinson's disease confined to the substantia nigra can cause dementia. In practice, extranigral pathology is almost always found on postmortem examination, both subcortical, affecting a range of neurotransmitter systems, and cortical. Pathology includes both Lewy bodies and Alzheimer-type senile plaques (sp) and neurofibrillary tangles (nft) (Jellinger 1999). In demented patients, such cortical pathology is found in almost all cases *post mortem* (Lieberman 1997) and appears to be significantly associated with neuropsychiatric complications.

Cognitive impairment and other neuropsychiatric symptoms

Although cognitive decline is a necessary condition for the clinical diagnosis of dementia, whatever the pathology, alone it does not define the dementia. It is rare to find cognitive deterioration in the absence of at least one so-called 'non-cognitive', neurobehavioural or neuropsychiatric symptom in any dementing condition including PD dementia or Alzheimer's disease. In a community-based sample of 42 patients with PD dementia (excluding DLB), 19 suffered hallucinations, 17 depression and 13 anxiety (Aarsland *et al.* 2001). Other major symptoms present in more than 25% of the sample were delusions and apathy. It is unlikely that these diverse symptoms have a single pathological or pathophysiological substrate, e.g. apathy was a more dominant feature in patients expressing significant cognitive impairment in the early stages of PD and became less frequent with progression of the motor symptoms, whereas delusions showed the reverse pattern, being associated with increasing disease severity.

The frequent co-morbidity among cognitive impairment, psychosis, depression and apathy make it impossible to consider the management of cognitive impairment in isolation from these other psychiatric features. The clinical link between dementia and psychosis is particularly strong. Dementing patients are much more likely to experience psychotic symptoms in response to anti-parkinsonian medication, and early psychotic features such as hallucinations tend to be predictive of subsequent cognitive deterioration. Not surprisingly, therefore, much of the literature relevant to the clinical management of dementia in PD comes from studies into the management of psychosis (see Chapter 6), although few have explicitly examined the impact on cognitive impairment (see below).

Approaches to the management of cognitive impairment

A number of potential strategies are available for the management of dementia in PD:

- The role of conventional anti-parkinsonian medication.
- The minimisation of adverse cognitive and neuropsychiatric side effects of anti-parkinsonian treatment.
- The direct treatment of neuropsychiatric symptoms associated with dementia.
- The direct treatment of cognitive impairment.
- Family and carer-based interventions.

Does conventional anti-parkinsonian treatment have a role in the management of cognitive impairment?

Before discussing the impact of anti-parkinsonian drugs on dementia, it is worth considering the evidence for its effect on cognitive function in non-demented patients. Early reports from the era of levodopa mentioned clear awakening or alerting effects of treatment (Marsh *et al.* 1971; Sacks 1973) on the patient's mental state. Such effects, however, tended to be transient and often came from patients with relatively advanced disease, who were started on levodopa for the first time. With the almost universal use of dopa-based drugs in PD from the point of diagnosis, we have less opportunity to assess the acute impact of levodopa on developed cognitive impairment, although there is a significant literature on the cognitive impact of treatment in *de novo* patients. The remaining evidence comes from studying the effect of acute drug administration on cognition, either after a period of short-term withdrawal or during naturally occurring 'wearing-off' periods. Kulisevsky (2000) has recently reviewed the evidence from these three classes of study, and concludes that each is associated with its own pattern of results. In *de novo* patients, some early but incomplete cognitive improvement may be observed in a range of cognitive domains, but particularly on tests of executive function and memory. In patients with more advanced disease, but still with a stable treatment response, dopa drugs may improve the speed of response but tend not to have either a significant or consistent effect on other aspects of cognitive function. Finally in patients starting to suffer wearing-off effects, the increasing doses of drug required to produce a therapeutic response tend to be associated with deterioration in cognitive function, particularly on more demanding tasks. Kulisevsky (2000) and others (Gotham *et al.* 1988) have speculated that such patterns, as well as individual variations in response, may reflect differences in the degree of dopamine depletion in the putamen, relative to the caudate nucleus and/or prefrontal cortical regions. Titrating drug levels against the motor response alone may lead to an effective under-dosing or over-dosing of other systems which may contribute to cognitive impairment.

When it comes to dementing patients, there seems to be little evidence for any positive role for conventional anti-parkinsonian medication in managing the cognitive symptoms. This would be consistent with the hypothesis that a major cause of the cognitive disturbance is the extrastriatal and particularly cortical pathology. At best, dopa-based drugs appear to have no effect on ameliorating cognitive problems in such patients, and at worst exacerbate the impairment either directly or through a worsening of co-morbid psychotic symptoms.

Although dopa-based drugs may continue to have a valuable role in the management of the motor symptoms of demented patients with PD, other treatments are clearly contraindicated. Anticholinergic medication can produce cognitive problems, even in young individuals without neurological disorder (Frith *et al.* 1984). In PD, they can exacerbate an existing mild problem and cause frank confusional states in patients with more severe deficits (De Smet *et al*. 1982). Surgical treatments, whether lesions or deep brain stimulation, are also contraindicated in demented patients (Trepanier *et al*. 2000). In part this is at the risk of worsening the existing dementia. More generally, however, it is because such patients tend to show a reduced clinical motor response and have an increased risk of complications. There is certainly no evidence for any positive effect of current surgical approaches on cognitive or neuropsychiatric function in demented patients.

The minimisation of adverse treatment effects

As noted above, when a patient has a clinically significant cognitive impairment, he or she is more likely to suffer co-morbid neuropsychiatric complications to treatment, particularly psychosis. It is usually in response to these latter symptoms, rather than to the cognitive decline itself, that clinicians opt to reduce dosage or to switch to a less 'toxic' drug.

All anti-parkinsonian medication has the potential for producing adverse responses in patients, particularly those with dementia. However, some drugs carry increased risk. As noted already, anticholinergic drugs such as benzhexol or orphenadrine should be avoided if significant cognitive impairment is found, whether or not there are co-morbid psychiatric symptoms. Selegiline and amantadine also commonly cause problems, followed by the dopa agonists. Fortunately, for most patients, levodopa appears to be the least problematic drug, offering some opportunity for managing the motor problems. However, with any dose reduction/drug switching regimen, the minimisation of drug-related side effects may be at the expense of reduced motor symptom control. Decisions about the balance between symptom control and minimisation of adverse effect can only be taken after full and informed discussion with patients and their families.

The direct treatment of associated neuropsychiatric symptoms

With the arrival of the newer classes of atypical antipsychotic drugs, including clozapine, quetiapine and olanzapine, direct treatment of psychotic symptoms has become possible for the first time in PD. The impact of such drugs on psychosis is considered in Chapter 6. Surprisingly, given the frequent co-morbidity between psychosis and dementia, little attention has been paid to the impact of such drugs on cognitive function. Where data are even available, there is little evidence that antipsychotics have a positive beneficial effect on cognition (e.g. Aarsland *et al*. 1999b). In only one study has cognitive change been assessed as a potential outcome measure (Juncos *et al*. 2000). This study involved an open label trial of quetiapine in a sample of 29 patients who had previously failed treatment with other atypical antipsychotics. In addition to the impact on psychiatric symptoms, quetiapine led to significant improvement in working memory and long-term verbal memory, although overall cognitive status as assessed by the Mini-Mental State Examination (MMSE) did not improve.

Although the focus of the discussion so far has been on co-morbidity between dementia and psychosis, patients with PD present with increased risk of depression and anxiety. Although anxiety is not a primary cause of cognitive impairment, it can have a significant indirect effect on a patient's overall level of functioning, including the cognitive domain. In contrast, major depressive illness can directly lead to significant cognitive impairment and/or exacerbate coexisting problems (Brown *et al.* 1994). This is particularly true in elderly people in whom so-called 'depressive dementia' can closely mimic the type of cognitive impairment associated with subcortical pathology (Cummings & Benson 1984). Critically, however, the cognitive disorder can show a positive response after the effective treatment of the primary mood disturbance. Therefore, quite apart from the clinical need to treat the depression and reduce patient suffering (see Chapter 6), the effective management of depression is one of the more obvious approaches to tackling a possible cause or contributing factor to a coexistent dementia.

The direct treatment of dementia

To this point the chapter has considered only indirect interventions, treating neuropsychiatric problems that may cause or exacerbate cognitive dysfunction. Unfortunately research into therapeutic options to manage cognitive impairment in PD directly has barely begun. In Alzheimer's disease, there have been huge efforts made to develop novel drugs to provide symptomatic relief and slow the rate of progression. These so-called 'cognitive enhancers', such as donepezil, rivastigmine and galantamine, have now been made more widely available to people with mild-to-moderate Alzheimer's disease. Given that their primary mode of action is on the cholinergic system, there is a natural caution in using such agents in patients with PD dementia because of the risk of worsening their motor symptoms, although there is little evidence of marked extrapramidal side effects from their use in DLB (see below). Furthermore, experience with the atypical neuroleptics suggests that combining drugs with seemingly opposing pharmacological actions should not be discounted without further investigation. To date, however, there are no published data on which to guide clinical recommendation. Of other existing drugs, methylphenidate has been suggested to have a potential role in the treatment of cognition and negative symptoms in Alzheimer's disease and vascular dementia (Galynker *et al.* 1997), but again there is no published evidence of its possible role in PD dementia.

In contrast, cognitive enhancing agents are becoming more widely employed in the treatment of DLB where reduced cortical cholinergic activity makes it a rational treatment option. Shea *et al.* (1998) reported a series of nine patients treated with donepezil over an 8- to 24-week period. Mean MMSE score rose from 15.4 to 19.9, and overall improvements were made by seven patients. The impression of carers was very positive. A recent randomised controlled trial of rivastigmine (McKeith *et al.* 2000) failed to find any significant improvement in cognition as measured by the

MMSE, although as a group, the patients were less impaired than those reported by Shea and colleagues. Nevertheless, there was a significant improvement in a composite measure of speeded cognitive function. A suggestion of broader cognitive benefit was also given, but not reported in any detail. Perhaps more important were the significant reductions in neuropsychiatric symptoms, particularly delusions, hallucinations, anxiety and apathy.

Family and carer-based intervention

Dementia, whatever the underlying pathology, is a social as much as a medical problem. In the context of PD, the combination of cognitive impairment, movement disorder and neuropsychiatric symptoms places a considerable burden on the families and carers. This can lead to significant problems in achieving the aim of most patients to remain in their own home for as long as possible and avoid the need for institutional care. Effective management of dementia therefore needs to address how the burden of care can be reduced. Although medical management of symptoms is obviously a central approach, it is rarely sufficient on its own. Despite this, we have to turn once again to Alzheimer's disease to look for systematic research into psychological approaches to management. Although there have been only a small number of published studies the results are encouraging, e.g. Teri *et al.* (1997) employed behavioural techniques to treat depressive symptoms in patients, with therapy delivered through carers. This led to a significant and persisting reduction in depression in the patients, with a similar improvement in psychological health of carers themselves. Perhaps even more significantly, Mittleman *et al.* (1996) demonstrated how a family-based intervention could help to delay the need for nursing home placement. In this country, Marriott *et al.* (2000) also report a randomised controlled trial using a carer-based cognitive–behavioural intervention. Once again, there was a significant reduction in carer morbidity. Significantly, the patients also showed a reduction in behavioural disturbance at follow-up and an increase in activities at 3 months.

Conclusions

Cognitive impairment and its associated neuropsychiatric problems are an important component of the overall disease burden of PD, to the patient, the carers and the NHS. Treatment of the motor symptoms alone is often inadequate, and can become increasingly difficult in some patients as the disease progresses and non-motor symptoms come to dominate the clinical picture. We are only just beginning to tackle these issues through the development of new and more rational treatment approaches. Dose reduction and drug switching remain an important weapon in the armoury, but are valuable only to the extent that an acceptable balance can be found between minimising neuropsychiatric symptoms and maintaining mobility. Direct treatment of associated neuropsychiatric symptoms offers promise, particularly with the advent of atypical neuroleptics. More, however, could probably be done in the assertive treatment of depression, particularly where it may be contributing directly to cognitive decline. Finally, we are still very much in the dark when it comes to the direct management of cognitive deficits. Potential pharmacological approaches need to be rigorously investigated, and more needs to be done to assess behavioural approaches shown to be valuable in reducing the overall disease burden in other neurodegenerative dementias.

References

Aarsland D, Larsen JP, Karlsen K, Lim NG, Tandberg E (1999a). Mental symptoms in Parkinson's disease are important contributors to caregiver distress. *International Journal of Geriatric Psychiatry* **14**, 866–874

Aarsland D, Larsen JP, Lim NG, Tandberg E (1999b). Olanzapine for psychosis in patients with Parkinson's disease with and without dementia. *Journal of Neuropsychiatry and Clinical Neuroscience* **11**, 392–394

Aarsland D, Cummings JL, Larsen JP (2001). Neuropsychiatric differences between Parkinson's disease with dementia and Alzheimer's disease. *International Journal of Geriatric Psychiatry* **16**, 184–191

Brown RG, Scott LC, Bench CJ, Dolan RJ (1994). Cognitive function in depression: Its relationship to the presence and severity of intellectual decline. *Psychological Medicine* **24**, 829–847

Carter JH, Stewart BJ, Archbold PG *et al*. (1998). Living with a person who has Parkinson's disease: The spouse's perspective by stage of disease. *Movement Disorders* **13**, 20–28

Cummings JL & Benson DF (1984). Subcortical dementia. Review of an emerging concept. *Archives of Neurology* **41**, 874–879

De Smet Y, Ruberg M, Serdaru M, Dubois B, Lhermitte F, Agid Y (1982). Confusion, dementia and anticholinergics in Parkinson's disease. *Journal of Neurology, Neurosurgery, and Psychiatry* **45**, 1161–1164

Frith CD, Richardson JT, Samuel M, Crow TJ, McKenna PJ (1984). The effects of intravenous diazepam and hyoscine upon human memory. *Quarterly Journal of Experimental Psychology* A **36**, 133–144

Galynker I, Ieronimo C, Miner C, Rosenblum J, Vilkas N, Rosenthal R (1997). Methylphenidate treatment of negative symptoms in patients with dementia. *Journal of Neuropsychiatry and Clinical Neurosciences* **9**, 231–239

Gotham AM, Brown RG, Marsden CD (1988). 'Frontal' cognitive function in patients with Parkinson's disease 'on' and 'off' levodopa. *Brain* **111**, 299–321

Jellinger K (1999). Neuropathological correlates of mental dysfunction in Parkinson's disease: an update. In Wolter E, Scheltens P, Berendse H (eds) *Mental Dysfunction in Parkinson's Disease II*. Utrecht: Academic Pharmaceutical Productions, pp 82–105

Juncos JL, Evatt ML, Jewart RD *et al*. (2000). Tolerability, safety and cognitive effects of quetiapine in patients with Parkinson's disease treated for psychotic symptoms. *European Neuropsychopharmacology* **10**, S307

Kulisevsky J (2000). Role of dopamine in learning and memory: implications for the treatment of cognitive dysfunction in patients with Parkinson's disease. *Drugs and Aging* **16**, 365–379

Lieberman AN (1997). Point of view: Dementia in Parkinson's disease. *Parkinsonism and Related Disorders* **3**, 151–158

McKeith I, Del Ser T, Spano P *et al.* (2000). Efficacy of rivastigmine in dementia with Lewy bodies: a randomised, double-blind, placebo-controlled international study. *Lancet* **356**, 2031–2036

Marriott A, Donaldson C, Tarrier N, Burns A (2000). Effectiveness of cognitive-behavioural family intervention in reducing the burden of care in carers of patients with Alzheimer's disease. *British Journal of Psychiatry* **176**, 557–562

Marsh GG, Markham CM, Ansel R (1971). Levodopa's awakening effect on patients with Parkinsonism. *Journal of Neurology, Neurosurgery, and Psychiatry* **34**, 209–218

Mittelman MS, Ferris SH, Shulman E, Steinberg G, Levin B (1996). A family intervention to delay nursing home placement in patients with Alzheimer's disease: a randomized controlled trial. *Journal of the American Medical Association* **276**, 1725–1731

Sacks O (1973). *Awakenings*. London: Duckworth

Shea C, MacKnight C, Rockwood K (1998). Donepezil for treatment of dementia with Lewy bodies: a case series of nine patients. *International Psychogeriatrics* **10**, 229–238

Teri L, Logsdon RG, Uomoto J, McCurry SM (1997). Behavioral treatment of depression in dementia patients: A controlled clinical trial. *Journals of Gerontology Series B-Psychological Sciences, Social Sciences* **52**, P159–P166

Trepanier LL, Kumar R, Lozano AM, Lang AE, Saint-Cyr JA (2000). Neuropsychological outcome of GPi pallidotomy and GPi or STN deep brain stimulation in Parkinson's disease. *Brain and Cognition* **42**, 324–347

PART 4

Uroneurology

Chapter 10

Scientific evidence and expert clinical opinion for the investigation and management of incontinence and sexual dysfunction

Kristian Winge and Clare J Fowler

Parkinson's disease and the bladder

Prevalence

There is a general perception that bladder control can be a major problem in patients with Parkinson's disease (Tanner *et al.* 1987; Kirby & Fowler 1988). The prevalence of urinary disturbances has been claimed to be between 38% and 71% (Porter & Bors 1971; Hald & Bradley 1982; Andersen 1985; Berger *et al.* 1987; Hattori *et al.* 1992), although a substantial number of these papers included elderly patients, and many of the studies were published before the diagnosis of multiple system atrophy (MSA) was recognised. Furthermore, they were largely based on patients presenting to urology clinics with urinary symptoms. A recent study on Parkinson's disease (PD) patients diagnosed according to modern criteria, however, found the prevalence of urinary symptoms to be 27% (Araki *et al.* 2000).

Typically patients present with long-standing neurological disease, the bladder symptoms coming on some years after treatment for PD was started (Chandiramani *et al.* 1997; Araki *et al.* 2000). Although it was thought to be unclear whether the symptoms related to the patient's age, the duration of the disease or the severity of the disease (Aranda *et al.* 1983; Gray *et al.* 1995), Araki and Kuno (2000) have recently shown a clear correlation with the neurological disability.

Nature of complaints

Patients complain of urgency and frequency, which may be severe, and urge incontinence particularly if poor mobility compounds their bladder disorder (Araki *et al.* 2000; Lemack *et al.* 2000). Urodynamics studies of several series of patients with urinary symptoms have found that the most common abnormality is detrusor hyperreflexia, the incidence in patients with PD and urinary complaints varying from 45% to 93% (Pavlakis *et al.* 1983; Fitzmaurice *et al.* 1985; Berger *et al.* 1987; Christmas *et al.* 1988; Hattori *et al.* 1992; Araki *et al.* 2000), but areflexia may occur.

Many male patients with PD will be in the age group in whom bladder outflow obstruction caused by benign prostatic hyperplasia (BPH) is a common coexistent disorder. Those with outflow obstruction complain of difficulties of voiding such as hesitancy and poor flow, and furthermore may also have urgency because the obstruction itself can cause detrusor overactivity.

However, female patients with urinary complaints seem to be similarly affected and approximately 70% complain of urgency with or without urge incontinence. The remaining female patients have mixed irritative and obstructive or purely obstructive symptoms. Urodynamic evaluation demonstrates detrusor hyperreflexia in 70–80% of female patients. However, women with Parkinson-related syndromes demonstrated detrusor hypocontractility or areflexia in 20–30% of cases, and electromyography reveals sphincteric dysfunction in 30–50% of patients (Dmochowski 1999).

Possible neurogenic causes of bladder symptoms in Parkinson's disease

There are several possible neurogenic causes of bladder symptoms in PD. Some authors have suggested that an impaired relaxation or 'bradykinesia' of the urethral sphincter can result in voiding dysfunction as a result of bladder outflow obstruction (Galloway 1983; Christmas et al. 1988), and hence to hyperactive detrusor. However, studies using cystometry found that obstructive voiding patterns are not common in PD patients (Dmochowski 1999; Araki et al. 2000), indicating that other mechanisms play a more significant role.

The hypothesis that has been most widely proposed is that in healthy individuals the basal ganglia have an inhibitory effect on micturition reflex and, with cell loss in the substantia nigra, detrusor hyperreflexia develops. Experimental evidence of an inhibitory role for the basal ganglia comes from animal MPTP (1-methyl-4-phenyl-1,2,3,6-tetrahydropyridine) models (Albanese et al. 1988) and cats (Lewin et al. 1967; Yoshimura et al. 1990). The role of the globus pallidus and the substantia nigra have been evaluated in cats, in particular, but studies done on humans indicate that the mechanism is more complex than a simple inhibition of the pontine micturition centre (Fitzmaurice et al. 1985).

In addition to cystometry, recent studies have also indicated (Arak & Kuno 2000; Lemack et al. 2000) that urinary symptom scoring systems are useful. However, they are not specific and cannot differentiate between symptoms caused by neurological disorders and those caused by BPH. A group of PD patients with mild-to-moderate PD was evaluated using validated symptom questionnaires, and compared with an age- and sex-matched control group (Lemack et al. 2000). The investigators were not able to demonstrate significant differences between male PD patients and patients with symptomatic BPH; PD patients scored higher scores only in frequency and urgency questions. In the female group, PD patients scored less than patients presenting for urological evaluation as a result of lower urinary tract symptoms. However, in the male group, the PD patients were almost 10 years older than the non-PD group, whereas in the female group the difference was only 2.2 years. The value of scoring systems is in the screening of patients and an early assessment of the severity of bladder dysfunction. Another recent study (Araki *et al.* 2000) has found that the complaints of the patients, as evaluated using the International Prostate Symptom Score (IPSS), correlates with the degree of neurological disability.

It is also possible that antiparkinsonian medication may affect the bladder function, but studies that have looked at the effect of L-dopa or apomorphine on bladder behaviour in patients with PD have produced conflicting results. In one small study, hyperreflexia improved after administration of apomorphine and to a lesser extent after L-dopa (Aranda & Cramer 1993), but in another patients showing 'on–off' phenomena, hyperreflexia on cystometry, showed a lessening with L-dopa in some patients and a worsening in others (Fitzmaurice *et al.* 1985). A similar effect was found on detrusor hyperreflexia when subcutaneous apomorphine was given; bladder outflow resistance was reduced and voiding improved in 9 of 10 patients (Christmas *et al.* 1988). It was proposed that this intervention be used to demonstrate the reversibility of outflow obstruction in men with PD before prostatic surgery is undertaken – an excellent suggestion but unfortunately rarely done.

A recent study on rats (Seki *et al.* 2001) has indicated that tonic activation of dopamine D_1-receptors is seen in conscious rats, which inhibits the micturition reflex, and activation of dopamine D_2-receptors stimulates micturition. Therefore, degeneration of dopaminergic neurons in the substantia nigra and a subsequent loss of striatal dopamine concentration may lead to detrusor hyperactivity, by an inability to activate the tonic inhibition executed by D_1-receptors. Administration of D_2-receptor agonists might therefore theoretically worsen the problems, but further studies need to be performed.

A single small study using the dopamine agonist pergolide mesylate, which acts on both D_1- and D_2-receptors, reported a significant improvement both symptomatically and urodynamically (Yamamoto 1997). In monkeys treated with MPTP selective dopamine D_1-receptor agonist depresses detrusor hyperreflexia, whereas subcutaneous injections of a dopamine D_2-receptor agonist and apomorphine, a dopamine D_1- and D_2-receptor agonist, slightly but significantly reduced the volume threshold of the bladder for the micturition reflex in both normal and MPTP-treated groups (Yoshimura *et al.* 1993).

Treatment

The neurogenic bladder is generally well treated (Andersson 2000) with anticholinergics such as oxybutynin chloride and tolterodine tartrate, but no double-blind, placebo controlled, studies have been done specifically in patients with PD. This therapy is usually tried in patients with urgency and frequency because it reduces the parasympathetic effect on the bladder. It is important to evaluate post-micturitional residual urine during treatment, because this may increase. Side effects of otherwise prescribed anticholinergic drugs (given to control tremor in PD) may, however, be aggravated. It is a clinical experience that the patients generally tolerate the drugs well and benefit from the treatment.

As it is likely that a number of the earlier studies on 'Parkinson's disease' and the bladder included patients with MSA, the view that patients with PD have a poor outcome after prostatic surgery may be misleading. Urological intervention is not contraindicated in men with PD, but it is reasonable to try these patients on anticholinergic medication first if storage symptoms are prominent. If conservative measures fail, a voiding cystometrogram to demonstrate obstructed voiding must be performed before transurethral resection of prostate is considered (Chandiramani *et al.* 1997).

The importance of ensuring the correct neurological background of urinary complaints in parkinsonian syndromes is emphasised by the fact that a number patients, first diagnosed as having PD, may turn out to have MSA. The onset of urinary symptoms in relation to other neurological symptoms in MSA is fundamentally different from that which occurs with PD. The prevalence is significantly higher, rating between 45% and > 95% (Kirby *et al.* 1986; Singer *et al.* 1992; Sakakibara *et al.* 1993, 2000; Beck *et al.* 1994; Tison *et al.* 2000), and the complaints differ; both urgency and frequency as well as incontinence and sometime large volumes of post-micturitional residual urine may develop. Urogenital symptoms in MSA may precede other and more evident neurological involvement as well as other autonomic features by several years (Beck *et al.* 1994; Sakakibara *et al.* 2000).

In the early stages, the two conditions may be difficult to differentiate, but in Table 10.1 the urogenital features of MSA are outlined. Several studies have indicated that sphincter EMG may also be helpful in order to differentiate the two conditions. However, this issue is currently subject to some debate, although a recent paper concluded that both specificity and sensitivity are high when thresholds for detecting abnormality are set optimally (Tison *et al.* 2000). Table 10.2 lists the studies to date.

Table 10.1 Urogenital criteria in favour of multiple systems atrophy

Urinary symptoms preceding or presenting with parkinsonism
MED preceding or presenting with parkinsonism
Urinary incontinence
Significant post-micturition residue (>100 ml)
Worsening bladder control after urological surgery

Sexual dysfunction in Parkinson's disease

Prevalence

As other symptoms in the PD patient are still better treated and the life expectancy of patients increases, it is becoming clearer that a proportion of patients with this disease also suffer from sexual dysfunction. Again, it is important to recognise patients with MSA, because it is now clear that erectile dysfunction (ED) can precede other symptoms in that condition by several years. Little is known about the sexual dysfunction of women with MSA.

Table 10.2 Studies on sphincter EMG and multiple systems atrophy

Studies suggesting that sphincter EMG is useful in the diagnosis of MSA	Studies suggesting that sphincter EMG is not useful in the diagnosis of MSA
Eardley *et al.* (1989)	Schwartz *et al.* (1997)
Pramstaller *et al.* (1995)	Libelius & Johanson (2000)
Palace *et al.* (1997)	Giladi *et al.* (2000)
Stocchi *et al.* (1997)	
Chandiramani *et al.* (1997)	
Tison *et al.* (2000)	
Sakakibara *et al.* (2000)	

Estimates of the prevalence of ED in men with PD show that it is a significant problem, affecting 60% of a group of men compared with an age-matched, healthy, non-parkinsonian group, in whom the prevalence was 37.5% (Singer *et al.* 1989). Typically, the problem affects men only some years after the neurological disease has been established. A survey of young patients with PD (mean age 49.6 years) and their partners revealed a high level of dysfunction, with the most severely affected couples being those in which the patient was male. Erectile dysfunction and premature ejaculation were complaints in a significant proportion, although in general terms sexual dysfunction appeared to be multifactorial with no simple single cause identified. In a recent study from 2000, the wider terms of sexuality in younger patients (mean age 45), including both male and female patients with PD, was examined (Jacobs *et al.* 2000), showing that PD patients were less active and less satisfied with the their sexual relationships than age- and sex-matched control persons.

Possible causes of erectile dysfunction in Parkinson's disease

The cause of ED in PD is unclear but it may possibly be the result of a central deficiency of dopaminergic systems. There is experimental evidence that dopaminergic mechanisms are involved both in determining libido and in causing penile erection (Heaton 2000). Some men using subcutaneous injections of apomorphine to treat complicated motor fluctuations in PD have also benefited from the treatment in respect of their sexual function (O'Sullivan & Hughes 1998).

An increase in libido in some patients with PD treated with L-dopa is a recognised problem (Uitti *et al.* 1989), but the true prevalence of this problem is not known. In one study aimed at determining sexual dysfunction in PD, although not asked specifically about this issue, 5 members of 44 couples stated that a high frequency was a problem, but it was not clear whether this was the result of an increase in activity (Brown *et al.* 1990).

Treating sexual dysfunction in PD can be difficult because so many other parkinsonian symptoms may have an impact on this part of life. A small-scale, open-label study of sildenafil citrate in the treatment of men with ED and PD parkinsonism

(Zesiewicz *et al.* 2000) found that 10 men with PD responded well, with no adverse effects to the medication, and one recent, still unpublished, double-masked study on parkinsonism found that 11 of 12 men with PD also responded well, but three of six men with MSA developed severe hypotension on the active medication, causing the study to be terminated (Hussein *et al.* 2001). In practical terms, lying and standing blood pressure should be measured before prescribing sildenafil to men with parkinsonism to identify unrecognised autonomic failure, which appears to predispose to the development of this adverse effect. In parkinsonian patients with orthostatic hypotension, local treatment may have an effect, but no placebo-controlled studies have been put forward. The medication was, however, effective in all the men with MSA, indicating that ED in men with MSA cannot be caused by hypotension.

References

Albanese A, Jenner P, Marsden CD, Stephenson JD (1988). Bladder hyperreflexia induced in marmorsets by 1-methyl-4-phenyl-1,2,3,6-tetrahydropyridine. *Neuroscience Letters* **87**, 46–50

Andersen JT (1985). Disturbances of bladder and urethral function in Parkinson's disease. *International Urology and Nephrology* **17**, 35–41

Andersson KE (2000). Treatment of overactive bladder: other drug mechanisms. *Urology* **55**, 51–57

Araki I & Kuno S (2000). Assessment of voiding dysfunction in Parkinson's disease by the international prostate symptom score. *Journal of Neurology, Neurosurgery, and Psychiatry* **68**, 429–433

Araki I, Kitahara M, Oida T, Kuno S (2000). Voiding dysfunction and Parkinson's disease: urodynamic abnormalities and urinary symptoms. *Journal of Urology* **164**, 1640–1643

Aranda B & Cramer P (1993). Effects of apomorphine and L-dopa on the parkinsonian bladder. *Neurourology and Urodynamics* **12**, 203–209

Aranda B, Perrigot M, Mazieres L, Pierrot-Deseilligny E (1983). Bladder sphincter disorders in Parkinson's disease. *Revue Neurologique (Paris)* **139**, 283–288

Beck RO, Betts CD, Fowler CJ (1994). Genitourinary dysfunction in multiple system atrophy: clinical features and treatment in 62 cases. *Journal of Urology* **151**, 1336–1341

Berger Y, Blaivas JG, DeLaRocha ER, Salinas JM (1987). Urodynamic findings in Parkinson's disease. *Journal of Urology* **138**, 836–838

Brown RG, Jahanshahi M, Quinn NP, Marsden CD (1990). Sexual function in patients with Parkinson's disease and their partners. *Journal of Neurology, Neurosurgery, and Psychiatry* **53**, 480–486

Chandiramani VA, Palace J, Fowler CJ (1997). How to recognize patients with parkinsonism who should not have urological surgery. *British Journal of Urology* **80**, 100–104

Christmas TJ, Kempster PA, Chapple CR *et al.* (1988). Role of subcutaneous apomorphine in parkinsonian voiding dysfunction. *The Lancet* **ii**, 1451–1453

Dmochowski RR (1999). Female voiding dysfunction and movement disorders. *International Urogynecology Journal of Pelvic Floor Dysfunction* **10**, 144–151

Eardley I, Quinn NP, Fowler CJ *et al.* (1989). The value of urethral sphincter electromyography in the differential diagnosis of parkinsonism. *British Journal of Urology* **64**, 360–362

Fitzmaurice H, Fowler CJ, Rickards D *et al.* (1985). Micturition disturbance in Parkinson's disease. *British Journal of Urology* **57**, 652–656

Galloway NT (1983). Urethral sphincter abnormalities in Parkinsonism. *British Journal of Urology* **55**, 691–693

Giladi N, Simon ES, Korczyn AD *et al.* (2000). Anal sphincter EMG does not distinguish between multiple system atrophy and Parkinson's disease. *Muscle and Nerve* **23**, 731–734

Gray R, Stern G, Malone-Lee J (1995). Lower urinary tract dysfunction in Parkinson's disease: changes relate to age and not disease. *Age and Ageing* **24**, 499–504

Hald T & Bradley WE (1982). Neurological diseases and the urinary bladder. In Hald T & Bradley WE (eds) *Neurological Diseases and the Urinary Bladder*. Baltimore: Williams & Wilkins

Hattori T, Yasuda K, Kita K, Hirayama K (1992). Voiding dysfunction in Parkinson's disease. *Japanese Journal of Psychiatry and Neurology* **46**, 181–186

Heaton JPW (2000). Central neuropharmacological agents and mechanisms in erectile dysfunction: the role of dopamine. *Neuroscience and Biobehavioral Review* **24**, 561–569

Hussain IF, Brady C, Swinn MJ, Mathias CJ and Fowler CJ (2001). Exacerbation of orthostatic hypotension with sildenafil citrate (Viagra) in patients with autonomic failure due to multiple system atrophy (MSA). *Journal of Neurology, Neurosurgery and Psychiatry* **71**, 371–374

Jacobs H, Vieregge A, Vieregge P (2000). Sexuality in young patients with Parkinson's disease: a population based comparison with healthy controls. *Journal of Neurology, Neurosurgery, and Psychiatry* **69**, 550–552

Kirby R, Fowler C, Gosling J, Bannister R (1986). Urethro-vesical dysfunction in progressive autonomic failure with multiple system atrophy. *Journal of Neurology, Neurosurgery, and Psychiatry* **49**, 554–562

Kirby RS & Fowler CJ. (1988). Bladder and sexual dysfunction in diseases affecting the autonomic nervous system. In Bannister R (ed.) *Bladder and Sexual Dysfunction in Diseases Affecting the Autonomic Nervous System* 2. Oxford: Oxford University Press, pp 413–431

Lemack GE, Dewey RB, Roehrborn CG, O'Suilleabhain PE, Zimmern PE (2000). Questionnaire-based assessment of bladder dysfunction in patients with mild to moderate Parkinson's disease. *Urology* **56**, 250–254

Lewin RJ, Dillard GV, Porter RW (1967). Extrapyramidal inhibition of the urinary bladder. *Brain Research* **4**, 301–307

Libelius R & Johanson JF (2000). Quantitative electromyography of the external anal sphincter in Parkinson's disease and multiple system atrophy. *Muscle and Nerve* **23**, 1250–1256

O'Sullivan JD & Hughes AJ (1998). Apomorphine-induced penile erections in Parkinson's disease. *Movement Disorders* **13**, 536–539

Palace J, Chandiramani VA, Fowler CJ (1997). Value of sphincter electromyography in the diagnosis of multiple system atrophy. *Muscle and Nerve* **20**, 1396–1403

Pavlakis AJ, Siroky MB, Goldstein I, Krane RJ (1983). Neurourologic findings in Parkinson's disease. *Journal of Urology* **129**, 80–83

Porter RW & Bors E (1971). Neurogenic bladder in parkinsonism: effect of thalamotomy. *Journal of Neurosurgery* **34**, 27–32

Pramstaller PP, Wenning GK, Smith SJ, Beck RO, Quinn NP, Fowler CJ (1995). Nerve conduction studies, skeletal muscle EMG, and sphincter EMG in multiple system atrophy. *Journal of Neurology, Neurosurgery, and Psychiatry* **58**, 618–621

Sakakibara R, Hattori T, Tojo M, Yamanishi T, Yasuda K, Hirayama K (1993). Micturitional disturbance in multiple system atrophy. *Japanese Journal of Psychiatry and Neurology* **47**, 591–598

Sakakibara R, Hattori T, Uchiyama T *et al.* (2000). Urinary dysfunction and orthostatic hypotension in multiple system atrophy: which is the more common and earlier manifestation? *Journal of Neurology, Neurosurgery, and Psychiatry* **68**, 65–69

Schwarz J, Kornhuber M, Bischoff C, Straube A (1997). Electromyography of the external anal sphincter in patients with Parkinson's disease and multiple system atrophy: frequency of abnormal spontaneous activity and polyphasic motor unit potentials. *Muscle and Nerve* **20**, 1167–1172

Seki S, Igawa Y, Kaidoh K, Ishizuka O, Nishizaw, O, Andersson KE (2001). Role of Dopamine D1 and D1 receptors in the micturition reflex in conscious rats. *Neurology and Urodynamics* **20**, 105–113

Singer C, Weiner WJ, Sanchez-Ramos JR, Ackerman M (1989). Sexual dysfunction in patients with Parkinson's disease and their partners. *Journal of Neurology and Rehabilitation* **3**, 199–204

Singer C, Weiner WJ, Sanchez-Ramos JR (1992). Autonomic dysfunction in men with Parkinson's disease. *European Neurology* **32**, 134–140

Stocchi F, Carbone A, Inghilleri M *et al.* (1997). Urodynamic and neurophysiological evaluation in Parkinson's disease and multiple system atrophy. *Journal of Neurology, Neurosurgery, and Psychiatry* **62**, 507–511

Tanner GM, Goetz CG, Klawans HL (1987). Autonomic nervous system disorders. In Koller WC (ed.) *Autonomic Nervous System Disorders*. New York: Marcel Dekker, pp 145–170

Tison F, Arne P, Sourgen C, Chrysostome V, Yeklef F (2000). The value of external anal sphincter electromyography for the diagnosis of multiple system atrophy. *Movement Disorders* **15**, 1148–1157

Uitti, RJ, Tanner, GM, Rajput, AH, Goetz, CG, Klawans, HL (1989). Hypersexuality with antiparkinsonian therapy. *Clinical Neuropharmacology* **12**, 373–383

Wermuth L & Stenager E (1995). Sexual problems in young patients with Parkinson's disease, *Acta Neurologica Scandinavica* **91**, 453–455

Yamamoto M (1997). Pergolide improves neurogenic bladder in patients with Parkinson's disease. *Movement Disorders* **12**, 328

Yoshimura N, Mizuta E, Kuno S, Yoshida O (1990). The mechanism for inducing detrusor hyperreflexia in the primate model of parkinsonism. *Neurology and Urodynamics* **9**, 371

Yoshimura N, Mizuta E, Kuno S, Sasa M, Yoshida O (1993). The dopamine D1 receptor agonist SKF 38393 suppresses detrusor hyperreflexia in the monkey with parkinsonism induced by 1-methyl-4-phenyl-1,2,3,6-tetrahydropyridine (MPTP). *Neuropharmacology* **32**, 315–321

Zesiewicz TA, Helal M, Hauser RA (2000). Sildenafil citrate (Viagra) for the treatment of erectile dysfunction in men with Parkinson's disease. *Movement Disorders* **15**, 305–308

PART 5

Developing the efficiency and effectiveness of the clinical service: I

The evidence base for nursing intervention: the development, function and utility of the role of the Parkinson's disease clinical nurse specialist

Douglas MacMahon, Sue Thomas and Lynne Osborne

Background

The role of the clinical nurse specialist is now well established in many areas both nationally and internationally in, for example, areas such as stoma care, diabetes and rheumatology. Patients in these areas demonstrate increased satisfaction as well as more confidence to manage their conditions through specialist nursing support (Wade & Moyer 1989).

The development of the Parkinson's disease nurse specialist (PDNS) is relatively recent despite long-standing evidence that people with Parkinson's disease often have many simple problems that are neither recognized nor managed effectively by professionals (Oxtoby 1982; Mutch *et al.* 1986; Clarke *et al.* 1995; Findley 1999).

The first PDNS was initially appointed as a research post in 1987, and later appointed within the NHS in 1989 in Cornwall, in a multidisciplinary clinic set in a geriatric day hospital (MacMahon *et al.* 1990). Following the success of this initiative and in response to a need to improve standards and services for people with Parkinson's disease (Royal College of Physicians 1990; Neurological Charities 1992), the Parkinson's Disease Society of the UK (PDS-UK) set up a study for further evaluation of the concept. This study was performed to compare the effects of follow-up by a PDNS compared with consultant neurologist-led care at three outpatient centres using a randomised evaluative design (Reynolds *et al.* 2000). In this study, five PDNSs worked in selected district general hospitals in association with medical teams to establish Parkinson's disease clinics and network with other healthcare professionals involved in the care of people with the disease. The results were really inconclusive, for a variety of reasons. Only two (of 22) differences were found where physical functioning and general health improved more in the control (i.e. neurologist care) group. PDNSs for patients with Parkinson's disease did not appear to be cost-effective, although medical and nursing specialists valued their complementary expertise, and patient and carers valued their contributions. Indeed it is perhaps the satisfaction and increased confidence levels in Parkinson's disease patients and carers that led the Parkinson's Disease Society on to spearhead development of the PDNS to bring about greater equity of service provision for this client group.

In November 1994, the PDS-UK launched the Parkinson's Disease Society nurse specialist project in the House of Commons and, since that date, differing practice models have evolved according to local circumstance and need. The effectiveness of their intervention has been measured in a large community-based trial by Professor Sir Brian Jarman. To date, around 120 PDNSs are in post in varying parts of the UK. The benefit of the PDNS has been apparent to patients and carers from the outset but a lack of resources within the Neurology and Elderly Care Directorates, and a poor understanding of their role by commissioners, has been a major limiting factor for development. This lack of resources has led to a variety of funding initiatives, including commercial, charitable and NHS contributions – all working in partnership with the aim of delivering improved care for people with Parkinson's disease.

The function and utility of the PDNS

PDNSs work in a holistic way and are often the fulcrum of the multidisciplinary team. Their roles are diverse and they must exercise high levels of judgement, discretion and decision-making in clinical care. They monitor and improve standards of care through both supervision and audit. They provide skilled professional leadership and develop Parkinson's disease management through teaching, application of research-based practice, and giving support to colleagues in other disciplines. Patient education, support, and the identification and anticipation of care needs are important factors in ensuring quality of life and preventing complications in Parkinson's disease. Breakdown of care in the community may be precipitated by ignorance of self-management strategies in Parkinson's disease (Thomas 1994). This is enormously expensive in financial, work and psychological terms. PDNSs are thus ideally placed to help with the problems that the disease can present (Table 11.1).

A literature review demonstrates how diverse the role of the PDNS can be: Noble (1998) described how the PDNS could work as part of the multidisciplinary team caring for patients at every stage of the disease; she stated that they are:

> Fundamental in co-ordinating targeted case management and community care; acting as a resource for information; providing direct access to advice and effective case management and as a catalyst for improved public awareness.

Other authors have suggested the diversity of patient and carer interaction within this role: Calne (1994) suggests that the nurses have a major role to play in patient education, emotional and lifestyle counselling, and information services. She also comments on issues such as sexual dysfunction, something that patients rarely discuss with physicians. The unique role of this nurse, she suggests, is in the co-ordination of services and in pharmacotherapy as part of the care team.

Whitehouse (1994) suggests that the nurse can act as a link for the patient, hospital and community services to meet the needs of both patient and carer. Taira (1992) concentrates on educational and emotional support, diet, medication and exercise,

Table 11.1 Patient priorities from four-stage management scale for Parkinson's disease

---

Diagnostic phase
Achieve acceptance of diagnosis
Reduce distress
Control symptoms and improve prognosis

Maintenance phase
Prevention of complications
Maintenance of function and self-care

Complex phase
Maintenance/restoration good health
Management of drugs
Address disease-related problems
Consider surgical intervention
Support for carers

Palliative phase
Relief of symptoms and distress in patients and carers
Avoidance of treatment-related problems

From MacMahon & Thomas (1998).

whereas Vernon (1989) suggests that the role of the nurse includes health assessment, medication instruction, monitoring and liaison with other members of the healthcare team and the patient and family.

Fitzsimmonds and Bunting (1993) stress the contribution that nurses can make to the fulfilment of quality of life, life satisfaction, self-esteem and physical health, and also the importance of goal setting with the family.

Clinical nurse specialists have been criticised by many for following the medical model whereas others (nurses) have been developing their nursing role and expertise. Much confusion and controversy still arises about what should be the correct criteria for a clinical nurse specialist and in which direction the role should progress. In some areas, posts have been initiated without due consideration of the service framework or level of support required for the effective operation of the individual specialist nurse. This can then lead to dissatisfaction from the specialist nurse, the NHS and the service user. There is a need for wider awareness of what the role of the PDNS entails among clinical and managerial colleagues, and for careful planning of support mechanisms and appropriate resources before such posts are set up.

The PDNS is a specialist practitioner whose essential skills are:

> . . . clinical leadership, research awareness, development of nursing knowledge, acting as consultant, educator, change agent, and evaluating care.

The UK Central Council for Nurses, Midwives and Health Visitors (UKCC) (now the NMC) has described the specialist practitioner as one who: 'exercises higher levels of judgement and discretion in clinical care' (UKCC 1994). These definitions assume concepts of patient advocacy and expert practice. Such nurses use their specialist knowledge, skills, experience and understanding of Parkinson's disease and its impact on the individual to determine what level of care is needed, and to direct resources accordingly. Nurse specialists can generally spend more time with the patient and have a more meaningful discussion about a wider range of problems, and can thus effectively reduce consultant/ GP consultation time. By adopting a holistic, collaborative and co-ordinated approach, they can enable people with Parkinson's disease to achieve their maximal potential in self-management and can maintain contact between consultations by telephone, thus giving greater reassurance to their patients. Their expertise is predominantly within secondary care, although people with Parkinson's disease are generally cared for in the community, i.e. a primary care setting. Thus, the PDNS can help to bridge the gap between the two and in essence he or she is a potential key worker in co-ordinating service provision for those living with Parkinson's disease. The application of the skills and knowledge of this nurse can be a cost-effective way to enhance care, and can effect appropriate referral for interventions from other therapists particularly physiotherapists, occupational therapists, speech and language therapists, and dietitians (Bhatia *et al.* 2001).

The ability of a nurse to assess the signs of parkinsonism (by modified UPDRS) was assessed by Bennett (1997). The ratings by nurse clinicians after appropriate training, corresponded closely to those of a neurologist with expertise in movement disorders and showed good inter-rater agreement and consistency.

PDNS evaluation studies

A 1-year follow-up study (Reynolds *et al.* 2000) of 108 randomised patients with Parkinson's disease at three centres was performed to investigate differences between care provided by a hospital-based PDNS and that provided by the consultant neurologist (control). The only two (of 22 differences) found were where physical functioning and general health improved in the control group. Provision of PDNSs for patients with Parkinson's disease could not be recommended in this study solely on cost effectiveness because of similar outcomes, but increased costs were associated with the PDNS providing additional care. However, medical and nursing specialists valued their complementary expertise and patients 'and carers' responses to consultation reflect that PDNSs had a particular contribution; further studies have been undertaken to research this area.

The largest community study to date (Jarman 1998) has evaluated health outcomes and costs of community-based PDNSs in nine areas of England. Patients were randomly assigned to a PDNS or ordinary care through a GP. Invitations went to 3,124 patients with 1,859 consenting to participate; 818 were assigned to GP care and 1,041 to care by a PDNS. The nurse visited at 8-weekly intervals. After the first year, the nurse group demonstrated better care measured by reduce excess mortality, fractures, falls and hospital inpatient time. There were marginal increases in drug costs but reduced nursing home and hospital costs, giving a net saving of £300 per annum overall cost in year 1.

In a later presentation of the data (Jarman *et al.* 2002) responses to the global questionnaire were significantly better from the nurse group ($p = 0.006$). Stand-up group 2 (unable to stand without help) demonstrated a highly significant difference in mortality in favour of the nurse group ($p < 0.001$). In this group nurses were also more successful in keeping patients at home instead of moving them into institutions, which was reflected in a saving in institutional costs of borderline significance ($p = 0.07$). The authors' interpretation of the data was that, although nurses did not improve on ordinary care in mild or advanced disease, they did have a significant positive effect among patients with moderate disease.

When seeking to establish causality, there is an accepted hierarchy of strength of evidence which goes from anecdotal evidence through consensus to double-masked, controlled randomised trials. This, however, ignores the catalytic effects that emanate from good practice.

Perhaps the best way of identifying what difference the PDNS can make is to illustrate nurse intervention using a four-stage disease management paradigm developed to act as a lingua franca in Parkinson's disease (MacMahon & Thomas 1998). The paradigm known as 'Pathways' (Figure 11.1) has been developed with the aim of ensuring effective care management at every stage of the progression of the disease.

> Managed care is an uncomfortable notion for many but unmanaged care seems much worse.
>
> Bowman (1998)

The four stages of the management paradigm (Figure 11.2) identify the main areas of difficulty in Parkinson's disease and are categorised as diagnostic, maintenance, complex and palliative phases. By understanding what the patient requires during each stage and addressing needs effectively, the specialist nurse may improve the quality of life of the patient and carers (MacMahon 1999).

Exemplars of the roles of the PDNS at the four stages

Case history: 'diagnosis' phase

A woman aged 61 years was diagnosed in May 2000, after symptoms of a frozen shoulder for 6 months. On assessment, mask-like facies, decreased right arm swing, slight right arm rigidity, good fine finger movements and a resting tremor were observed; she was clearly frightened about the future.

Figure 11.1 Model of care.

Nurse intervention

Parkinson's disease and its management were explained and literature given. Symptoms were not disabling and no treatment was wanted. Reassurance, discussion and education were given (there is a growing evidence base for improved outcomes

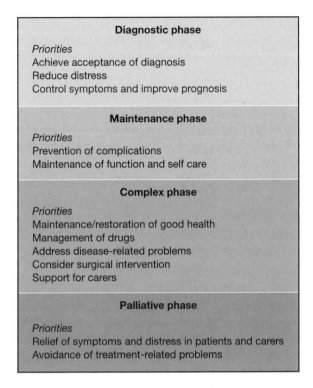

Diagnostic phase

Priorities
Achieve acceptance of diagnosis
Reduce distress
Control symptoms and improve prognosis

Maintenance phase

Priorities
Prevention of complications
Maintenance of function and self care

Complex phase

Priorities
Maintenance/restoration of good health
Management of drugs
Address disease-related problems
Consider surgical intervention
Support for carers

Palliative phase

Priorities
Relief of symptoms and distress in patients and carers
Avoidance of treatment-related problems

Figure 11.2 Patient priorities from four-stage management scale for Parkinson's disease. (From MacMahon & Thomas 1998.)

after appropriate telling of and support at diagnosis – Findley 1999). She was referred to a physiotherapist.

Information about car driving and motor insurance was given and she was advised to inform her insurers and the Driver and Vehicle Licensing Agency of the diagnosis. A telephone contact number was given to her, and a review appointment made.

Case history: 'maintenance' phase

A man aged 58 years had been diagnosed 5 years previously. Left-sided bradykinesia, rigidity and minimal tremor were evident despite his current medication of Sinemet-Plus (co-careldopa) four times daily and Sinemet CR at night. He was functionally independent, but a little slower at some of the activities of daily living requiring dexterity (e.g. buttons, tooth-brushing).

Nurse intervention

His medication and its timing was reviewed for maximal efficacy, and the 'pros' and 'cons' of adding dopamine agonist/COMT inhibitor were discussed. A baseline

UPDRS was assessed. Both GP and patient were offered information. Benefit entitlements were checked; and regular telephone contact and review were established.

Case history: 'complex' phase

A man aged 67 was diagnosed 10 years previously. His current medication was Madopar 62.5 in the morning, Madopar CR five tablets daily, and pergolide 1 mg four times daily. On assessment, there was a build-up of dyskinesia with wearing-off symptoms after 3 hours – freezing occurred at unpredictable times; he was found on direct enquiry to have erectile failure and occasional speech difficulty.

Nurse intervention

Drug timings were reviewed – and dispersible and standard Madopar (co-beneldopa) were tried. A catechol O-methyltransferase (COMT) inhibitor, surgical referral and other multidisciplinary team involvement were discussed with a Parkinson's disease medical specialist. Carer support was investigated (carer strain was measured), and he was referred to speech and occupational therapy and a sexual dysfunction clinic.

Case history: 'palliative' phase

A man aged 79 had his Parkinson's disease diagnosed in 1980. His current problems were of increasing confusion, hallucinations (mainly visual – mostly in the evening), intermittent immobility and frequent falls. Current medication was Madopar dispersible 62.5 four times daily and half Sinemet CR twice daily. On assessment, he displayed severe bradykinesia, rigidity and tremor, poor speech and impaired swallowing. An abbreviated mental state test was 5/10 using a mental test score (Hodkinson 1972).

Nurse intervention

Consider changing medication timings, consider reducing L-dopa to reduce confusion and hallucinations and maintain safety. Speech and language therapy referral and Mini-Mental State questionnaire was performed (21/30). Multidisciplinary team discussed his needs and those of his carer, and a psychiatric referral was made. Power of attorney was suggested, other accommodation needs were discussed and regular contact was maintained thereafter.

Evidence for an effect on service delivery

After a nurse appointment, an audit of existing outpatient and inpatient resources showed deficits in clinics and educational resources, and inequality of service provision. A range of developments has progressively occurred, including nurse-led clinics, exercise classes, courses for nurses and other disciplines, study days for multidisciplinary teams and improved telephone contact through a team secretary.

Further service development is anticipated in response to professional, patient and carer views acquired through re-audit against agreed standards.

The most recent UK treatment guidelines now recommend the use of nurse specialists as part of the Parkinson's disease team, often working as key workers at all stages of the disease (Bhatia *et al*. 2001; PDS-UK Primary Care Task Force 1999).

Conclusion

In conclusion, PDNSs are still in an evolutionary phase. With the experience gleaned from their progress over the past decade, the evidence base is slowly accumulating of their benefits. Many of the adverse effects of Parkinson's disease can be mitigated by the proper use of modern drug therapy and by marshalling timely interventions from a range of health and social agencies. This dictates the need for effective liaison among patients, doctors and other health professionals in both primary and secondary health care, and social services. The application of the skills and knowledge of a specialist nurse often working as a 'key worker' can be a cost-effective way to enhance care, and can effect appropriate referral for interventions from other disciplines. This includes physiotherapists, occupational therapists, speech and language therapists, and dietitians. PDNSs are proving crucial in effecting this liaison, and their effects on other professional and lay interventions are becoming clearer with recent research.

The most recent treatment guidelines allude to their importance and their roles as co-ordinators and 'key workers'. They have established a set of specialist nursing skills because they work directly in patient care in both the community and hospital settings (outpatient and inpatient). They also act as patients' advocates – establishing change in the practice of other professionals with whom Parkinson's disease patients need to relate. As with many professional activities, the levels of evidence are not yet scientifically incontrovertible, but the evidence of effect at anecdotal, district and societal level has stimulated the appointment of more than 120 nurses in the UK in the last decade, and this number is planned to double in the near future. There is general agreement that treatment and care of patients have improved as a consequence of their appointment.

The effects of PDNSs may therefore ultimately prove to be at least as much as catalysts and educators as direct practitioners of nursing care.

References

Bennett DA, Shannon KM, Beckett LA, Goetz CG, Wilson RS (1997). Metric properties of nurses' ratings of parkinsonian signs with a modified Unified Parkinson's Disease Rating Scale. *Neurology* **49**, 1580–1587

Bhatia K, Brooks DJ, Burn DJ *et al*. (2001). Updated guidelines for the management of Parkinson's disease. *Hospital Medicine* **62**, 456–470

Bowman C (1998). Take a team approach to PD. *Health and Ageing* November 24–26

Calne S (1994). Nursing care of patients with idiopathic Parkinsonism. *Nursing Times* **90**(24), 38–39

Clarke CE, Zobkiw RM, Gullaksen E (1995). Quality of life and care in Parkinson's disease. *British Journal of Clinical Practice* **49**, 288–293

Findley LJ (1999). Quality of life in Parkinson's disease. *International Journal of Clinical Practice* **53**, 404–405

Fitzimmons B & Bunting LK (1993). Parkinson's disease. Quality of life issues. *Nursing Clinics of North America* **28**, 807–818

Hodkinson HM (1972). Evaluation of a mental test score for assessment of mental impairment in the elderly. *Age and Ageing* **1**, 233–238

Jarman B (1998). The Community Nurse Specialist Project. Conference presentation. British Geriatrics Society Special Interest Group Meeting, London

Jarman B, Hurwitz B, Cook A, Bajekal M, Lee A (2002). The effects of community-based Parkinson's disease nurse specialists on health outcomes and costs: a randomised controlled trial. *British Medical Journal* **324**, 1072–1075

MacMahon D (1999). Parkinson's Disease Nurse Specialists. An important role in disease management. *Neurology* **52**(suppl 3), S21–S25

MacMahon DG & Thomas S (1998). Practical approach to quality of life in Parkinson's disease: the nurses role. *Journal of Neurology* **245**(suppl 1), S19–S22

MacMahon DG, Maguire R, Fletcher PJ for the Parkinson's Disease Clinic (1990). A focal Point for multi-disciplinary care. *Care of the Elderly* **2**, 406–411

Mutch WJ, Dingwall-Fordyce I, Downie AW, Paterson JG, Roy SK (1986). Parkinson's disease in a Scottish city. *British Medical Journal* **296**, 534–536

Neurological Charities (1992). *Living with a Neurological Condition. Standards of service for quality of life*. London: Parkinson's Disease Society

Noble C (1998). Parkinson's disease and the role of nurse specialists. *Nursing Standard* **12**(22), 32–33

Oxtoby M (1982). *Parkinson's Disease Patients and their Social Needs*. London: Parkinson's Disease Society

Parkinson's Disease Society UK Primary Care Task Force (1999). *Parkinson's Aware in Primary Care*. London: Parkinson's Disease Society

Reynolds H, Wilson-Barnett J, Richardson G (2000). Evaluation of the role of the Parkinson's disease nurse specialist. *International Journal of Nursing Studies* **37**, 337–49

Royal College of Physicians (1990). Standards of Care for patients with neurological disease. A consensus report of a working group. *Journal of the Royal College of Physicians of London* **24**(2), 90–97

Taira F (1992). Facilitating self-care in clients with Parkinson's disease. *Home Healthcare Nurse* **10**, 23–27

Thomas S (1994). Managing Parkinson's disease. *Community Nurse* **4**(6), 15–20

United Kingdom Central Council for Nurses, Midwives and Health Visitors (1994). *Standards of Education and Practice following Registration*. London: UKCC

Vernon G (1989). Parkinson's disease. *Journal of Neuroscience in Nursing* **21**, 271–284

Wade B & Moyer A (1989). An evaluation of clinical nurse specialists: implications for education and the organisation of care. *Senior Nurse* **9**, 11–16

Whitehouse C (1994). A new source of support. The nurse practitioner role in Parkinson's disease and dystonia. *Professional Nurse* **9**, 448–451

Further reading

Royal College of Physicians of London (1992). *Standard Assessment Scales for elderly people.* London: Royal College of Physicians

Parkinson's Disease Society, UK (1999). *Parkinson's and the Nurse.* London: Parkinson's Disease Society

Playfer JR, Hindle JV (eds) (2001). *Parkinson's disease in the older patient.* London: Arnold

Thomas S, MacMahon DG, Henry S (1999). *Moving and Shaping – the Future. Commissioning Services for People with Parkinson's Disease.* London: Parkinson's Disease Society

Scientific evaluation of community-based Parkinson's disease nurse specialists on patient outcomes and healthcare costs

Brian Hurwitz, Brian Jarman, Adrian Cook and Madhavi Bajekal

Introduction

There are a large number of Parkinson's disease nurse specialists (PDNSs) in the UK working in community settings. As with diabetes nurse specialists (who preceded them by more than a decade) the role of these specialist nurses evolved initially in a context of hospital clinics as described by MacMahon in Chapter 11.

In common with many conditions of low prevalence but high medical complexity, the primary care of Parkinson's disease (PD) poses UK general practitioners (GPs) particular problems. With a prevalence of about 1.6 per 1,000, the average GP with a list of 1,900 patients is responsible for the care of only three patients with the condition (Mutch *et al.* 1986; Ben-Shlomo & Sieradzan 1995; Schrag *et al.* 2000), too small a number to gain the requisite range and depth of clinical experience required to manage the condition optimally. Yet surveys suggest that up to 70% of PD patients have no regular contact with consultants with a specialist interest in PD, and rely entirely on GPs for the medical care of their condition (Parkinson's Disease Society 1993; College of Health 1994; Ridsdale 1995). This scenario offers a powerful rationale for development of community-based PDNSs, who can assume responsibility for the care of large numbers of PD patients across many general practices in a locality.

Few definitive evaluations of the effectiveness of nurse specialists have been undertaken (Wilson-Barnett & Beech 1994). A small controlled study involving a PDNS attachment to the PD clinic at the National Hospital, Queen Square, in London, indicated that nurses who undertook two home visits and five telephone contacts over a 6-month period had a positive effect on information provided to patients, and were also subjectively valued, although they had no detectable benefit on patient psychosocial functioning (Jananshahi *et al.* 1994). A more recent hospital-based, randomised controlled trial of 185 PD patients found little firm evidence of a PDNS effect on a range of patient self-reported health outcomes (Reynolds *et al.* 2000).

Our study set out to test the effectiveness of community-based PDNSs working with GPs in a randomised controlled trial design. The formal null hypothesis tested was that there is no difference in health outcome, or in net healthcare costs, between patients who receive community-based PDNS care and those who receive standard GP care.

Study design

We aimed to undertake the trial in parts of the UK that are reasonably representative of the country as a whole, but where community PDNS services were not already well developed and offering the very service we wished to study. We selected study areas only from English health authorities ($n = 57$), which in 1995 were co-terminal with local authorities (to ensure optimal relationships between health carers and social services) and from areas that did not already have well-developed community-based PDNS services. These 57 health authorities became the sampling frame from which we randomly selected nine areas to take part in the trial (Figure 12.1). The health authorities were first stratified by three factors that we knew had a strong influence on the service organisation and accessibility of community health services: size, population density (an indicator of rurality, which has a large impact on accessibility) and area deprivation score (Jarman 1983, 1984). Each of the 57 eligible authorities was allocated to one of nine strata, from which one authority area was chosen randomly (Figure 12.1). The nine health authorities selected all agreed to participate but, because recruitment of practices in one area proved difficult, it was decided to withdraw the study from this locality and to approach the second randomly selected health authority in that stratum which agreed to participate. Approval for the trial was obtained from each of the relevant nine local research ethics committees.

All general practices in the nine selected areas were approached and asked to ascertain, from their own information sources (disease registers, GP and receptionist memory) and repeat prescribing data, patients with a diagnosis of PD. Eligible patients had to be taking one or more anti-parkinsonian medications and to have had either a hospital or GP diagnosis of PD. Patients aged 17 years or younger, or with severe mental illness or cognitive impairment sufficient (in the view of their GP) to preclude valid informed consent, were not eligible to join the trial. Depending on how actively involved in the recruitment process practices wished to be, patients were invited to take part in the study by letter either from their GP or from us as study organisers. Written consent was obtained from every patient who participated.

Statistical power and randomisation

The statistical power of this study would be reduced if there were significant inter-nurse variability of effectiveness; if present, such variability would increase the statistical variance of a combined nurse effect in the intervention arm. To minimise the chances of inter-nurse variability in clinical skill and access to patients, all the nurses undertook the same educational and clinical specialist training (see below), and efforts were made to equate their workload by taking account of differences in geography and deprivation between the selected health authority areas. This was achieved by varying the patient randomisation ratios in each health authority area, from a 50:50 ratio of PDNS:control group in Gloucestershire, to a 70:30 split in Bromley. In each health authority area, the randomisation ratio was determined by the

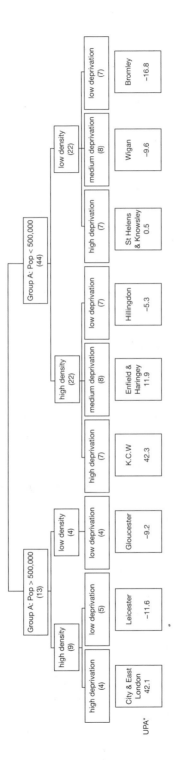

* Amended under-privileged area score (excludes under-5s component).

Figure 12.1 Sampling frame for selection of study areas (number in each stratum in brackets).

total number of patients recruited, deprivation, geographical factors, such as nurse travel time and ease of parking, and the number of whole-time equivalent nurses who could be made available to a health area (Table 12.1). Most areas were allocated one PDNS, but Leicestershire and Gloucestershire shared three, whereas Kensington, Chelsea and Westminster, City and East London and Hillingdon shared two nurses among them.

Table 12.1 Geographic distribution of PDNSs and study patients

Health authority	Patients randomised	UPA score[a]	Patients per PDNS	Number of PDNS	PDNS patients	Control patients
Bromley	194	−16.8	135	1	135	59
Leicestershire	406	−11.6	146	1.4	204	202
Wigan	206	−9.6	124	1	124	82
Gloucestershire	443	−9.2	139	1.6	223	220
Hillingdon	106	−5.3	114	0.5	57	49
St Helen's & Knowsley	159	0.5	95	1	95	64
Enfield & Haringey	156	11.9	94	1	94	62
City and East London	102	42.1	68	0.9	61	41
Kensington, Chelsea & Westminster	87	42.3	80	0.6	48	39
Total	**1,859**			**9**	**1,041**	**818**

[a] Amended under-privileged area score (excludes under fives component); higher score is socially more deprived.

With an expected dropout rate of 15% in each year of the trial, a total initial sample size of 1600 patients would be sufficient to detect a 10% change in a categorical outcome (such as stand-up group) of initial prevalence of 50%, with 80% power at the 5% significance level. In fact, a total of 1,836 patients were randomised, 1028 (56%) to the PDNS group and 808 (44%) to the control group (see Figure 12.2).

Randomisation

Patients were randomised within practice, using block randomisation lists reflecting the randomisation ratio of the health authority area described above. Where numbers permitted, patients were stratified within practice by age (< 70, 70–77, > 77 years), sex and disease duration (< 5, 5–9, > 9 years), separate lists being used in each stratum. Randomisation was performed between January and March 1996 by an independent social survey organisation, Social and Community Planning Research, now renamed the National Centre for Social Research.

PDNS intervention

Nine nurses were employed by the study organisers, supplied with a leased car and a mobile telephone, and offered an administrative base in the relevant health authority area. None of the nine nurses recruited had previously worked as a community-based PDNS, but several had formerly gained experience of PD nursing on hospital neurology wards. At the start of the study, the nurses were seconded to the Nursing and Midwifery School of the University of Sheffield, to study on course A43 of the English National Board, 'Meeting the Special Needs of People with Parkinson's Disease and their Carers' (School of Nursing and Midwifery 2000). All nine nurses gained this nursing certificate within 12 months of joining the study team.

During the trial, the clinical position of each PDNS in the community was advisory to GPs rather than clinically autonomous. The nurses assumed the following areas of responsibility under the guidance of an already experienced PDNS manager:

- Counselling and educating patients and carers about PD – in their homes, at health centre and GP clinics, in hospital outpatients and on the telephone.
- The provision of drug information to patients under the auspices of GPs and consultants.
- Monitoring clinical well-being and response to treatment (minimum of two assessments per year), reporting to GPs and consultants where appropriate.
- Instigating respite and day hospital care where appropriate; seeing patients in hospital if admitted, and liaising with hospital staff when discharged.
- Assessing social security benefit entitlement.
- Liaison with members of local multidisciplinary primary care teams for ongoing assessment and therapy where appropriate.

PDNSs were not empowered to change patient medication unilaterally but could (and did) make suggestions to GPs about altering dose regimens, change in medication preparation and addition of new drugs. During the trial, the working pattern of PDNSs was characterised by a time use study in which the nurses kept a diary of their daily work over two 1-week periods separated by 6 months. Patients allocated to the control group were not provided with additional services until the end of the 2-year intervention when each was offered one PDNS assessment.

Baseline and follow-up assessments of patients

A detailed questionnaire was developed and piloted, to be administered to patients face to face by trained lay interviewers employed by the National Centre for Social Research. Study patients were interviewed in their homes or place of residence, information relevant to health outcome and costs being collected at baseline, after 1 and 2 years (Table 12.2). Before each interview, patients were also sent a self-completed questionnaire eliciting information about their self-perceived health status.

Table 12.2 Trial outcomes

Primary outcome	Source of information
Clinical	
Stand-up test group	Patient interview
Dot-in-square score	Patient interview
Mortality	NHS Central Registry
Proportion sustaining fracture	Patient interview
Patient well-being	
PDQ-39 questionnaire	Patient completed
EuroQoL	Patient interview
Global subjective well-being question	Patient completed
Healthcare costs	
Institutional, respite, hospital, day care, medication, community and GP care, social security benefits, home aids and adaptations	Patient interview
PDNS	Costs based on NHS scales
Secondary outcome	
Medication	
Median dose L-dopa	Patient interview
Proportion patients on L-dopa controlled release preparation	Patient interview
Proportion patients on more than monotherapy	Patient interview
Referral	
Proportion patients referred to ancillary therapy	Patient interview
Proportion of patients referred to PD specialist	Patient interview

The self-completed questionnaire included a validated instrument for measuring the functioning and well-being of PD patients, the PDQ-39 questionnaire (Jenkinson *et al.* 1995, 1998; Peto *et al.* 1995), and the EuroQoL health-related quality-of-life measure (score range: -0.59 to $+1$, where a higher value represents better quality of life) (Williams 1995). The PDQ-39 is a disease-specific measure that scales patients' responses to aspects of morbidity known to be affected by PD: mobility, activities of daily living, emotional well-being, self-perceived stigma, social support, cognition, communication and bodily discomfort. It has a score range of 0–100 (where a higher score represents worse function).

The 1- and 2-year follow-up questionnaires also included a self-perceived global health question, asking patients about change in their general health over the preceding 12 months. The five possible responses to this question were: much better = 0, better = 1, same = 2, worse = 3, much worse = 4. As response at year 2 is influenced by response at year 1, a single value was derived that represented an individual's change in health over the 2-year study period which ranged from 0 (best) to 8 (worst); details of this score derivation are given in the appendix.

Patient interviews

Face-to-face interviews addressed assessment of clinical outcome measures, use of health and social services, and personal characteristics (age, sex, social class, employment, income and household circumstances). Clinical assessment was based on patients' questions eliciting information on duration and severity of disease, a test of patients' ability to put dots in a grid of 90 squares over a 30-second period, which measures visuomotor coordination and is influenced by tremor and bradykinesia (Gerstenbrand *et al.* 1973). The Columbian Rating Scale was used to test patients' ability to arise from sitting on a wooden chair (Wade 1994). Results were classified as follows: able to stand up normally, slowly or needing two attempts (group 1); tended to fall back and/or took more than two attempts, but eventually got up without help (group 2); and could not rise without holding on to something, or unable to stand up (group 3). Adverse events such as fractures were also recorded, together with information relevant to secondary outcome (see Table 12.2).

Mortality as a primary outcome

We endeavoured to flag all patients recruited to the trial for death and cause of death at the NHS Central Registry. The Registry provided monthly reports on deaths, thereby freeing the study from reliance on GP-reported deaths. The flagging also allowed mortality monitoring to be extended for a period after the PDNS intervention had ceased, allowing possible longer-term differences in mortality between intervention and control groups to be examined.

Costs

Services, aids and home adaptations received by PD patients were valued using standard sources of information from the Personal Social Services Research Unit (Netten & Denett 1996), costed at 1996 prices. Medication use was costed by reference to the Monthly Index of Medical Specialities (1996) net ingredient costs. For all these elements, average costs were calculated by summing the unit cost per patient, averaging for the year where appropriate and dividing the total by the number of patients in the study. Costs incurred by carers could not be calculated accurately because their hours of involvement with patients were markedly skewed (varying from less than an hour a day to 24 hours a day), and we were unable to discern precisely differing degrees of carer involvement – from being 'on call' to being actually required to assist patients – which arguably should be costed at significantly different rates.

Statistical methods

We compared the nurse and control groups for outcomes at the end of the 2-year trial. Between-group differences were estimated from regression models, including ordinal logistic regression for progression on stand-up test, logistic regression for bone fracture, ordinary linear regression for dot-in-square scores and quality-of-life measures, and Cox regression for mortality. Terms initially included to model variability between nurses were found to be unnecessary and therefore removed.

Changes in healthcare cost (excluding carer and Social Security Benefit costs) over the 2-year trial were calculated for each patient, and unpaired *t*-tests used to compare differences in the mean change of the nurse and control groups. Parametric confidence intervals for differences are reported. Data were highly skewed and all results were checked using 2000 bootstrapped samples, a method of sampling with replacement (Thompson & Barber 2000). Costs of apomorphine are not included in the main analysis because their extreme values when averaged across a year relate to only a very small number of patients who took the drug on 'an as-required basis'. Wide fluctuations in the frequency of apomorphine use makes a cost analysis based on such values unreliable.

Results

Of 863 eligible general practices in the nine randomly selected health authorities, 438 (51%) agreed to participate. The practices ascertained 3,392 patients with PD, of whom 3,124 were eligible to take part in the study and of these 1,859 (60%) agreed to participate (Figure 12.2). As a result of 23 deaths during the recruitment period, only 1,836 patients were present when the intervention began.

Seventeen of the 1836 patients were not traced at the NHS Central Registry and are therefore not included in mortality analyses. At baseline, no marked differences were observed between treatment groups with respect to age, sex, accommodation, social class, disease duration, disease severity or medication (Table 12.3) and follow-up during the study was very similar in the groups.

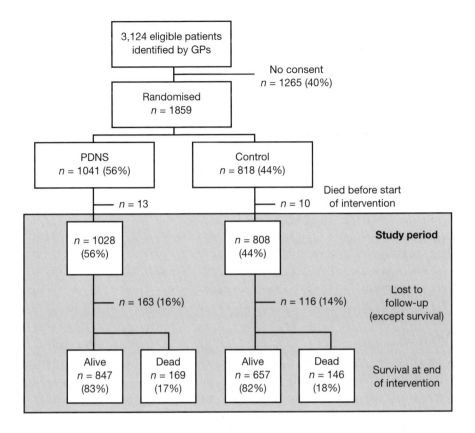

Figure 12.2 Patient flow before and during study period.

Table 12.3 Characteristics of participants at beginning of study, by treatment group

		PDNS (n = 1028)[a]	Control (n = 808)[a]
Sociodemographic characteristics			
Age (years)	< 70	354 (34)	256 (32)
	70–77	359 (35)	290 (36)
	> 77	315 (31)	262 (32)
Sex	Male	588 (57)	456 (56)
Accommodation	Free-living	916 (89)	716 (89)
	Sheltered	47 (5)	41 (5)
	Institution	65 (6)	51 (6)
	If free-living:		
	have a main carer	631 (69)	489 (68)
Social class	Manual	462 (46)	382 (49)
PD-related health measures			
Duration since	0–4	517 (53)	400 (52)
diagnosis (years)[a]	5–9	211 (22)	183 (24)
	> 9	247 (25)	187 (24)
Stand-up group[c]	No problems	453 (46)	344 (43)
	Without holding on	187 (19)	155 (19)
	Unable or had to hold	353 (36)	299 (37)
Bone fracture	Incident in last 12 months	55 (5)	50 (6)
Dot-in-square test	Best hand score	45.6 (21.7)[b]	45.0 (21.8)
Medication	L-dopa	869 (85)	695 (86)
	L-dopa + anticholinergic	98 (10)	62 (8)
	L-dopa + dopamine agonist	84 (8)	45 (6)
	L-dopa (mg daily)	300 (150,550)[d]	300 (150,500)
EuroQoL	Score	0.43 (0.35)[b]	0.43 (0.36)
PDQ-39	Summary score	37.9 (21.8)[b]	38.2 (21.8)

[a] Results are the number (percentage).
[b] Results are the mean (standard deviation).
[c] Small amount of missing data from patients refusing test or being unaware of time since diagnosis.
[d] Results are p50 (p25, 75).

Comparative data are not available for participants and those who declined to take part. However, the study sample as a whole was representative of the PD population of England and Wales in terms of duration of PD and age, except for slight under-representation of patients aged 85 or more, which was probably the result of the cognitive impairment exclusion criterion (Figures 12.3 and 12.4 compare the age distribution of patients in our study with that of patients consulting GPs in the fourth national survey of morbidity in general practice (McCormick *et al.* 1995) and with the age of patients in Mutch *et al.*'s total ascertainment study (1986) up-rated for the population of England) (Hurwitz *et al.* 1999).

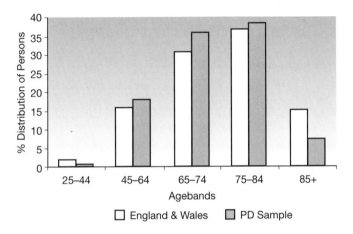

Figure 12.3

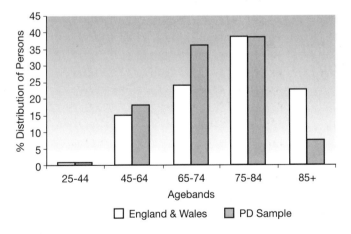

Figure 12.4

As would be expected, all the patients in the study showed a decline in their PD health status (Table 12.4). Patients were significantly more likely to perform poorly in the stand-up test and dot-in-square test, and scores in the EuroQoL and in each item of the PDQ-39 also showed a worsening of health. At the end of the study, average self-perceived health score as assessed in the global health question was 4.89, which is also indicative of deterioration (as unchanged self-perceived health over 2 years would score 4 on this question – see appendix).

Table 12.4 Deterioration of participants during study period – paired comparison of outcome measures at baseline and 2-year assessment in 1,254 participants present on both occasions

		Baseline	Two years	Change (95%CI)	p
Stand-up group	No problems	606 (49)	469 (38)		<0.001
	Without holding on	242 (20)	196 (16)		
	Unable or had to hold	391 (32)	576 (46)		
Dot-in-square, best hand score[b]		47.6 (21.9)	45.61 (21.1)	–2.6 (–3.7 to –1.5)	<0.001
EuroQoL tariff[b,c]		0.47 (0.35)	0.38 (0.35)	–0.10 (–0.12 to –0.08)	<0.001
PDQ-39[d]					
Mobility[b]		49.9 (33.4)	60.5 (32.3)	11.7 (10.2–13.1)	<0.001
Activities of daily living[a]		42.2 (28.4)	52.1 (29.2)	10.8 (9.5–12.1)	<0.001
Emotional well-being[a]		31.2 (23.8)	34.6 (25.2)	4.1 (2.9–5.3)	<0.001
Stigma[a]		29.4 (27.9)	30.7 (28.0)	1.7 (0.4–3.1)	0.013
Social support[a]		11.6 (18.8)	15.0 (21.5)	3.5 (2.0–4.9)	<0.001
Cognition[a]		34.8 (22.7)	38.7 (23.8)	4.8 (3.7–5.9)	<0.001
Communication[a]		22.5 (22.8)	28.6 (24.7)	6.8 (5.6–7.9)	<0.001
Bodily discomfort[a]		43.1 (25.5)	44.6 (25.0)	1.7 (0.4–3.0)	0.011

[a] Results are the number (percentage).
[b] Results are the mean (standard deviation).
[c] High score is good.
[d] High score is bad.

Primary outcomes

Objective measures of health

At the end of 2 years, severity of PD was not significantly different in the nurse and control group as shown by the results of the stand-up and dot-in-square tests (Table 12.5). There were also no differences detected in the proportion of each group who sustained a fracture over the trial period. The 2-year mortality rate was 17% with no differences between nurse and control patients overall; 4 years after randomisation, no between-group difference in mortality was seen (Table 12.5).

Table 12.5 Clinical outcomes at study end

		PDNS (n = 696)	Control (n = 558)	PDNS vs control (odds ratio [95%CI])	p
Stand-up test group[a,b]	No problems	248 (36)	221 (40)		
	Without holding on	114 (17)	82 (15)	1.15 (0.93–1.42)	0.19
	Unable or had to hold	329 (48)	247 (45)		
Bone fracture during study[a]		92 (13)	62 (11)	1.20 (0.85–1.69)	0.31
Dot-in-square test, best hand[c]		45.3 (21.2)	46.0 (21.1)	–0.70 (-3.25–1.84)[d]	0.59
Mortality		PDNS (n = 1016)	Control (n = 803)	Hazard ratio	
Died by 1/1/1998 (2 years)		169 (17)	146 (18)	0.91 (0.73–1.13)	0.38
Died by 1/1/2000 (4 years)		353 (35)	307 (38)	0.89 (0.76–1.03)	0.12

[a] Results are number (percentage).
[b] Results are mean (standard deviation).
[c] Small amount of missing data from patients refusing test.
[d] Regression coefficient and confidence interval from linear regression model.

Patient well-being

Table 12.6 shows the results of patient self-assessments at the end of the study. No differences between groups were observed in average EuroQoL scores or in any scores on PDQ-39 dimensions of morbidity. However, when asked about change in general health in the global health question, the combined scores from years 1 and 2 differ between treatment groups, with PDNS patients doing significantly better (difference in means –0.23, 95%CI –0.4 to –0.06, $p = 0.008$).

Table 12.6 Quality-of-life measures at study end[a]

	Nurse (n = 696)	Control (n = 558)	PDNS vs control (difference [95%CI])	p
Global health[b]	4.79 (1.50)	5.02 (1.38)	–0.23 (–0.40 to –0.06)	0.008
Euroqol tariff[c]	0.37 (0.35)	0.39 (0.35)	–0.02 (–0.06 to 0.02)	0.30
Parkinson's Disease Questionnaire[b]				
Mobility	61.1 (31.9)	59.8 (32.9)	1.38 (–2.57 to 5.34)	0.49
Activities of daily living	52.4 (28.6)	51.7 (29.9)	0.71 (–2.73 to 4.14)	0.69
Emotional well-being	34.7 (24.7)	34.5 (25.8)	0.21 (–2.79 to 3.20)	0.89
Stigma	30.6 (27.5)	30.8 (28.7)	–0.14 (–3.44 to 3.16)	0.93
Social support	15.9 (22.1)	13.7 (20.8)	2.21 (–0.66 to 5.08)	0.13
Cognition	39.3 (23.2)	38.0 (24.4)	1.30 (–1.52 to 4.11)	0.37
Communication	28.6 (24.4)	28.7 (25.1)	–0.10 (–3.02 to 2.82)	0.95
B odily discomfort	45.4 (24.8)	43.7 (25.3)	1.68 (–1.26 to 4.62)	0.26
PDQ-39 summary index	39.7 (21.2)	39.2 (22.1)	0.47 (–2.72 to 3.66)	0.77

[a] Results are mean (standard deviation). [b] High score is bad. [c] High score is good.

Costs

Provision of PDNS care and all associated car hire and administrative charges were calculated to cost £200 per patient per year. Increased total cost of health care (institutional, respite, hospital, day care, medication excluding apomorphine, community care and cost of PDNSs) found during the study period reflects the progressive nature of PD. Among PDNS patients, the mean annual cost per patient rose from £4,050 in the year preceding the study to £5,860 in the second year of the study, and from £3,480 to £5,630 in controls; the difference in mean increase between groups was not statistically significant (Table 12.7). The mean costs of different components of health care were similar in each group during the second year of the trial. At baseline 16 of 1,836 patients were taking apomorphine at an average cost of £6,900 per patient; at the end of the study 20 of 1,254 patients used apomorphine at the greatly increased average yearly cost of £54,700 each.

Table 12.7 NHS and local authority costs (excluding benefits)

	PDNS (n = 1028)	Control (n = 808)	p	95%CI
Year preceding study[a]	4.05 (55.4)	3.48 (35.0)		
Year 2[b]	5.86 (39.1)	5.63 (33.1)		
Individual mean increase[b]	2.54 (34.6)	2.80 (31.6)	0.47[c]	(-0.98 , 0.45)[d]
Cost components – year 2[b]				
PDNS	0.20			
Institutional cost	2.86 (20.6)	3.31 (20.6)		
Respite care	0.09 (12.8)	0.08 (7.98)		
Hospital cost	0.79 (17.9)	0.74 (22.3)		
Primary health care	0.15 (6.34)	0.19 (6.34)		
Therapy	0.10 (4.33)	0.10 (4.71)		
Drugs[e]	0.70 (25.3)	1.12 (3.74)		
Home help	0.34 (2.50)	0.30 (2.50)		

Results are in thousands of pounds mean (maximum).
[a] All patients entering study.
[b] Patients present at study end.
[c] Unpaired *t*-test with unequal variances, checked using 2000 bootstrapped samples.
[d] Checked with 2000 bootstrapped samples.
[e] Excluding apomorphine.

Secondary outcome

Medical treatments

During the study, the median daily dose of L-dopa rose from 300 to 400 mg, but with no significant between-group difference. The proportion of patients taking a controlled release form of L-dopa rose differentially between groups, from a third of each treatment group at baseline, to 53% of PDNS and 45% of control patients ($p = 0.016$). Also apparent was a greater tendency for PDNS patients taking selegiline to discontinue doing so: among 581 patients with complete follow-up and taking selegiline at baseline, 72% of the PDNS group had discontinued use after 2 years, compared with 55% of control patients ($p < 0.001$). No differences were found between PDNS and controls in the proportion of patients taking anticholinergics, dopamine agonists or apomorphine, or in the average number of different types of anti-PD medication prescribed. During the intervention period, the proportion of patients in each group referred to hospital outpatients, day centres or ancillary therapists (including speech, physio- and occupational therapists) did not vary significantly between PDNS patients and controls.

Nurse activity

The time use study revealed that patients in the intervention group received on average eight nurse assessments per year. PDNSs assessed an average of 13.7 patients per week, 75% at home, 14% on GP premises and 11% in hospital consultant clinics. In a typical week, the nurses made five visits to GPs, two to carers and one to a consultant to discuss patient care. Apart from face-to-face contact, considerable amounts of nurse time were spent each week on administration, letter writing, telephoning patients (6 hours) and travelling (8.4 hours).

Discussion

Our study is by far the largest of its kind to date and the only scientific evaluation of PDNSs based in primary care. During the study, the health status of participants as a whole showed a clear decline over the 2-year period (see Table 12.4), mirrored by an increase in median daily dose of levodopa. Between PDNS and control groups, however, only small differences in health outcome were observed, and the significantly better responses to the global health question indicate that PDNSs helped preserve patients' sense of well-being. Information about subjective well-being was collected via a health question often used by clinicians specialising in PD, to help them gauge patient perception of differences in well-being between hospital clinic visits. The benefit in subjective well-being found in the PDNS group was statistically significant, although the confidence interval around this difference is relatively wide and approaches zero at the lower end, implying, perhaps, that this could have been a chance finding. The positive benefit in well-being also needs to be interpreted in the light of the lack of accompanying positive changes in health status revealed by the disease-specific PDQ-39 or by EuroQoL score. Healthcare costs of PD patients were comparable to those of other studies (MacMahon *et al.* 2000), and lack of differences in health service usage between PDNS and control groups resulted in no significant differences in net health costs.

Although our study took place in primary care, our findings are in broad agreement with those of the earlier hospital-based study by Jahanshahi *et al.* (1994), which found that patients subjectively valued PDNS although their psychosocial functioning did not measurably improve, and are also in line with the recent hospital-based randomised trial by Reynolds *et al.* (2000) which found no evidence of a nurse specialist effect on a range of self-reported health outcomes in 185 patients with Parkinson's disease.

In our study, we did observe differences in process of care measures between the PDNS and control groups, but, with the exception of the case of subjective well-being, these were not accompanied by detectable differences in health outcome, e.g. greater use among PDNS patients of controlled-release L-dopa medication suggests that PDNSs were aware of (and could implement) current good practice. Close to the start of this trial, the UK PD Research Group (Lees 1995) published a finding of excess mortality in patients on combined levodopa and selegiline therapy since when selegiline use has fallen dramatically, a trend clearly observable in our study. However, in our study, reduction of selegiline over 2 years was significantly greater in the PDNS group, which again suggests that the nurses were more responsive than GPs to emerging scientific evidence.

Possible reasons for little health benefit

As with any trial in which patients are randomised within general practice and which inevitably results in many practices caring for patients in both arms of the trial, contamination of controls from the spill-over effects of nurse intervention (via the educative effects of PDNSs working with GPs and practice nurses) cannot be entirely excluded. If present, this would diminish the power of the study to detect PDNS efficacy. Contamination of controls by the intervention is more likely to take place in large practices containing many study patients. PDNSs certainly had a lot of contact with members of primary care teams, but they reported rigorously avoiding contact with, or conversation about, patients for whom they were not responsible.

In the analysis, we looked specifically for evidence of contamination by examining within-patient changes in the mobility dimension of the PDQ-39. One PDNS and one control patient were randomly selected from each participating practice and their scores on the mobility dimension regressed on practice size (on the assumption that the larger the number of study patients from each practice the greater the likelihood that contamination would have occurred), but no significant difference between PDNS and control groups was found.

The trial intervention involved nurses who required 'on the job' training in PD specialist nursing, who were therefore on a professional learning curve and who may not have been optimally effective in specialist nursing at least in the initial stages of the study; they may also not have been representative of experienced British PDNSs as a whole. It is not easy to see how we could have guarded against this aspect of the trial. At the time the study was planned, 1994–1995, we did not wish to deplete the number of PDNSs working within the NHS and it would have been hard to recruit experienced specialist nurses, occupying secure NHS posts, to a temporary 2-year research project.

Another limitation of our study stems from the pragmatic nature of the trial, which relied on finding PD patients from GP records and information systems. A cross-sectional prevalence survey of idiopathic PD conducted in 15 general practices across London indicates that this approach to case ascertainment has its limitations. Among patients whose records contained a diagnosis of Parkinson's disease or parkinsonism, prescription of anti-parkinsonian drugs, or mention of tremor after the age of 50 years, 22% were found to be suffering from no form of parkinsonism after formal testing in a tertiary care institution (Schrag *et al.* 2000). In our study it is likely that some non-PD patients entered the trial, but randomisation would minimise the likelihood of bias resulting from this limitation, as such patients should be distributed proportionately in both arms. Nevertheless, recruitment of non-PD sufferers could weaken the power of the study to detect differences in health outcome in patients with genuine parkinsonism.

Conclusion

Our study found no significant differences in health outcome between PDNS and control patients except in the subjective well-being of PD patients which significantly benefited from care by recently trained community-based PDNSs. The trial was of sufficient size to detect important changes, and the measured decline of health in the group as a whole confirms that the research instruments we used to measure PD health status were appropriate (Peto *et al.* 2001).

We believe that the benefit in subjective well-being is an important finding especially in a disease such as PD where decline is generally relentless (Marsden 1994). Moreover, this benefit was achieved without an increase in healthcare costs.

Acknowledgements

This chapter is based on our report of the study published in the *British Medical Journal* (Jarman *et al.* 2002). We would like to thank all the participating patients and GPs, and Ruth Jones, Debbie Hart, Chris Leigh of the research team, and the PDNSs: Jane Stewart, Janet Barton, Elizabeth Carter, Jaqueline Chamberlain, Joanne Evans, Katherine Gray, Karen Harris, Kate Madden, Lynne Osborne and Katie Richards. Thanks also to Susan Purdon, Julie Barber and Caroline Dore for statistical advice and comments on earlier drafts of the paper, and to Nish Chaturvedi, Konrad Jamrozik and Sasha Shepperd for comments on later drafts; to Gerald Stern, Doug MacMahon and Niall Quinn for Parkinson's disease advice; and to the PDNS Steering Group of the study, in particular, Mary Baker, Leslie Findley, Beverley Castleton, David Hutchinson, James Cornford and Jennifer Wilson-Barnett.

The project was funded by the Paul Hamlyn Foundation (40%), the Parkinson's Disease Society (30%) and Britannia Pharmaceuticals Limited (30%).

References

Ben-Shlomo Y & Sieradzan K (1995). Idiopathic Parkinson's disease: epidemiology, diagnosis and management. *British Journal of General Practitioners* **45**, 261–268

College of Health (1994). *The Needs of People with Parkinson's Disease*. London: College of Health

Gerstenbrand F, Grunberger J, Schubert H (1973) Quantitative testmethoden zur objecktivierung des effekts einer L-Dopalangzeittherapie beim Parkinson-syndrom. *Nervenarzt* **44**, 428–433

Hurwitz B, Bajekal M, Jarman B (1999). Evaluating community-based Parkinson's disease nurse specialists – rationale, methodology and representativeness of patient sample in a large randomised controlled trial. In: Stern G (ed), *Advances in Neurology, Vol 80, Parkinson's disease*. Philadelphia: Lippincott Williams & Wilkins, pp. 431–439

Jahanshahi M, Brown C, Whitehouse C, Quinn N, Marsden CD (1994). Contact with a nurse practitioner: A short-term evaluation study in Parkinson's disease and dystonia. *Behavioural Neurology* **7**, 189–196

Jarman B (1983). Identification of underprivileged areas. *British Medical Journal* **312**, 1705–1709

Jarman B (1984). Underprivileged areas: validation and distribution of scores. *British Medical Journal* **289**, 1587–1592

Jarman B, Hurwitz B, Cook A, Bajekal M, Lee A (2002). The effects of community-based Parkinson's disease nurse specialists on health outcomes and costs: a randomised controlled trial. *British Medical Journal* **324**, 1072

Jenkinson C, Peto V, Fitzpatrick R, Greenhall R, Hyman N (1995). Self-reported functioning and well-being in patients with Parkinson's disease: a comparison of the short-form health survey (SF-36) and the Parkinson's disease questionnaire (PDQ 39). *Age and Ageing* **24**, 505–509

Jenkinson C, Fitzpatrick R, Peto V (1998). *The Parkinson's Disease Questionnaire*. Oxford: Health Services Research Unit, Department of Public Health, University of Oxford

Lees AJ (1995). On behalf of the Parkinson's Disease Research Group of the United Kingdom. Comparison of therapeutic effects and mortality data of levodopa and levodopa combined with selegiline in patients with early, mild Parkinson's disease *British Medical Journal* **311**, 1602–1607

McCormick A, Fleming D, Charlton J (1995). *Morbidity Statistics from General Practice. Fourth national study, 1991–1992*. London: HMSO

MacMahon DG, Findley L, Holmes J, Pugner K (2000). The true economic impact of Parkinson's disease: a research survey in the UK. *Movement Disorders* **15**(suppl 3), 861.

Marsden CD (1994). Parkinson's disease. *Journal of Neurology, Neurosurgery, and Psychiatry* **57**, 672–681

MIMMS (1996). *The Monthly Index of Medical Specialities 1996 net ingredient costs*. London: Haymarket Medical Ld

Mutch WJ, Dingwall-Fordyce I, Downie AW, Paterson JG, Roy SK (1986). Parkinson's disease in a Scottish city. *British Medical Journal* **292**, 534–536

Netten A & Denett J (1996). *Unit Costs of Health and Social Care*. Canterbury: Personal Social Services Research Unit

Parkinson's Disease Society (1993). *Parkinson's disease and the nurse.* London: Parkinson's Disease Society 1999.Calne DB. Treatment of Parkinson's disease. *New England Journal of Medicine* **329**, 1021–1027

Peto V, Jenkinson C, Fitzpatrick R, Greenhall R (1995). The development and validation of a short measure of functioning and well-being for individuals with Parkinson's disease. *Quality Life Research* **4**, 241–248.

Peto V, Jenkinson C, Fitzpatrick R (2001). Determining minimally important differences for the PDQ-39 Parkinson's disease questionnaire. *Age and Ageing* **30**, 299–302

Reynolds H, Wilson-Barnett, Richardson G (2000). Evaluation of the role of the Parkinson's disease nurse specialist. *Nursing Studies* **37**, 337–349

Ridsdale L (1995). Community care for patients with idiopathic Parkinson's disease. *British Journal of General Practitioners* **394**, 226–227

School of Nursing and Midwifery (2000). *Knowledge Based Practice for People with Parkinson's Disease and Their Carers.* Sheffield: School of Nursing and Midwifery, Northern General Hospital

Schrag A, Ben-Shlomo Y, Quinn NP (2000). Cross sectional prevalence survey of idiopathic Parkinson's disease and Parkinsonism in London. *British Medical Journal* **321**, 21–22

Thompson SG & Barber A (2000). How should cost data in pragmatic randomised trials be analysed? *British Medical Journal* **320**, 1197–1200

Wade DT (1994). M*easurement in Neurological Rehabilitation.* Oxford: Oxford University Press

Williams A (1995). *The Measurement and Validation of Health: A chronicle.* York: Centre for Health Economics, Discussion paper 136, University of York

Wilson-Barnett J & Beech S (1994). Evaluating the clinical nurse specialist. A review. *International Journal of Nursing Studies* **31**, 561–571

Appendix

An area-under-the-curve method was used to combine global subjective well-being responses over the 2-year study period, e.g. patients at intersection (0,0) at baseline move 1 unit to the right on the x axis in year 1 of the study. Movement on the y axis is determined by the global subjective response: 'much better' stays on the axis (1,0), 'better' rises by 1 unit (1,1), 'same' rises by 2 units, 'worse' rises by 3 units and 'much worse' rises by 4 units. During year 2 of the study, patients move another unit along the x axis, with movement on the y axis once again dependent on global subjective response in the same manner as year 1. Patients who were much better in each successive year do not rise up the y axis but move from (0,0) to (2,0) on the axis; at the end of the intervention they have an area under the curve of 0 units. Patients who were 'much worse' in each year move from (0,0) to (2,8) and have an area under the curve of 8 units at the end of the intervention. Patients who get much better in year 1 but stay the same in year 2 of the study arrive at the same point (2,2) as someone staying the same and then getting much better, but the former patient has a lower score of 1 compared with the latter who has a score of 4 which reflects the earlier benefit.

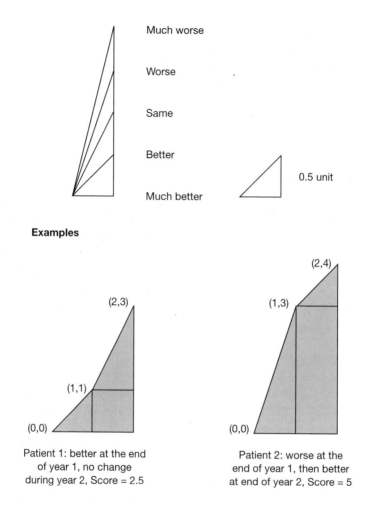

Examples

Patient 1: better at the end
of year 1, no change
during year 2, Score = 2.5

Patient 2: worse at the
end of year 1, then better
at end of year 2, Score = 5

Figure A12.1 Area-under-the-curve method used to combine global question responses

Chapter 13

Physiotherapy and Parkinson's disease: a review of the evidence

Diana Jones and Rowena Plant

Introduction

The evidence base in relation to physiotherapy and Parkinson's disease has to be able to satisfy a range of information seekers. Individuals with Parkinson's disease want to know what physiotherapy has to offer them, what to expect and how to access the service. Consultants, GPs and other referrers to physiotherapy ask whether the evidence supports referral to physiotherapy. They want to know when individuals should be referred, for what reasons and how to go about referring. Physiotherapists want to know about the best evidence in relation to treatment approaches, measurement of effectiveness and service delivery patterns. Researchers want to know how best to evaluate the impact of physiotherapy.

Currently, referral rates to physiotherapy for people with Parkinson's disease are low and have changed little over the past 20 years (Oxtoby 1982; Mutch *et al.* 1986; Chesson *et al.* 1996; Yarrow 1999). This remains in spite of the increasing prevalence of Parkinson's disease with age (Thomas *et al.* 1999) and demographic trends reflecting increasing numbers of older people in the population, often aspiring to maintaining active lives. The evidence base compounds such low referral rates. Although there is an increasing knowledge base in relation to physiotherapy and Parkinson's disease, its variety, in relation to research designs, treatment approaches and outcome measures used means that there are difficulties synthesising results to inform practice (de Goede *et al.* 2001; Deane *et al.* 2001a, 2001b).

This chapter addresses four key questions in relation to physiotherapy and Parkinson's disease. First, it asks what evidence there is for the effectiveness of physiotherapy and Parkinson's disease. Recent systematic reviews in the field (de Goede *et al.* 2001; Deane *et al.* 2001a, 2001b) will be discussed. Second, it asks what the nature of the evidence base is. Comparison is made among the stated aims, methods and outcomes used in two types of research studies: those studies evaluating general packages of physiotherapy treatment and those evaluating specific physiotherapy techniques. Third, it asks what the nature of physiotherapy in Parkinson's disease is. The outcomes of the Parkinson's Disease: Physiotherapy Evaluation Project UK (Plant *et al.* 2000) are discussed. Last, it asks what the relationship is between areas of difficulty experienced by people with Parkinson's disease and the scope of physiotherapy practice. Implications for clinical practice and research are discussed.

What is the evidence of effectiveness?

Two systematic reviews that aimed to compare (1) the efficacy and effectiveness of physiotherapy with placebo interventions and (2) standard physiotherapy with novel physiotherapy, in people with Parkinson's disease, have recently been undertaken under the auspices of the Movement Disorders Group of the Cochrane Collaboration (Deane *et al.* 2001a, 2001b). Only randomised or quasi-randomised controlled trials were included in the reviews. Eleven trials comparing physiotherapy with placebo or no treatment in 280 patients, and seven trials comparing two forms of physiotherapy in 142 patients were identified (Table 13.1). Most of the outcomes measured were reported to have improved as a result of the primary therapy under study. The numbers involved in the trials were small, and physiotherapy techniques, duration and location of treatment, and outcome measures varied considerably. The results were therefore reviewed qualitatively rather than undertaking a quantitative meta-analysis. The conclusion drawn was that there was insufficient overall evidence to affirm or deny the efficacy of physiotherapy in Parkinson's disease, but that this did not imply a lack of effect, rather that further work using strict methodological guidelines (Begg *et al.* 1996) was required.

Table 13.1 Trials of physiotherapy interventions included in the Cochrane (Deane *et al.* 2001b) and de Goede *et al.* (2001) reviews

Cochrane review physiotherapy vs placebo	Cochrane review type A vs type B	de Goede et al. *(2001)*
Gibberd *et al.* (1981)		
Hurwitz (1989)		
Cerri *et al.* (1994)		
Comella *et al.* (1994)		Comella *et al.* (1994)
Forkink *et al.* (1996)		
Katsikitis & Pilowsky (1996)		
Patti *et al.* (1996)		Patti *et al.* (1996)
Schenkman *et al.* (1998)		Schenkman *et al.* (1998)
Chandler and Plant (1999)		
Thaut *et al.* (1996)	Thaut *et al.* (1996)	Thaut *et al.* (1996)
Homann *et al.* (1998)	Homann *et al.* (1998)	
	Palmer *et al.* (1986)	Palmer *et al.* (1986)
	Hirsch (1996)	
	Mohr *et al.* (1996)	Mohr *et al.* (1996)
	Shiba *et al.* (1999)	
	Marchese *et al.* (2000)	
		Gauthier *et al.* 1987)[a]
		Formisano *et al.* (1992)
		Kamsma *et al.* (1995)
		Dam *et al.* (1996)
		Muller *et al.* (1997)
		Nieuwboer (1999)

[a]Included in Cochrane Occupational Therapy and Parkinson's Review (Deane *et al.* 2000c).

A research synthesis of studies evaluating the effects of physiotherapy on neurological signs, activities of daily living and walking ability has also recently been completed (de Goede *et al.* 2001). de Goede *et al.* (2001) included both true and quasi-experiments in their research synthesis (Table 13.1); a true experiment comprised a control condition and randomisation, and a quasi-experiment included non-randomised procedures with control. When the estimated effect size and the summary effect size were calculated for each outcome measure under study, there were significant results in relation to activities of daily living, walking speed and stride length, but not in terms of neurological signs. The authors highlighted the need to assess whether the statistically significant results were clinically significant, and in common with the Cochrane reviewers commented on methodological weakness in the evidence base.

The reviews in this section have underlined that in relation to physiotherapy and Parkinson's disease, the evidence base is not of the robustness or type necessary to mount rigorous evaluation using meta-analysis and systematic review methodology. Questions remain about what the studies were measuring and if what was measured was really the effect of physiotherapy. It is therefore important to consider what the aims of studies evaluating physiotherapy in Parkinson's disease are, and how these relate to the aims of physiotherapy in practice. In addition, it is important to establish what measures of outcome are chosen, and whether these outcomes are able to measure a physiotherapy effect.

What is the nature of the evidence base?

With the purpose of identifying links among the stated aims of studies, the types of physiotherapy intervention employed and levels of outcome measurement, our research group reviewed studies that sought to evaluate physiotherapy treatment approaches in Parkinson's disease published between 1980 and 2001. The full range of methodologies was included from case reports to randomised controlled trials. Studies were identified through regular searches of literature databases and immersion in the field of study over a period of 10 years. Two distinct groups of studies were discernible (Table 13.2). The first was composed of those studies evaluating a general package of physiotherapy using a range of techniques – active exercises, passive mobilisation, relaxation, training of gait, balance and transfers, in addition to pain relief, advice and education. The second group of studies addressed particular problem areas encountered by the client group using specific physiotherapy treatment techniques. These included compensatory movement strategies, cueing, a targeted focus on trunk or balance work, and the use of treadmill training.

The aims and outcomes of the studies reviewed were related to a framework based on the *International Classification of Functioning and Disability, Beta-2 draft* (ICIDH-2 – World Health Organization 1997) classification of impairment, activity and participation, informed by discussion of classification of outcome measures in

Wade (1992) and Shumway-Cook and Woollacott (1995). From our review, we were able to determine the physiotherapy-related aims and outcomes for each level of the ICIDH-2. Impairment level aims and outcomes were related to body structure or function, e.g. motor impairments such as joint mobility and muscle force, and impairments of cognitive or respiratory function. At the level of activity, in relation to, for example, mobility or bathing, aims and outcomes were related (1) to ability, as measured by degree of difficulty, assistance given or time taken, and (2) to performance, which focused on how the activity was actually undertaken. Participation level aims and outcomes were related to involvement in all aspects of everyday life, such as using public transport to take part in social and other activities.

Table 13.2 Studies using a package of physiotherapy and those using a specific approach

Package of physiotherapy	Specific approach
Gibberd et al. (1981)	Banks and Caird (1989)[a]
Palmer et al. (1986)	Yekutiel et al. (1991)[b]
Hurwitz (1989)	Bagley et al. (1991)[c]
Pederson et al. (1990)	Weissenborn (1993)[c]
Formisano et al. (1992)	Chan et al. (1993)[a]
Comella et al. (1994)	Kamsma et al. (1995)[b]
Cerri et al. (1994)	Morris et al. (1996)[c]
Patti et al. (1996)	Mohr et al. (1996)[c]
Viliani et al. (1999)	Dam et al. (1996)[c]
Chandler and Plant (1999)	Thaut et al. (1996)[c]
	Forkink et al. (1996)[d]
	Hirsch (1996)[d]
	Nieuwboer et al. (1997)[c]
	Bridgewater and Sharpe (1997)[a]
	Shenkman et al. (1998)[a]
	Moore and Robertson (1998)[c]
	Homann et al. (1998)[a]
	Nieuwboer (1999)[b,c]
	Shiba et al. (1999)[c]
	Marchese et al. (2000)[c]
	Miyai et al. (2000)[e]

Package of physiotherapy – active exercises, passive mobilisation, relaxation, training, e.g. of gait, cueing and sequencing, in addition to pain relief, advice and education.

Specific approaches:
[a]Trunk focus.
[b]Compensatory movement strategies.
[c]Cueing (verbal, visual, auditory).
[d]Balance focus.
[e]Treadmill.

Studies evaluating a general package of physiotherapy treatment

In relation to the studies evaluating a package of physiotherapy, there were marked imperfections in the match between stated aims and levels of measured outcome (Figure 13.1). Aims were mainly articulated in relation to motor impairments – improvement of joint range, strength and balance, the reduction of rigidity and the prevention of contractures. However, outcomes were largely measured at the level of activity relating mainly to the ability to undertake daily activities. Extensive use was made of both focal (e.g. Nine Hole Peg Test) and global (e.g. Functional Independence Measure) disability scales, activity of daily living scales (e.g. Barthel Index), Parkinson's disease-specific scales (e.g. Northwestern University Disability Scale) and timed tests (e.g. 10-m walk). Such a poor linkage of aims and outcomes is likely to predispose to equivocal results (Ashburn *et al.* 1993).

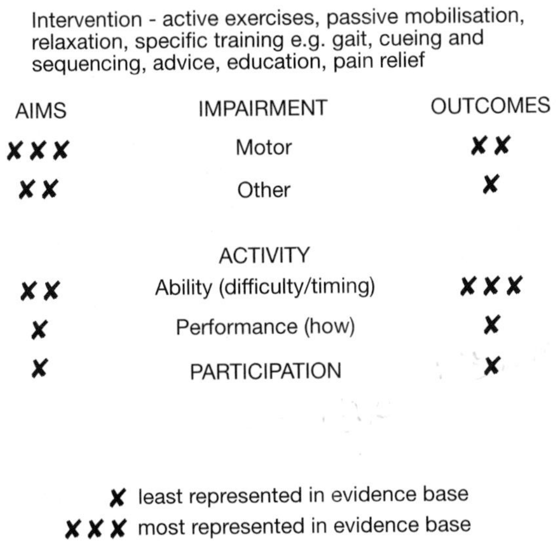

Intervention - active exercises, passive mobilisation, relaxation, specific training e.g. gait, cueing and sequencing, advice, education, pain relief

AIMS	IMPAIRMENT	OUTCOMES
✗ ✗ ✗	Motor	✗ ✗
✗ ✗	Other	✗
	ACTIVITY	
✗ ✗	Ability (difficulty/timing)	✗ ✗ ✗
✗	Performance (how)	✗
✗	PARTICIPATION	✗

✗ least represented in evidence base

✗ ✗ ✗ most represented in evidence base

Figure 13.1 Relationship between stated aims of treatment and levels of measured outcome in studies of packages of physiotherapy.

Studies evaluating specific physiotherapy treatment techniques

In those studies that sought to evaluate specific physiotherapy evaluations, there was a clearer and closer linking of treatment techniques and aims of intervention to the level at which the primary outcomes were being measured (Figure 13.2). Two principal categories emerged within specific intervention studies, one group of studies focusing at the level of impairment in an attempt to improve neuromusculoskeletal body functions (WHO 1997) affecting movement, and the other focusing at the level of activity to promote movement strategies that improve functional performance, e.g. in studies investigating compensatory movement strategies there was clear articulation of the nature of the technique. The stated aim was to promote effective movement strategies, and the primary outcomes focused at the level of performance of movement strategies, with extensive use of observational, video and electronic movement analysis. A similar logical linkage between aims and outcome measures was observed in studies of cueing techniques. In relation to trunk and balance work, there was a focus on impairment level aims but, unlike the general package, multiple technique studies, targeted techniques and primary outcomes relating to impairments that matched these aims. These included dynamometry and computerised dynamic posturography. The closer match between aims and outcomes in evaluations of specific techniques suggest that design and results of such studies are likely to be far more informative about the effect of physiotherapy intervention.

So far in this overview of the evidence for physiotherapy in Parkinson's disease, our working conclusion is that there is a lack of robustness in the evidence base, contributed to by a lack of congruence between the stated aims of intervention studies and measured outcomes. However, a body of more recent work on specific physiotherapy techniques demonstrates greater congruence between aims and outcomes (see Table 13.2 and Figure 13.2). A key question, however, still remains unanswered. Are our conclusions to date based on studies and reviews that were evaluating physiotherapy, or something else? All good research demands definition of the subject. In this case, what is the purpose and definition of treatment using physiotherapeutic methods in Parkinson's disease? It is important to know the precise nature of physiotherapy in Parkinson's disease to be sure that the interventions and outcomes that are being measured will ensure the evidence has implications, both for the everyday clinical practice of physiotherapists and for the everyday lives of individuals with Parkinson's disease. It is a not a question to be asked lightly, nor one that many professions have asked of themselves in specific practice.

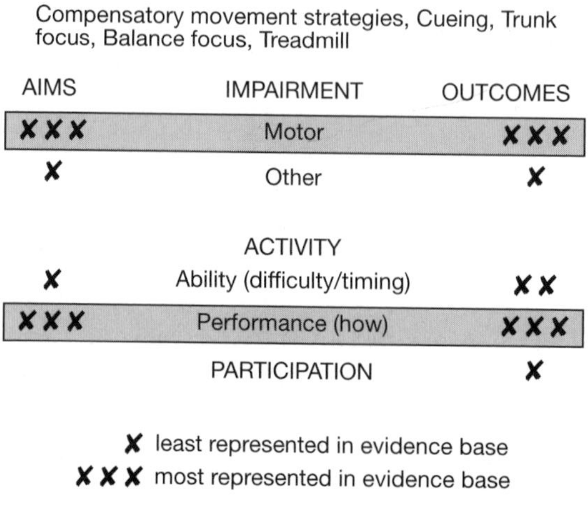

Compensatory movement strategies, Cueing, Trunk focus, Balance focus, Treadmill

AIMS	IMPAIRMENT	OUTCOMES
X X X	Motor	X X X
X	Other	X
	ACTIVITY	
X	Ability (difficulty/timing)	X X
X X X	Performance (how)	X X X
	PARTICIPATION	X

X least represented in evidence base
X X X most represented in evidence base

Figure 13.2 Relationship between stated aims of treatment and levels of measured outcome in studies of specific physiotherapy techniques.

What is the nature of physiotherapy and Parkinson's disease?

In the late 1990s, through their extensive international networks, the Parkinson's Disease Society and the European Parkinson's Disease Association became aware of the threat to the purchasing of physiotherapy services for Parkinson's disease as a result of the perceived paucity of the evidence base. Under the auspices of these organisations, which were aware of how much their members valued physiotherapy, an exploratory study was designed to build baseline knowledge about practice and service delivery (Plant *et al.* 2000). Glaxo Wellcome funded the study and its aims were to develop:

- a consensus on best practice physiotherapy management in Parkinson's disease
- a validated model for describing and analysing physiotherapy
- robust baseline knowledge to enable meaningful future evaluations of physiotherapy.

There were two stages to the study: data from a Delphi survey in the first stage were used to develop a case study approach adopted in the second stage.

The Delphi approach was selected because of its consensus methodology designed to use knowledge and insights from experts through an iterative process (Jones & Hunter 1995). There were three phases, a review of the evidence followed by two postal rounds to specialist therapists ($n = 49$). Thirty-two statements about physiotherapy for people with Parkinson's disease were constructed from the literature review. The statements were rated on a scale of 1–9 – an approach similar to that used previously by the Intercollegiate Stroke Working Party (Irwin 1997). The statements were linked to four topic domains:

1. The context of physiotherapy (how it should be organised).
2. The reasons for physiotherapy (why it should be undertaken).
3. The actions undertaken in physiotherapy (what approaches should be used).
4. The effects of physiotherapy (what outcomes should be measured).

The context domain was rated desirable/undesirable and does/does not happen, with the other domains rated agree/disagree. Results illustrated the variability in actual provision for people with Parkinson's disease even among specialist therapists, and consensus on the best context for practice, which included multidisciplinary team working and a commitment to a community focus and on-going review. On the basis of a consensus, the role of physiotherapy in Parkinson's disease was defined as: the maximisation of functional ability and the minimisation of secondary complications through movement rehabilitation within the context of education and support for the whole person.

There was a strong consensus among the specialist physiotherapists that an eclectic approach to treatment (i.e. using techniques drawn selectively from a variety of approaches) had the best effect. Results indicated that the effect of physiotherapy should be measured in relation to clearly specified aims of treatment, and principally in relation to effect on functional performance.

To ground the consensus gained in stage 1 in the reality of professionals' and patients' experience, case study methodology was adopted for stage 2 of the project (Yin 1994). Multiple sources of evidence are used in a case study approach and the data generated are triangulated to gain greater understanding of a range of issues. Nine trusts were selected as cases. Physiotherapists from these trusts had taken part in the Delphi survey and were chosen because they indicated in the survey that many of the positive statements about practice happened in their service. They were also the physiotherapists who felt most strongly that these aspects were desirable. Case studies were of two kinds: direct and indirect. Three geographically distant sites in the UK were chosen for direct case study. Direct case study sites were visited by a member of the research team who conducted face-to-face structured interviews with senior physiotherapists (eight), clinical service managers (six) and members of the multidisciplinary team (three). Ethical permission was gained for patient interviews. Ten patients who had recently completed a course of physiotherapy were identified by the senior physiotherapist and asked to participate in a face-to-face semi-structured interview about their treatment. Their case notes were subject to documentary analysis. The remaining six sites were termed indirect case study sites. Here semi-structured telephone interviews were conducted with senior physiotherapists (six) and their clinical service managers (six). The computer-aided data analysis software package NUD*IST (QSR 1994) was employed to manage and integrate the different data sources. Drawing on the results of stage 1 and 2 of the project, 12 recommendations were proposed. Table 13.3 highlights the main areas covered by the recommendations.

Table 13.3 Areas of recommendation from Parkinson's Disease Physiotherapy Evaluation Project UK (Plant *et al.* 2000)

Areas of recommendation
Use of knowledge generated within study for future evaluations
Use of model of physiotherapy (Figure 13.3) to maximise physiotherapy contribution to management
Development of guidelines on timing and source of referral
Identification of optimal patterns of contact and review
Identification of battery of measurement tools
Investigation of natural history of functional performance in Parkinson's disease
Development of concept of METERS (**m**ovement **e**nablement **t**hrough **e**xercise **r**egimens and **s**trategies)
Development of group work
Development of mechanisms to link intervention to home context
Establishment of the needs and role of carers
Development of physiotherapy-specific evidence-based education packages

The proposed model of physiotherapy in Parkinson's disease (Figure 13.3) is central to future work in the area. Situated within the context of overall Parkinson's disease management, the model highlights the core areas of practice that multidisciplinary team members can look to physiotherapy to evaluate and help manage on an ongoing basis throughout an individual's illness trajectory. These core areas relate to gait, balance, posture (including range of movement) and transfers. They are principally addressed through a treatment concept that has been termed METERS – **m**ovement **e**nablement **t**hrough **e**xercise **r**egimens and **s**trategies. To be congruent with intervention aimed at the promotion, maintenance and use of quality functional performance, measurement should also be targeted at this level.

The model can also be used to guide referral to physiotherapy, enabling early identification of treatment options. Patients in the study who had been diagnosed between 1 and 5 years ago had a mean time before referral to physiotherapy of 2.4 years; if diagnosed between 6 and 10 years ago their mean referral time was 6 years; if diagnosed over 10 years ago mean referral time was 17 years. Given an average disease duration of 15 years, timely referral would seem to be key. Professional physiotherapy opinion strongly favoured early referral (Plant *et al.* 2000).

The Parkinson's Disease Physiotherapy Evaluation Project (PEP) UK has explored and articulated the nature of physiotherapy in Parkinson's disease. Follow-up action on the recommendations should help ensure that the evidence base is strengthened by investigation of intervention in core areas of practice evaluated through the use of matched outcome measures. Guidelines on the use of physiotherapy in Parkinson's

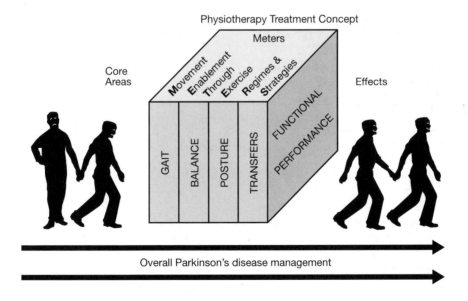

Figure 13.3 Model of physiotherapy and Parkinson's disease (Plant *et al.* 2000).

disease, which have emerged from the PEP project, will be pivotal in informing, developing and evaluating practice.

It is interesting to note that none of the studies identified in Table 13.2 measured the effect of physiotherapy in terms of achieving outcomes negotiated as goals with individuals. Importantly there remains a lack of theoretical understanding of the meaning of movement in everyday life and of quality indicators of meaningful movement. One approach to identifying where physiotherapy may be expected to impact on individuals' lives may be to look at the levels of reported problems in relation to movement and functional activities.

Problems of Parkinson's disease and the scope of physiotherapy practice

Despite optimal pharmacology individuals with Parkinson's disease continue to experience major difficulties in everyday life (Clarke *et al.* 1995). In a recent update by Yarrow (1999) of the Oxtoby (1982) survey of the members of the Parkinson's Disease Society, the extent to which functional and additional problems faced by people with Parkinson's disease and their carers fall within the remit of physiotherapy practice is highlighted. In relation to walking, 62% reported difficulty even during their best performance time. Respondents reported difficulties at their worst time in relation to turning over in bed (63%), getting in and out of a chair (57%), gait initiation (50%), freezing (46%), climbing steps or stairs (46%), negotiating doorways or walking in confined spaces (40%), and getting to the toilet (28%). Parkinson's disease was often complicated by coexisting morbidity such as anxiety (48%) and arthritis (43%). For the majority of respondents their carer was their spouse or partner. Turning over in bed was a task needing help from 38% of carers, and getting a good night's sleep was rated as very important by 69% of carers. Carers themselves experienced multiple pathology, again with high levels of anxiety (33%) and arthritis (48%). Assessment of the individual needs of carers is important (Thomas *et al.* 1999). An increase in parkinsonian symptoms has been documented in the spouses of individuals with Parkinson's disease (Kirollos *et al.* 1993), and Weller *et al.* (1992) reported reduced axial rotation in this group compared with controls.

User perceptions of therapy were evaluated as part of a study of the availability of access routes to, and delivery of, therapy services in Scotland in the 1990s (Chesson *et al.* 1996): 62% of questionnaire respondents with Parkinson's disease reported problems with daily activity, 60% with mobility and 43% with walking; 38% had received physiotherapy. The reasons given for this were to improve mobility and walking, to have exercise and to reduce pain. Only a third reported that their expectations of physiotherapy had been met; however, this did not stop a quarter of this group expressing possible future needs for physiotherapy. The highest fulfilment of expectations for physiotherapy, at 40%, related to improved mobility and walking, and this percentage was much lower than for core activities related to occupational therapy and speech and language therapy. It is not possible to know how expectations in relation to physiotherapy were engendered. However, late referrals when disabilities were likely to be established were the norm and unrealistic expectations of physiotherapy may have been held. A quarter of respondents cited improvement in mobility as the single thing that would most improve their quality of life. Many carers cited improvement in therapy provision as something that would improve their quality of life as well as that of those for whom they cared.

Perceptions of quality of life and congruence with therapists' perceptions were the subject of a second study by Chesson *et al.* (1997). Getting about, enjoying life, being able to do what they did before and being independent were key aspects identified by individuals in relation to quality of life. Therapy was a source of support and social interaction. Therapists perceived psychological benefits from therapy but these were not considered as worthwhile as functional gains. Most therapists were concerned with physical aspects of the disease and felt that improving these aspects would improve quality of life. Chesson *et al.* (1997) suggest that one way forward may be greater emphasis on psychological aspects of disability, information and advice, and a focus on patients' self-management strategies.

Individuals and carers value physiotherapy as a positive contribution to managing a deteriorating condition, and they are proactive in seeking physiotherapy through their GPs and consultants (Plant *et al.* 2000). The core areas of physiotherapy identified in the study of best practice physiotherapy – gait, balance, posture (including range of movement) and transfers (Plant *et al.* 2000) – map directly on to areas in which individuals and carers experience high levels of difficulty. Key issues for physiotherapy are the involvement of individuals in decision-making about the goals of physiotherapy, in addition to the gaining of understanding and development of measures that inform about the impact of physiotherapy on meaningful movement.

Future implications for clinical practice and research

Building on the recommendations of the Parkinson's Disease: Physiotherapy Evaluation Project UK (see Table 13.3), physiotherapists and information specialists have come together with funding from the Parkinson's Disease Society to develop guidelines for intervention by physiotherapists in Parkinson's disease (Guidelines Group 2001). Structured under six main headings – Referral, Physiotherapy Services, Assessment and Outcome, Physiotherapy Management, Team Approach and Information – the guidelines attempt to answer the questions of practising physiotherapists based on the best available evidence, e.g. questions relating to Referral are:

- What can physiotherapy offer to people with Parkinson's disease and their carers?
- When should people be referred for physiotherapy?
- How are people referred for physiotherapy?

Because the guidelines are addressing a wide range of questions from when to refer, to how to treat and how to structure service delivery, conventional hierarchies of evidence and strength of recommendation are inappropriate. To capture the full range of sources of evidence that make up the knowledge base relating to physiotherapy and Parkinson's disease, a methodological key has been devised which provides a description of the overall approach or specific research design used to generate the evidence. Each statement in the text is supported by a reference categorised according to a methodological key.

These guidelines will enable other initiatives to build on best evidence. They are accessible through the internet at: http://online.unn.ac.uk/faculties/hswe/research/ Rehab/Guidelines/Intro.htm.

One current study contributing to the evidence base is RESCUE – Rehabilitation in Parkinson's Disease: The Strategy of Cueing. This is an international, multicentre trial (Plant *et al.* 2001). Cueing is an oft-used method of treatment and self-management. Cues are predetermined external stimuli or internal self-instruction that result in the triggering and improvement of the quality of functional motor tasks. The objectives of the project are to determine optimal cue types, learning and transfer procedures, and self-management in everyday life.

Conclusion

This chapter asked four key questions in relation to physiotherapy and Parkinson's disease, relating to effectiveness, the nature of the evidence base, the nature of physiotherapy, and areas of difficulty for individuals in relation to the scope of practice. Relatively recent systematic reviews in the field (de Goede *et al.* 2001; Deane *et al.* 2001a, 2001b) have highlighted methodological weakness of a particular type of evidence base. However, within that body of knowledge, important studies that build therapeutic intervention on a developing understanding of neuroscience have been identified (Thompson & Playford 2001). It is just such a link between the basis of intervention techniques, the aims of interventions and the level at which their effects are measured that is required to ensure a joined-up and meaningful knowledge base. Evidence from practice has highlighted core areas of practice, key interventions and optimum level of outcome. However, more work is needed to link this to the experience of movement in the everyday lives of individuals with Parkinson's disease. Physiotherapists in Parkinson's disease have risen to the challenge of putting their 'evidence house in order' by learning from best practice (Plant *et al.* 2000) and developing practice guidelines based on the best of current evidence (Guidelines Group 2001). These actions should enable future evidence to be strengthened and the contribution of physiotherapy treatment to self-management, surgical intervention, pharmacology and social care to be maximised.

Acknowledgements

Co-members of the Parkinson's Disease Physiotherapy Evaluation Project UK team: Professor Ann Ashburn, Professor of Rehabilitation, Southampton General Hospital; Dr Brenda Lovgreen, Senior Lecturer, Manchester School of Physiotherapy, Manchester; Felicity Handford, Secretary, Association of Physiotherapists in Parkinson's Disease (Europe), Brussels; Eleanor Kinnear, Integrated Neurological Services, London. This paper was written in March 2001.

References

Ashburn A, Partridge C, De Souza L (1993). Physiotherapy in the rehabilitation of stroke: a review. *Clinical Rehabilitation* **7**, 337–345

Bagley S, Kelly B, Tunnicliffe N *et al.* (1991). The effect of visual cues on the gait of independently mobile Parkinson's disease patients. *Physiotherapy* **77**, 415–420

Banks MA & Caird FI (1989). Physiotherapy benefits patients with Parkinson's disease. *Clinical Rehabilitation* **3**, 11–16

Begg C, Cho M, Eastwood S *et al.* (1996). Improving the quality of reporting of randomized controlled trials. The CONSORT statement. *Journal of the American Medical Association* **276**, 637–639

Bridgewater KJ & Sharpe MH (1997). Trunk muscle training and early Parkinson's disease. *Physiotherapy Theory and Practice*, **13**, 139–153

Cerri CG *et al.* (1994). Physical exercise therapy of Parkinson's disease. *Movement Disorders* **9**(suppl 1)., 68

Chan J, Lee J, Neubert C (1993). Physiotherapy intervention in Parkinsonian gait. *New Zealand Journal of Physiotherapy* April, 23–28

Chandler C & Plant R (1999). A targeted physiotherapy service for people with Parkinson's disease from diagnosis to end stage: a pilot study. In Percival R & Hobson P (ed.). *Parkinson's Disease: Studies in psychological and social care*. London: BPS Books, pp 256–269

Chesson R, Cockhead D, Maehle V (1996). *Availability of Therapy Services to People with Parkinson's Disease Living in the Community*. Aberdeen: The Robert Gordon University

Chesson R, Romney-Alexander D, Maehle V (1997). *Health Related Quality of Life. A comparative study of professionals' views, and people with Parkinson's Disease own perceptions*. Aberdeen: The Robert Gordon University

Clarke CE, Zobkiw RM, Gullaksen E (1995). Quality of life and care in Parkinson's disease. *British Journal of Clinical Practice* **49**, 288–293

Comella CL, Stebbins GT, Brown-Toms N *et al.* (1994). Physical therapy and Parkinson's disease. *Neurology* **44**, 376–378

Dam M, Tonin P, Casson S *et al.* (1996). Effects of conventional and sensory-enhanced physiotherapy on disability of Parkinson's disease patients. In Battistin L, Scarlato G, Caraceni T *et al.* (eds) *Advances in Neurology*. Philadelphia: Lippincott-Raven Publishers, pp 551–555

de Goede CJT, Keus SHJ, Kwakkel G *et al.* (2001). The effects of physical therapy in Parkinson's disease: a research synthesis. *Archives of Physical Medicine and Rehabilitation* **82**, 509–515

Deane KHO, Jones D, Clarke CE *et al.* (2001a). *Physiotherapy for Patients with Parkinson's Disease*. The Cochrane Library, Oxford: Update Software, Issue 3

Deane KHO, Jones D, Ellis-Hill C *et al.* (2001b). *A Comparison of Physiotherapy Techniques for Patients with Parkinson's Disease*. The Cochrane Library, Oxford, Update Software, Issue 1

Deane KHO, Ellis-Hill C, Clarke CE *et al.* (2001c). *Occupational Therapy for Patients with Parkinson's Disease*. The Cochrane Library, Oxford, Update Software, Issue 3

Forkink A, Toole T, Hirsch MA *et al.* (1996). *The Effects of a Balance and Strengthening Program onEquilibrium in Parkinsonism*, Vol. PI-96–33. Florida State University, Tallahassee, FL: Pepper Institute on Aging and Public Policy

Formisano R, Pratesi L, Modarelli FT *et al.* (1992). Rehabilitation in Parkinson's disease. *Scandinavian Journal of Rehabilitation Medicine* **24**, 157–160

Gauthier L, Dalziel S, Gauthier S (1987). The benefits of group occupational therapy for patients with Parkinson's disease. *American Journal of Occupational Therapy* **41**, 360–365

Gibberd FB, Page NRG, Spencer KM *et al.* (1981). Controlled trial of physiotherapy and occupational therapy for Parkinson's disease. *British Medical Journal* **282**, 1196

Guidelines Group (2001). *Guidelines on Physiotherapy and Parkinson's Disease*. Newcastle upon Tyne: Institute of Rehabilitation

Hirsch M (1996). Activity dependent enhancement of balance following strength and balance training, Doctoral thesis, Florida State University

Homann CN, Crevenna R, Hojnig H *et al.* (1998). Can physiotherapy improve axial symptoms in parkinsonian patients A pilot study with the computerized movement analysis battery Zebris. *Movement Disorders* **13**(suppl 2), 234

Hurwitz A (1989). The benefit of a home exercise regimen for ambulatory Parkinson's disease patients. *Journal of Neuroscience Nursing* **21**(3), 180–184

Irwin P (1997). Assessing the level of external consensus with expert derived criteria for a national multi-disciplinary stroke audit package. MSc thesis, University of Birmingham

Jones J & Hunter D (1995). Consensus methods for medical and health services research. *British Medical Journal* **311**, 376–380

Kamsma YPT, Brouwer WH, Lakke JPWF (1995). Training of compensational strategies for impaired gross motor skills in Parkinson's disease. *Physiotherapy Theory and Practice* **11**, 209–229

Katsikitis M & Pilowsky I (1996). A controlled study of facial mobility treatment in Parkinson's disease, *Journal of Psychosomatic Research* **40**, 387–396

Kirollos C, O'Neill CJA, Dobbs RJ *et al.* (1993). Quantification of the cardinal signs of parkinsonism and of associated disability in spouses of sufferers. *Age and Ageing* **22**, 20–26

Marchese R, Diverio M, Zucchi F *et al.* (2000). The role of sensory cues in the rehabilitation of Parkinsonian patients: a comparison of two physical therapy protocols. *Movement Disorders* **15**, 879–883

Miyai I, Fujimoto Y, Ueda Y *et al.* (2000). Treadmill training with body weight support: its effect on Parkinson's disease. *Archives of Physical Medicine and Rehabilitation* **81**, 849–852

Mohr B, Muller V, Mattes R *et al.* (1996). Behavioral treatment of Parkinson's disease leads to improvement of motor skills and to tremor reduction. *Behavior Therapy* **27**, 235–255

Moore G & Robertson D (1998). The effect of a metronome on gait rhythm in Parkinson's disease. *Synapse,* **Autumn,** 3–4

Morris ME, Iansek R, Matyas TA *et al.* (1996). Stride length regulation in Parkinson's disease. Normalization strategies and underlying mechanisms. *Brain* **119**, 551–568

Muller V, Mohr B, Rosin R *et al.* (1997). Short-term effects of behavioral treatment on movement initiation and postural control in Parkinson's disease: a controlled clinical study. *Movement Disorders* **12**, 306–314

Mutch WJ, Strudwick A, Roy SK *et al*. (1986). Parkinson's disease: disability, review, and management. *British Medical Journal* **293**, 675–677

Nieuwboer A (1999). Functional disability and scope of rehabilitation in advanced Parkinson's disease. Thesis: Katholieke Universiteit

Nieuwboer A, Feys P, de Weerdt W *et al*. (1997). Is using a cue the clue to the treatment of freezing in Parkinson's disease? *Physiotherapy Research International* **2**, 125–134

Oxtoby M (1982). *Parkinson's Disease Patients and Their Social Needs*. London: Parkinson's Disease Society

Palmer SS, Mortimer JA, Webster DD *et al*. (1986). Exercise therapy for Parkinson's disease. *Archives of Physical Medicine and Rehabilitation* **67**, 741–745

Patti F, Reggio A, Nicoletti F *et al*. (1996). Effects of rehabilitation therapy on Parkinsonians' disability and functional independence. *Journal of Neurologic Rehabilitation* **10**, 223–231

Pederson SW, Oberg, B, Insulander A *et al*. (1990). Group training in parkinsonism: quantitative measurements of treatment. *Scandinavian Journal of Rehabilitation Medicine* **22**, 207–211

Plant RD, Jones D, Ashburn A *et al*. (2000). *Physiotherapy for People with Parkinson's Disease: UK best practice. Short report*. Newcastle upon Tyne: Institute of Rehabilitation

Plant RD, Nieuwboer A, Kwakkel G (2001). *Rehabilitation in Parkinson's Disease: The strategy of cueing*, European Framework V Quality of Life Research Programme

QSR (1994). *QSR NUD*IST*. Melbourne, Australia: Qualitative Solutions & Research Pty Ltd

Schenkman M, Cutson TM, Kuchibhatla M *et al*. (1998). Exercise to improve spinal flexibility and function for people with Parkinson's disease: a randomized, controlled trial. *Journal of the American Geriatrics Society* **46**, 1207–1216

Shiba Y, Obuchi S, Toshima H *et al*. (1999). *Comparison between Visual and Auditory Stimulation in Gait Training of Patients with Idiopathic Parkinson*. Japan: World Congress of Physical Therapy

Shumway-Cook A & Woollacott M (1995). *Motor Control. Theory and Practical Applications*. Baltimore, MA: Williams & Wilkins

Thaut MH, McIntosh GC, Rice RR *et al*. (1996). Rhythmic auditory stimulation in gait training for Parkinson's disease patients. *Movement Disorders* **11**, 193–200

Thomas S, MacMahon D, Henry S (1999). *Moving and Shaping – The Future. Commissioning services for people with Parkinson's disease*. London: Parkinson's Disease Society

Thompson AJ & Playford ED (2001). Rehabilitation for patients with Parkinson's disease [Commentary]. *The Lancet* **357**, 410

Viliani T, Pasquetti P, Magnolfi S *et al*. (1999). Effects of physical training on straightening-up processes in patients with Parkinson's disease. *Disability and Rehabilitation* **21**(2), 68–73

Wade D (1992). *Measurement in Neurological Rehabilitation*. Oxford: Oxford University Press

Weissenborn S (1993). The effect of using a two-step verbal cue to a visual target above eye level on the parkinsonian gait: a case study. *Physiotherapy* **79**, 26–31

World Health Organization (1997). *International Classification of Functioning and Disability. Beta-2 draft,* Full version. Geneva: WHO

Yarrow S (1999). *Survey of Members of the Parkinson's Disease Society*. London Parkinson's Disease Society

Yekutiel MP (1991). A clinical trial of the re-education of movement in patients with Parkinson's disease. *Clinical Rehabilitation* **5**, 207–214

Yin RK (1994). *Case Study Research. Design and Methods*. Thousand Oaks, CA: Sage Publications

PART 6

Developing the efficiency and effectiveness of the clinical service: II

Chapter 14

Health economic evaluation and the financial burden of Parkinson's disease

Clive Bowman and Leslie Findley

Introduction

Health care in the UK, during the 1990s, was dominated by a variety of 'pressures' and 'targets' typified by waiting lists and initiatives for routine procedures such as hip replacement. Emerging new technology and treatments were nervously received by a service committed to short-term objectives and cost containment. Unsurprisingly, on this backdrop, the success story that is the ageing population became an unwelcome challenge rather than an opportunity for development. Ageism continues to be reflected in the very use of age as a diagnostic determinant for the purpose of service development and provision. Growing health and care needs arising from chronic disease and associated disability management continue to be obfuscated by defined 'priorities'; this organisational problem may be addressed by the radical modernisation programme. The epidemiology and complex interaction of the health and care required by sufferers of Parkinson's disease provide a useful model.

Here the results of an economic impact study of Parkinson's disease in the UK are reported, and information from a study of Parkinson's disease in nursing homes and the experience of a specialist Parkinson's disease care home are briefly described; to this the health and care service modernisation and partnership agenda are added to contextualise a proposal for an integrated health and care management model for Parkinson's disease.

The clinical severity and management stages of Parkinson's disease are commonly accepted to be in four broad groups: the diagnostic phase, maintenance phase, complex disease phase and finally a palliative stage (MacMahon & Thomas 1998). Individual outcomes are a complex product of health care in varying degrees at various stages, acknowledging a variety of other factors such as personal circumstances and preferences as well as co-morbidity. Clinical governance is established in secondary care and inevitably, with the principles of inclusiveness and equity (NHS Plan 2000) running through the modernisation of health care, will spread to chronic disease in the community (Department of Health 1999), rapidly becoming a major driving force in the shaping of clinical services. The individual and service outcomes of Parkinson's disease will be interdependent on health and care, as in other chronic disorders. The initial prejudice is therefore for service integration (Bowman *et al.* 1999).

The economic and quality-of-life impact of Parkinson's disease in the UK

This project sought to evaluate the costs of care and estimates the economic impact of Parkinson's disease in the community (the project members are listed in the acknowledgements). A multi-stage research approach led to hospital centres representative of the general population of Great Britain being determined. A random sample of general practices was selected from each centre and then all Parkinson's disease patients from those practices seen in the last 6 months were recruited. Data from patient interviews, records and self-report questionnaires were analysed in a standard manner. Here only the economic data from the study will be considered: 28 hospital centres were selected from which 76 associated individual general practices were identified. Of those general practices, 59% agreed to partake and 440 sets of usable data were obtained.

The population study was compared with the overall population density of the UK and, using the Jarman Deprivation Score, confirmed to be representative of the overall population. The sample age and sex characteristics are shown in Table 14.1 and the distribution of patients by age and the Hoehn and Yahr stage in Table 14.2.

Table 14.1 Sample age/sex characteristics

Age	Female	Male	Total
<65	34	38	72
65–74	62	71	133
75–84	72	93	165
85+	35	18	53
All	203	220	423

Patient age unknown for 13 respondents; patient sex unknown for 17 respondents.

Table 14.2 Sample distribution by patient age and Hoehn and Yahr (H&Y) stage (numbers)

Age group	H&Y 0 & I	H&Y II	H&Y III	H&Y IV	H&Y V	All
<65	23	19	16	11	1	70
65–74	36	35	33	25	3	132
75–84	40	31	50	35	9	165
85+	10	4	18	16	3	51
All	109	89	117	87	16	418

Patient age unknown for 5 respondents.
Stage 0 no signs; I, unilateral; II, bilateral disease; III, II+; IV, severe disease with marked disability; V, bedridden.

Before considering the costs of Parkinson's disease it is pertinent to note that in younger patients (those < 65), 76% had the diagnosis of Parkinson's disease made by a consultant, but this percentage fell to under 50% in those over 75 and down to 31% in the 85+ group. Conversely, GPs made the diagnosis only in 17% of younger patients under 65, but were responsible for the diagnosis in 51% of those over 85. Furthermore, the incidence of outpatient visits fell from 64% of younger patients to 31% in those over 85. Parkinson's disease nurses were associated with the care of approximately a quarter of the patients studied across all ages. These data indicate difficulties of access or, more worryingly, a degree of ageism in medical services. However, reviewing outpatient attendance and involvement of a specialist Parkinson's disease nurse by Hoehn and Yahr stage, it becomes apparent that outpatient visits are undertaken by 44% of Hoehn and Yahr stage 2, 55% of Hoehn and Yahr stage 3, falling to 39% Hoehn and Yahr stage 5, whereas the Parkinson's disease specialist nurse had a peak input of 30% to Hoehn and Yahr stage 4, falling back to 24% of Hoehn and Yahr stage 5. We conclude therefore that both escalating age and disease state are associated with a reduction of routine access to expertise. In addition, we recorded considerable co-morbidity as displayed in Figure 14.1.

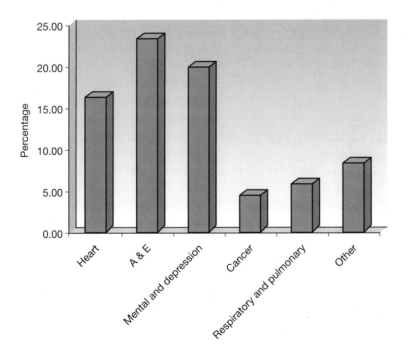

Figure 14.1 Percentage frequency of co-morbidity.

In analysing the costs of Parkinson's disease, we have determined direct costs including those provided by the health service, social services and funded privately, and indirect costs that we have variously considered as lost earnings, lost leisure time or carer replacement costs (the cost of the lost leisure at the cost of commercial care provision). Figure 14.2 describes the mean total cost of direct and indirect costs by patient age and Figure 14.3 the same figures by Hoehn and Yahr stage. The mean direct costs by patient age are shown in Figure 14.4 and by Hoehn and Yahr stage in Figure 14.5.

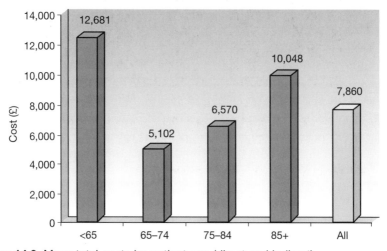

Figure 14.2 Mean total costs by patient age (direct and indirect).

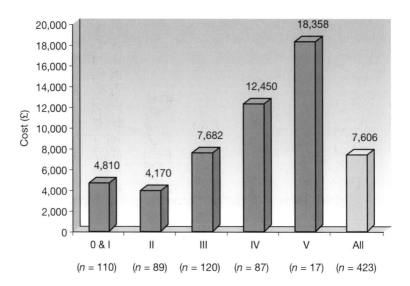

Figure 14.3 Mean total (direct and indirect) costs by Hoehn and Yahr (H&Y) stage.

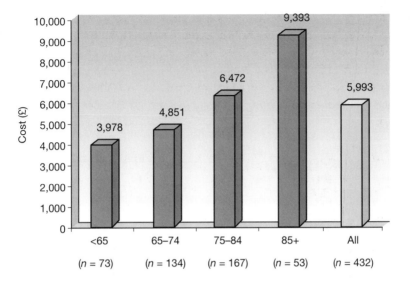

Figure 14.4 Mean total direct costs by patient age.

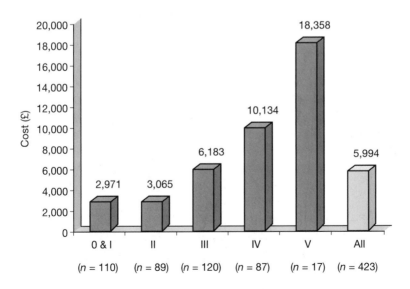

Figure 14.5 Mean total direct costs by Hoehn and Yahr (H&Y) stage.

Although age has a clear relationship to escalating cost, this is far more marked when considering stage of disease. Across all ages and disease stages the overall attribution of direct costs is demonstrated in Figure 14.6. It may be surprising for clinicians managing Parkinson's disease, who have difficulty gaining access to increased funding for new drugs and hospital beds for assessment and rehabilitation, to discover that more than 50% of overall direct costs are incurred by the social services and private care.

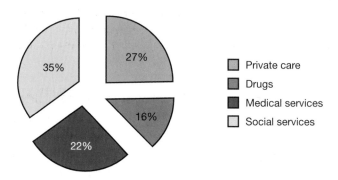

Figure 14.6 Breakdown of total direct costs. Mean total cost per patient per year: £5,992 (standard development £7,912).

Understanding the contribution of indirect costs is more difficult and three methods of computation were used:

1. The lost earnings approach estimates the actual income lost by patients and carers and produces an averaged figure of £1,668 per annum.
2. The lost leisure time, a measure that uses the caring time reported by carers at the rate of the minimum wage, yields a figure of £5,829 per patient per year.
3. The replacement cost determines the expense of funding of the same hours of lost leisure time at a commercial rate, producing a cost of £27,236 per person per annum.

To try to calculate the overall economic burden of Parkinson's disease, an understanding of the overall disease prevalence is necessary. This also has a wide range; Mutch *et al.* suggested in 1986 that there were 58,600 British citizens with Parkinson's disease, whereas, using the prevalence figures of Ashton from 1990, a figure of 100,000 patients seems likely. Anecdote from established movement clinics suggests a rising incidence of Parkinson's disease. Whether this is the result of a real epidemiological change or just improved diagnosis and an ageing population is unclear. Using our data, the lowest prevalence and the lowest estimation of indirect costs, the overall economic burden of Parkinson's disease in the UK is £449m per annum. Using the higher prevalence estimate and the most expensive indirect cost base produces a figure of £3,323m per annum. The economic burden of Parkinson's disease changes with age. Indirect costs tail off rapidly through retirement and similarly direct costs escalate, in particular through the use of care homes by older patients.

In summary, the economic study of the impact of Parkinson's disease confirms it to be a very expensive condition with lost earnings in younger patients and institutional care in older patients being of particular significance. Overall the stage of the disease is the most powerful determinant of cost. The most expensive patients are those at Hoehn and Yahr stages 4 and 5 in care homes. The intensity of professional management declines with escalating case cost!

Parkinson's disease and parkinsonism in nursing homes

Parkinson's disease and parkinsonism in nursing homes have not been the subject of many studies. The Parkinson's Disease Society sponsored the movement clinic at Weston-super-Mare General Hospital to undertake a survey of all residents in the catchment area of the hospital. A specialist nurse (Joan Beer) reviewed all case records prescribing data of the 1,220 nursing home residents and interviewed senior care staff. Subsequently a specialist registrar (Sarah Caine) reviewed all GP records; 135 patients were identified as having a clear diagnosis of parkinsonism or were on treatment for Parkinson's disease. Of this 135, 49 almost certainly had Parkinson's disease. This suggests a nursing home prevalence of around 7%, consistent with an American survey (Moghal *et al.* 1995). The reasons for admission of these 49 are displayed in Table 14.3.

Table 14.3 Reasons for nursing home admission of patients with idiopathic Parkinson's disease

Reason for admission	No. (49) (%)
Mental Impairment	16 (33)
Immobility	8 (16)
Following fracture (4 NOF)	8 (16)
Failure of care	4 (8)
To be near family	1 (2)
Intercurrent illness	1 (2)
Unknown	11 (22)

NOF, neck of femur

The Weston General Hospital movement clinic includes a specialist nurse for Parkinson's disease at the hospital (Bowman 1999). In addition to an interest in care home medical care, the follow-up arrangements of parkinsonian patients in care homes should therefore be good; however, of 49 nursing home residents with Parkinson's disease, only 16 had ongoing input from a consultant and/or specialist nurse; 44 patients had received 177 GP visits throughout the year, but five had no record of any medical contact for over a year. Of particular interest and concern was that only the 16 patients under review by the consultant or specialist nurse had any support from paramedical professionals and this is in the context of full access rights for GPs.

Mali Jenkins House Partnership in care

The Parkinson's Disease Society, in association with BUPA Care Services and the John Grooms Housing Association, operate the only home in the UK that focuses on the needs of Parkinson's disease patients. Mali Jenkins Home (named after the founder of the Parkinson's Disease Society) opened in 1996 and currently provides care for some 20 long-term residents. These are largely from the local community but the home has provided respite care to parkinsonian patients from all over the UK. The home has good operational links with a local GP, neurologist, geriatrician and specialist nurse services, but its greatest strength is its staff. The home is led by a nurse manager and has residential home status. It is clear that the healthcare assistants who have received training in the nature and needs of Parkinson's disease are very much more responsive and capable than those in generic 'care homes' as a consequence of their specialisation. It is the innate understanding and practical ability of the staff and the flexibility of drug rounds, assistance with slow eating and other common problems that provide the quality of care that is so evident on visiting.

Health and care modernisation

The modernisation of health and care services, especially the introduction of National Service Frameworks and new patterns of commissioning by primary care trusts and indeed care trusts, will need to satisfy demands to demonstrate health gain and 'best value'. The paradigm describing the stages of Parkinson's disease downgrades the economic burden of the late-stage patients; however, making diagnosis the key to entering an integrated system of care (Figure 14.7) focuses the system on integrated service delivery.

A venerable principle of geriatric medicine has been to acknowledge that long-term care represents the most expensive and unwanted outcome and that in consequence the management of complex cases demands considerable attention and co-ordination. This approach would promote an active response to the most frail and vulnerable patients, avoidable complications of severe disease and medication could be averted, a positive approach to needs created and a clearer recognition of the onset of the end-stage of disease, allowing a shift to a palliative stance to care.

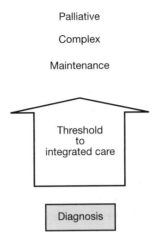

Figure 14.7 Integrated care.

Understanding the economic realities of Parkinson's disease makes an integrated health and care approach to Parkinson's disease, working from a dedicated community facility, evolve from a pipe dream to an entirely rational option.

After diagnosis patients could be enrolled into an integrated service. A nurse specialist would be assigned as their case manager supported by primary and secondary care. Considering the mix of cases, a specialist nurse could have 80–100 community-based patients, including 5–10 rehabilitation, intermediate and long-term care cases. Potentially the primary care trust serving 200,000 may need 6–8 specialist nurses for Parkinson's disease. In addition to providing a continued community case management, this team would provide an on-call service for a care home committed to Parkinson's disease. The specialist home would become a centre for rehabilitation of patients with Parkinson's disease and a suitable setting for treatment stabilisation with care staff well oriented to Parkinson's disease. In addition to clinical reviews, the specialist neurological and geriatric clinician would have a responsibility with nurse specialists and primary care to deliver clinical governance.

Although radical, this model builds on the experience of the Parkinson's disease specialist nurse outlined by MacMahon and the proposals for health and care management of care home residents made by the Royal College of Physicians of London, the Royal College of Nursing and the British Geriatrics Society (2000). The system of health and care outlined here opens the door to partnership arrangements, with independent providers potentially developing not only the care home base but also training and support for the specialist nurses, bringing national standards of service and governance albeit with a local commissioning and delivery of service. Finally, the provision and funding of specialist neurological centres undertaking evidenced interventions such as deep brain stimulation may be resolved through the impact on overall expenditure, reducing dependency on care.

Acknowledgements

Members of the economic burden of Parkinson's disease study steering committee: P Bain, M Baker, C Beech, CE Bowman, L Findley, J Holmes, DG MacMahon, V Peto, K Pugner, M Aujla. It was funded by an unrestricted grant by Dupont Pharma; the analysis was carried out by the Economists Advisory Group.

References

Bowman C (1999). Parkinson's disease: moving towards care management. *Parkinson's Disease* **1**(2), 1–3

Bowman C, Johnson MJ, Venables DA, Foote C, Kane RL (1999). Geriatric care in the UK: aligning services to needs. *British Medical Journal* **319**, 1119–1121

Department of Health (1999). Corporate Governance in primary care groups. Department of Health circular HSC1999/048. London: Department of Health

MacMahon DG & Thomas S (1998). A new paradigm for Parkinson's disease. *Journal of Neurology* **245**(suppl 1), s19–22

Moghal S, Rajput AH, Meleth R, D'Arcy C, Rajput R (1995). Prevalence of movement disorders in institutionalised elderly. *Neuroepidemiology* **14**, 297–300

Mutch WJ, Dingwall-Fordyce I, Downie AW, Paterson JG, Roy SK (1986). Parkinson's disease in a Scottish city. *British Medical Journal* **292**, 534–536

NHS Plan (2000). *The Government's Response to the Royal Commission on Long Term Care.* Department of Health Cm4818–II

Royal College of Physicians (2000). *The Health and Care of Older People in Care Homes A comprehensive interdisciplinary approach.* A report of a working party of the RCP, London, RCN and BGS. Royal College of Physicians of London, July

Common errors and service deficiencies in the investigation and management of Parkinson's disease

David J Burn

Introduction

An error is defined by the *Oxford English Dictionary* as a 'mistake, wrong opinion; sin', whereas a deficiency is stated as 'wanting or falling short in something; insufficient'. The consequences of an error may be permanent or temporary. A deficiency is either relative or absolute.

In this chapter a brief overview of errors and accidents is given, and how they apply to medicine in general. A classification for errors and deficiencies in the management and treatment of Parkinson's disease (PD) is presented and a number of examples provided. Finally, the potential role for clinical governance in reducing error and deficiencies in PD is discussed, as a means of improving overall quality of care in the UK.

Errors, adverse events and accidents

In the National Health Service (NHS) errors are linked inextricably with adverse events, clinical risk and clinical negligence. The annual cost of negligence to the NHS has been estimated as £200m (Secker-Walker 1999). Given the overall budget for the health service, this is a relatively small figure, but the concern lies in the rate of rise of this amount, and the increasing size of settlements for clinical negligence.

An adverse event may be defined as 'an unintended injury that was caused by medical management and that resulted in measurable disability' (Leape *et al.* 1991). Adverse events have previously been estimated to affect between 3.7% and 16.6% of admissions from studies carried out in the USA and Australia, respectively (Brennan *et al.* 1991; Wilson *et al.* 1995). In another study, based in Colorado, the rate was intermediate, but adverse events were more likely to occur in elderly people (Thomas & Brennan 2000). Most recently, a retrospective study based in the UK reported that 11.7% of hospitalised patients experienced an adverse event (Vincent *et al.* 2001). About half of these events were judged preventable with 'ordinary standards' of care. The authors extrapolated their findings to estimate that around 5% of the 8.5 million patients admitted to hospitals in England and Wales each year experience preventable adverse events. This would equate to an additional three million bed days and a cost to the NHS of around £1bn per year.

The frequency of and outcomes from errors are not always easy to quantify. Clearly 'hard' end-points such as operative mortality and morbidity are relatively easy to gather. In the study of Vincent *et al.* (2001), a third of the adverse events occurring in hospital led to 'moderate or greater disability', or death. The consequences of an error may of course be psychological as well as physical, and may affect not only the patient, but also the carers. Psychological consequences are harder to assess.

In industry, much time and effort have been devoted to modelling accidents. Within the organisation there may exist a corporate culture or processes, compounded by management decisions, that predispose to accidents occurring in the work place. In the latter, the conditions will then exist for the individual to commit an error. Safety mechanisms will be in place to detect such errors, although sometimes errors will not be detected, effectively breaching defences, leading to accidents (Reason 1995). Despite best intentions on the part of the individual, it is estimated that approximately 70% of accidents in health care result from human error (Secker-Walker 1999). Within medicine, anaesthetics is the only specialty to have significantly developed accident modelling along similar lines.

Parkinson's disease: characteristics of the condition

Before considering common errors and deficiencies in the management and treatment of PD in the UK, it is relevant to consider a number of disease-specific facts. These facts define the 'environment' in which errors and deficiencies occur.

Parkinson's disease is the second most common neurodegenerative disease, affecting approximately 200 per 100,000 of the population and one in every 100 people over the age of 65 years. Despite this, the average general practitioner (GP) will have only two or three patients with the condition on their register (Thomas *et al.* 1999). Parkinson's disease could not, therefore, be regarded as 'common' to the primary care physician. The condition is progressive, but the rate of progression may vary considerably from individual to individual. The phenotype of PD is also highly variable, ranging from a tremor-dominant form to a so-called postural–instability variety with gait difficulty. Although PD is defined by its excellent response to levodopa, this is not invariable. Furthermore, levodopa-induced complications such as dyskinesias appear after a variable latency of treatment. Non-dopaminergic complications, including depression, dementia, postural instability and autonomic dysfunction, occur in a substantial minority of patients. It is not possible, however, to predict which patients will develop these complications early in their disease course.

Parkinson's disease is predominantly managed on an outpatient basis at secondary and tertiary care levels. Multiple specialists may be involved in the management of PD. Given the wide age range of people presenting with the condition, and the variation in access to specialist services throughout the UK, the GP may refer to a neurologist, geriatrician or general physician. There is no diagnostic test available for PD; investigations such as brain imaging may be undertaken to exclude other pathologies, but the diagnosis of PD remains a clinical one.

Finally, the best medical management of PD remains uncertain. The evidence base for which drug to recommend *between* classes of dopaminergic agents at certain stages of the disease is either weak or non-existent. Furthermore, there have been few comparative trials of newer anti-parkinsonian drugs *within* classes of dopaminergic agents (e.g. the dopamine agonists).

Errors and deficiencies in Parkinson's disease

Table 15.1 lists a proposed classification for errors and deficiencies as they occur in the context of PD. As mentioned above, the outcome from an error may be permanent or temporary. An 'active' error implies a clearly identifiable (usually human) failing or mistake, whereas a 'latent' error refers more to a failing within the work environment and culture, e.g. a wrongly prescribed drug would constitute an 'active' error, whereas a failure to provide adequate education about use of the drug in general would represent a 'latent' error. Although the physical sequelae as the consequence of an error may be obvious and more readily quantified, psychological sequelae may also occur and may, in fact, be more long-standing and ultimately handicapping to the patient and the carer. Clearly, errors may be made in the diagnosis and management of PD by GPs and hospital specialists, and may affect either the newly diagnosed patient or the patient with an established diagnosis.

Table 15.1 Classification of errors and deficiencies in Parkinson's disease

Errors	Deficiencies
Permanent vs temporary	Absolute vs relative
Active vs latent	International, national, regional or local level
Physical vs psychological	Human (individual or corporate) vs economic
Primary, secondary, tertiary level of care	New vs established patient
New vs established patient	

A deficiency may be absolute or relative, e.g. in the latter situation, access to multidisciplinary resources in one area may compare unfavourably with another. An international or global deficiency could relate to a lack of knowledge or evidence base for treatment recommendations. Deficiencies may obviously be human, be they in an individual or at a more corporate level. Alternatively, they may be economic. As with errors, deficiencies may have a differential effect on the newly diagnosed or established patient.

Common errors

Table 15.2 provides a list of common errors in the diagnosis and management of PD and relates these errors to their likely cause and outcomes. The incorrect diagnosis of PD has recently been highlighted by a community-based study carried out in north

Wales by Meara *et al.* (1999). The authors identified 402 patients receiving anti-parkinsonian medication in primary care and found, on applying recommended clinical diagnostic criteria, that parkinsonism could be confirmed in only 64%. This was clinically probable PD in 53%. Of the 103 patients with a revised diagnosis, 48% had essential tremor, 36% vascular pseudo-parkinsonism and 16% Alzheimer's disease. Although this study used clinical criteria as the 'gold standard', earlier clinicopathological work by Hughes *et al.* (1992) reported that, of 100 cases diagnosed in life as PD, only 76% of this sample had Lewy body disease *post mortem*. Had clinical criteria been strictly applied, the proportion of PD cases correctly diagnosed would have increased to 93%. Although these papers refer to 'false-positive' diagnoses of PD, patients not diagnosed as PD who *do* have the disorder (i.e. 'false-negative' diagnoses) also frequently occur. In one study, 10% of patients confirmed as having typical pathological findings for PD were not considered to have this diagnosis in life (Hughes *et al.* 1993). These figures highlight the recommendation that patients with suspected parkinsonism be referred to a specialist in movement disorders (Bhatia *et al.* 1998). If diagnostic doubt still exists, it is probably best to admit uncertainty, rather than 'label' the patient inappropriately. The outcomes of incorrect diagnosis include not only inappropriate treatment and potential side effects, but also patient and carer stress and loss of confidence when the diagnosis ultimately has to be revised.

Table 15.2 Examples of common errors in diagnosis and management of PD

Error	Causes	Outcomes
Wrong diagnosis	Inexperience	Inappropriate treatment
	Failure to apply diagnostic criteria	Patient and carer stress
Diagnosis poorly explained	Individual factors	Patient and carer stress
	Time constraints	Long-term problems?
Inappropriate treatment	Suboptimal knowledge	Adverse events, hospitalisation
	Failure to refer	and institutionalisation
Failure to detect depression	Lack of awareness	Inappropriate drug treatment
	Inappropriate tools	Reduced patient and carer quality of life

One of the most common errors made in the overall management of PD has undoubtedly been a poor explanation of the diagnosis to the patient and the carer. There may be several reasons underpinning this, but the most likely relates to time constraints in the clinic. People with PD will often report that the experience of being given the diagnosis was not only traumatic but also perfunctory. Given the chronicity of the disease and potentially complex management issues involved, this adverse experience does nothing to empower the patient or to give him or her confidence in the future. A more detailed explanation of the diagnosis in an unhurried and accessible way should be done by a PD nurse specialist whenever possible.

Inappropriate drug treatment of PD may occur at all stages of the illness and at all levels of care. In some cases 'inappropriate' may be more a matter of opinion, rather than an incontrovertible fact. An example of this would include starting a young-onset PD patient on L-dopa therapy, rather than on a dopamine agonist. The weight of evidence at the present time, in the light of a number of recent double-masked studies, would favour the use of the agonist in order to delay the onset of disabling dyskinesias (Oertel 2000; Parkinson's Study Group 2000; Rascol *et al.* 2000). It could not be disputed, however, that the use of L-dopa would be an extremely effective symptomatic therapy. The use of an anticholinergic drug or selegiline in the frail elderly patient would be regarded as inappropriate by most, however, given the propensity of these agents to induce hallucinations and a toxic confusional state. As hallucinations are a major determinant of carer distress and nursing home placement, such inappropriate prescribing may also have significant health economic implications (Goetz & Stebbins 1993).

The final example given in Table 15.2 is the failure to detect depression in the person with PD. Depression occurs in 40–50% of people with PD, although this figure may be lower in community-based samples (Gotham *et al.* 1986). Recent studies have highlighted the fact that depression is the major determinant of quality of life in the person with PD, as well as in the carer (Findley *et al.* 2000; Kuopio *et al.* 2000; Schrag *et al.* 2000). The detection of depression in this context is, however, not easy. Patients may not actually appreciate that they are depressed and may attribute symptoms to their physical illness. In the Global Parkinson's Disease Survey, less than 10% of people surveyed actually recognised that they were depressed (Findley *et al.* 2000). The physician is handicapped by a lack of symptom specificity and the fact that several somatic symptoms, which are often reported by a person with depression, also overlap with symptoms of PD. Furthermore, assessment scales need to take such overlap into account, and to record depression rather than distress. The Geriatric Depression Scale and the Hospital Anxiety and Depression Scale may be useful screening tools which have defined cut-off points and take these problems into account. Failure to recognise depression not only reduces quality of life but may also lead to inappropriate drug prescribing for PD, because the patient and physician erroneously increase anti-parkinsonian drug treatment in the face of minimal motor disability, but a perception of 'not doing well'. In this context, the use of an antidepressant drug for an underlying affective disorder may be the most appropriate choice of therapy.

Common deficiencies

Table 15.3 gives a list of commonly perceived deficiencies in the diagnosis and management of PD and relates these deficiencies to their likely cause and outcomes.

Within the UK, there is considerable variation in the time taken to see a specialist with an interest in PD. Much of this variation relates to the local neurologist. Waiting times may vary from a few weeks to over a year. When the waiting time is lengthy, this may precipitate GPs to initiate treatment in a patient whom they believe to have PD and only refer to secondary care when complications or problems arise. From published guidelines, referral of a patient with suspected PD to a specialist in movement disorders is certainly encouraged and, where this does not (or cannot) occur, a deficiency may be perceived (Bhatia *et al.* 1998). The development of a more comprehensive PD service across the UK should certainly be encouraged to reduce the patient and carer stress associated with diagnostic delay, and also to improve diagnostic accuracy.

Table 15.3 Examples of common deficiencies in diagnosis and management of PD

Deficiency	Causes	Outcomes
Long delay to referral	Shortage of specialists Primary care attitudes	Patient and carer stress Primary care pressure
Ancillary investigations	Limited access or availability	Wrong diagnosis or missed co-morbidity
Nurse specialist	Local attitudes and priorities Lack of clinical 'lead'	Increased admissions and social service costs Suboptimal drug treatment
Multidisciplinary team	Clinical attitudes Local availability	Early complications and hospitalisation?

Most centres now have access to a computed tomography (CT) service. Where this is not available, co-morbidity such as coexistent cerebrovascular disease, or even the primary diagnosis, such as normal pressure hydrocephalus (causing so-called 'lower body parkinsonism'), may be missed. Limited access to other ancillary investigations such as magnetic resonance imaging (MRI), single photon emission computed tomography (SPECT) or sphincter electromyographic (EMG) studies may be regarded as a relative deficiency. Each technique may improve diagnostic accuracy, but has limited specificity and sensitivity. Furthermore, most studies that have evaluated the utility of these investigations have used clinical diagnosis, rather than pathological confirmation, as the diagnostic standard. Thus, whether they contribute significantly over and above an expert clinical assessment remains to be established.

It is widely perceived that access to a PD nurse specialist (PDNS) improves the quality of service provided to the person with PD and the family. Preliminary details from the PDNS intervention study, led by Professor Sir Brian Jarman, suggest that over the first year of this project the PDNS is cost-effective, saving approximately £300 per patient. Areas of saving include a reduced hospital admission rate secondary to fracture and also length of institutional care. The full report from this important study is eagerly awaited. As a result of the stratified design of this study, however, the results should be applicable to the rest of the UK. In another study, based in the south-east of England, the role of the PDNS was shown to be of significant benefit in 25% of patients. Medication benefits were maximised or side effects minimised in 30% of cases studied (Thomas *et al.* 1999).

Despite the subjective and objective benefits provided by the PDNS, there remain 'black holes' or 'voids' within the UK, where there is little or no patient access to this valuable resource. Such a glaring deficiency may relate to local attitudes and perceived priorities, but may also be the result of the absence of a lead clinician to drive the necessary business case.

On a similar theme, there is also evidence of very 'patchy' coverage within the UK for the patient with PD having access to multidisciplinary team (MDT) members, such as a physiotherapist and speech and language therapist. Traditionally, such teams have been well represented in the care of the elderly day hospital environment. It is essential for *all* specialists involved in the management of people with PD to appreciate the value of the MDT, and to refer earlier rather than later for appropriate advice, especially regarding the non-dopaminergic complications of the illness (such as postural instability and dysphagia).

Reducing error and deficiency in Parkinson's disease: quality and clinical governance

Clinical governance (CG) is a central theme underpinning the 10-year modernisation programme for the NHS (Department of Health 1997; Miles *et al.* 2001). The key aims of CG are to provide high-quality and dependable care to all patients. The key elements of CG are summarised in Figure 15.1. They include the development of clear lines of responsibility and accountability at all levels, the implementation of quality improvement programmes and the development of risk management. In essence, CG will ensure that each sector of the NHS will quality assure its own clinical decisions.

Improving quality should reduce error and deficiency in the management and treatment of people with PD. Quality is succinctly defined by Lilley (1999) as 'knowing what outcome you want and being sure you get it, every time, for as long as you want it'. Quality is, of course, an outcome not just a process, with its foundation in consistency. Our collective aim, in conjunction with CG, must be to increase the overall quality of care delivered to people with PD in the UK, thereby climbing the quality curve (Figure 15.2) (Lilley 1999). Figure 15.2 highlights that, although some centres will always be 'leading edge', the main thrust behind a climb in the quality curve is to raise the standard of care uniformly, not just in a few interested centres.

In the management of PD, there is clearly a continuum of care involved, with the focus of care shifting as the disease moves through the diagnostic, maintenance, complex and palliative phases (MacMahon & Thomas 1998). Implicit in the quality improvement process, therefore, is a close working partnership between primary and secondary health care services.

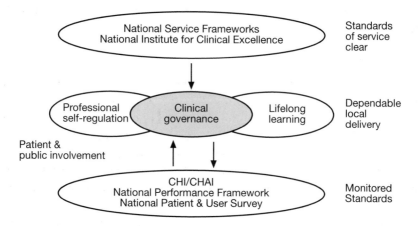

Figure 15.1 The clinical governance framework.

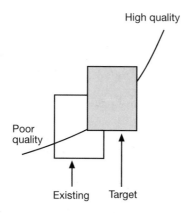

Figure 15.2 The 'new' NHS, quality and Parkinson's disease.

Clear national standards for PD are essential to reduce the variability and quality of care that currently prevails. A National Service Framework for chronic neurological illness, which will include PD, is not yet available. Documents such as *Moving and Shaping* (Thomas *et al.* 1999) and the development of drug monitoring and care guidelines (in close association with the Parkinson's Disease Society) can, however, make a significant and more immediate impact in this area. An improved evidence base to guide best treatment in *all* patients is also a prerequisite for quality improvement. The local delivery of quality services will be enhanced by ongoing, active professional education and development at all levels of service provision. Finally, patient groups, and user experience in general, will provide an essential barometer for the monitoring of services.

Conclusion

The 'cost' of errors and deficiencies in the investigation and management of people with PD is likely to be considerable and needs to be considered not only in terms of direct economic consequences. After all, a patient who suffers psychological trauma as the result of an error early in their management is not only likely to have less confidence in the medical profession, but may also be less likely to be compliant with future treatments. This article has proposed a classification for error and deficiency in the context of PD and has considered examples of commonly encountered errors and deficiencies.

Improving quality should lead to reduced errors and deficiencies in the management and treatment of PD. Until a National Service Framework is developed for chronic neurological illness, other components of CG offer the chance to improve overall quality of care the person with PD throughout the UK.

References

Bhatia K, Brooks DJ, Burn DJ *et al.* (1998). Guidelines for the management of Parkinson's disease. The Parkinson's disease consensus working group. *Hospital Medicine* **59**, 469–480

Brennan TA, Leape LI, Laird NM *et al.* (1991). Incidence of adverse events and negligence in hospitalised patients. Results of the Harvard medical practice study I. *New England Journal of Medicine* **324**, 370–376

Department of Health (1997). *The New NHS. Modern. Dependable.* London: The Stationery Office

Findley L, Peto V, Pugner K, Holmes J, Baker M, MacMahon DG (2000). The impact of Parkinson's disease on quality of life: Results of a research survey in the UK. *Movement Disorders* **15**, 179

Goetz CG & Stebbins GT (1993). Risk factors for nursing home placement in advanced Parkinson's disease. *Neurology* **43**, 2227–2229

Gotham AM, Brown RG, Marsden CD (1986). Depression in Parkinson's disease: a quantitative and qualitative analysis. *Journal of Neurology, Neurosurgery, and Psychiatry* **49**, 381–389

Parkinson's Study Group (2000). Pramipexole vs levodopa as initial treatment for Parkinson's disease. *Journal of the American Medical Association* **284**, 931–1938

Hughes AJ, Daniel SE, Kilford L, Lees AJ (1992). Accuracy of clinical diagnosis of idiopathic Parkinson's disease: a clinico-pathological study of 100 cases. *Journal of Neurology, Neurosurgery, and Psychiatry* **55**, 181–184

Hughes AJ, Daniel SE, Blankson S, Lees AJ (1993). A clinicopathologic study of 100 cases of Parkinson's disease. *Archives of Neurology* **50**, 140–148

Kuopio AM, Marttila RJ, Helenius H, Toivonen M, Rinne UK (2000). The quality of life in Parkinson's disease. *Movement Disorders* **15**, 216–223

Leape LI, Brennan TA, Laird NM *et al.* (1991). The nature of adverse events in hospitalised patients. Results of the Harvard medical practice study II. *New England Journal of Medicine* **324**, 377–384

Lilley R (1999). *Clinical Governance: A workbook for NHS doctors, nurses and managers.* Oxford: Radcliffe Medical Press

MacMahon DG & Thomas S (1998). Practical approach to quality of life in Parkinson's disease. *Journal of Neurology* **245**, S19–S22

Meara J, Bhowmick BK, Hobson P (1999). Accuracy of diagnosis in patients with presumed Parkinson's disease. *Age and Ageing* **28**, 99–102

Miles A, Hill AP, Hurwitz B (2001). Clinical governance and the NHS reforms. Aesculapius Medical Press, London

Oertel WH (2000). Pergolide vs levodopa (PELMOPET). *Movement Disorders* **15**, 4

Rascol O, Brooks DJ, Korczyn AD *et al.* (2000). A five-year study of the incidence of dyskinesias in patients with early Parkinson's disease who were treated with ropinirole or levodopa. *New England Journal of Medicine* **342**, 1484–1491

Reason J (1995). Understanding adverse events: human factors. *Quality Health Care* **4**, 80–89

Schrag A, Jahanshahi M, Quinn N (2000). What contributes to quality of life in patients with Parkinson's disease? *Journal of Neurology, Neurosurgery, and Psychiatry* **69**, 308–312

Secker-Walker J (1999). Clinical risk management. In Lugon M & Secker-Walker J (eds) *Clinical Governance: Making it happen.* London: Royal Society of Medicine Press Ltd, pp 77–91

Thomas EJ & Brennan TA (2000). Incidence and types of preventable adverse events in elderly patients: population based review of medical records. *British Medical Journal* **320**, 741–745

Thomas S, MacMahon D, Henry S, on behalf of the Parkinson's Disease Society Primary Care Task Force (1999). *Moving and Shaping: the future. Commissioning services for people with Parkinson's disease.* London: Parkinson's Disease Society

Vincent C, Neale G, Woloshynowych M (2001). Adverse events in British hospitals: preliminary retrospective record review. *British Medical Journal* **322**, 517–519

Wilson RM, Runciman WB, Gibberd RW, Harrison BT, Newby L, Hamilton JD (1995). The quality in Australia healthcare study. *Medical Journal of Australia* **163**, 458–471

PART 7

Quality of life and Parkinson's disease

Chapter 16

Factors influencing quality of life in Parkinson's disease

Leslie J Findley and Clive Bowman

Quality of life is a concept that has been introduced into medicine in an effort to quantify and measure change in conditions where current therapy cannot effect a cure. Parkinson's disease (PD) is a chronic, progressive, neurodegenerative disorder that is characterised by slowness of movement, rigidity, tremor of the limbs while at rest and abnormalities of posture (Bulpitt *et al.* 1985). As the disease progresses, patients with PD experience increasing difficulties in carrying out activities of daily living as movement and the control of movement decline (Marr 1991; Teulings *et al.* 1997). Patients who are given a diagnosis of PD face the prospect of increasing disability and dependence over a period of many years. They may become withdrawn, and those of working age retire prematurely with consequent economic loss and social isolation.

At this time, there is no cure for PD, and current pharmacological intervention is aimed at alleviating the symptoms of the disease by enhancing dopaminergic activity and reducing cholinergic activity in the brain (Coleman 1992). Similarly, surgical intervention has traditionally been undertaken with a view to controlling symptoms (Marsden 1990; Laitinen *et al.* 1992; Lang 2000), although some efforts to transplant fetal nigral cells have been undertaken (Lindvall *et al.* 1989; Spencer *et al.* 1992), so far without long-term success. Therefore, current medication choices and care strategies for patients with PD tend to focus on improving the motor symptoms of the disease rather than on the overall needs of the individual (Pentland *et al.* 1992).

With better understanding of the natural history of PD and related disorders, patients can now have a relatively normal life expectancy (Rajput *et al.* 1997). However, PD is a complex disease with effects on the autonomic nervous system and cognitive function, and with psychological symptoms including depression and anxiety.

Assessment of treatment for Parkinson's disease

As a reflection of the approaches taken to treat and assess PD, the most commonly used rating scales in this condition concentrate on measuring the physical signs and symptoms of the disease and the side effects of medication. Efforts to quantify disease severity began as early as 1956 (Riklan & Diller 1956).

A large range of well-established clinical scales is now in use and includes the Columbia Rating Scale (Hely *et al.* 1993), the Unified Parkinson's Disease Rating Scale (Fahn & Elton 1987) and the Schwab and England Activities of Daily Living score (Schwab & England 1969). These measures are completed by the clinician and focus mainly on the primary neurological symptoms of tremor, rigidity, bradykinesia and postural instability, and the resulting physical impairment, although most do have psychological dimensions to them. The most simple and popular, and hence the most widely used, severity scale is the 5-point Hoehn and Yahr scale (1967).

Each of the PD rating scales is used to measure signs and symptoms of the disease. However, although clinical assessment of symptoms is of importance to the clinician, it may be of less interest to the patient. Although it has been shown that motor disability (as measured by disease stage) impacts on quality of life (Chrischilles *et al.* 1998) and that alleviation of motor symptoms in PD should, therefore, improve quality of life, poor correlations between physical function and well-being have been found in conditions other than PD (Guyatt *et al.* 1993; Finlay and Coles 1995). Therefore, the assumption that alleviation of motor symptoms will improve quality of life cannot be made.

The importance of quality of life

Two patients with the same clinical characteristics may have very different attitudes to their condition and its treatment, and a patient's perception of the benefits obtained with a treatment may differ from those of the clinician. Therefore, it can be argued that health-related quality of life is the ultimate measure of any treatment, irrespective of the 'success' of therapy.

There is no clear definition of quality of life, particularly in relation to health care. The World Health Organization defines health as 'a state of complete physical, mental and social well-being' (WHO 1947). Using this definition in the context of medicine, it is reasonable to view health-related quality of life as the patient's perception of his or her own health in physical, mental and social terms. A suitable definition of quality of life is: 'a perceived state of well-being, which is influenced by physical, mental, functional, social and emotional factors'. It is individual, subjective and variable.

Irrespective of how quality of life is defined, it is clear that the aim of treatment in medical conditions for which there is no cure must primarily be to improve the patient's sense of well-being. Therefore, understanding the part played by the factors that influence quality of life is vital for creating a basis on which to establish management guidelines for PD. The patient's perceptions and concerns about their condition must be considered equally important to the control of symptoms. Quality-of-life assessments should focus on the patient's concerns and must not be assumed to be in line with the degree of disability (Shindler *et al.* 1993). This is particularly important in a chronic condition such as PD where the disability develops gradually over time and people cope in ways that are varied. It is possible that this variation occurs as the patients learn to adapt to their changing physical abilities. However, such adaptation may well be gained at an emotional cost.

Quality of life in Parkinson's disease

In recent years, a number of methods to assess the mental as well as the physical aspects of PD have been introduced. These methods vary but have in common that the assessment is made, and ultimately interpreted, by somebody external to the patient. It is reasonable to take the view that quality of life is inherently subjective and personal (Gill & Feinstein 1994). According to this view, the emphasis should be to assess how patients feel about their quality of life and how important they consider problems in quality of life to be. Furthermore, a structured review of evidence concluded that patients' and observers' ratings of patients' quality of life tend to differ (Sprangers & Aaronson 1992).

Parkinson's disease is a slowly progressing, life-changing condition that impacts on the life of the patient beyond the physical signs and symptoms – it affects their sense of well-being. As stated above, the successful management of PD is predominantly measured by the control of motor symptoms. Therefore, management protocols tend to focus on drug therapy. However, the patient's perception of quality of life cannot be simply equated with disease severity and patients at similar stages of PD can often have varying levels of perceived quality of life (Gotham *et al.* 1986).

Quality-of-life instruments fall broadly into two categories: generic and disease specific. Generic measures have the advantage of enabling comparisons between different conditions but tend not to have questions that would be relevant to a specific disease state. An example of such a question might be the social embarrassment that patients with Parkinson's disease might experience, which would not be expected with rheumatoid arthritis. However, the 36-item Short Form Health Survey (SF-36: Ware & Sherbourne 1992) has been found to have consistent strong associations with Hoehn and Yahr ratings (Chrischilles *et al.* 1998).

One of the most popular disease-specific quality-of-life questionnaires that is used in PD is the 39-Item Parkinson's Disease Questionnaire (PDQ-39: Peto *et al.* 1995). The PDQ-39 was generated from in-depth interviews with PD patients and subsequent shortening of the recorded 65-item list to 39. It is designed to assess the patient's perception of how the disease impacts on his or her functioning in eight different dimensions of PD. There are ten items in the questionnaire on mobility, six on activities of daily living, six on emotional well-being, four on stigma, three on social support, four on cognitions, three on communication and the remaining three items on bodily discomfort. It has been validated and found to have satisfactory internal and test–re-test reliability, and can be analysed either by the different domains or total score. The PDQ-39, in combination with the SF-36, has been shown to provide reproducible measurement of quality of life in patients with PD who have undergone surgical intervention (Gray *et al.* 2002).

Different symptoms of PD may impact on the patient's functioning in different ways. The PDQ-39 was used to explore the impact of various motor signs on different areas of patient-perceived functioning (Lyons *et al.* 1997). It was found that postural instability, gait difficulties and bradykinesia were the strongest predictors of the quality-of-life score whereas tremor and rigidity had less influence on the score. Motor fluctuations, particularly 'on/off' phenomena, may also affect quality of life, in that patients might withdraw socially because of the unpredictability of their functioning. Indeed, in one study it was reported that 48% of respondents avoided public situations that involved eating or drinking and 42% felt embarrassed in public because of their PD (Peto *et al.* 1997).

Relatively few studies have directly examined quality of life in PD. The emphasis has been on studying the impact of disease severity on functioning. In many studies, the severity of problems has been measured (De Boer *et al.* 1996; Brod *et al.* 1998; Wendell *et al.* 1999) but not the extent to which patients' lives are affected. The consequences to the patient of having feelings of embarrassment in company and withdrawing from social settings are likely to have an effect on his or her outlook and mood. Depression is assessed in the commonly used rating scales, but little if any consideration is given to the impact on a patient's participation in life.

The significance of depression in Parkinson's disease

It might be expected that mood, personality and coping styles would influence a patient's judgement about quality of life. There is no straightforward relationship between depression, disease severity and disability (Shindler *et al.* 1993). Indeed, it has been shown that patients with depression reported poorer quality-of-life scores than patients with severe or life-threatening physical diseases (Wells *et al.* 1989). Several studies have examined the relationship between quality of life and function (activities of daily living), but such relationships have been found inconsistently. This supports the view that quality of life extends beyond the ability of the patient to function on a day-to-day level.

Brown *et al.* (1989) assessed the accuracy of self-reported disability in patients with PD using the Beck Depression Inventory and the Mini-Mental State Examination to detect psychosocial dysfunction. The results suggested that depression did not affect the accuracy of self-reported disability and, although depression was associated with disability, it was not associated with symptom severity in patients with PD. Another study has shown that depression is higher in patients with PD than in healthy controls (Gotham *et al.* 1986). Therefore, there is evidence to suggest that the focus of treatment for the patient with PD should not be exclusively targeted at motor symptom control.

A recently published, cross-sectional, multinational (seven-country) survey (GPDS 2002) identified those elements of the management of people with PD that have the greatest effect on quality of life. In this survey, which was conducted by the European Parkinson's Disease Association and supported by the WHO, the primary hypothesis was that the quality of life of patients with PD is affected by factors other than disease severity and anti-PD medication. In a series of pre-pilot studies, six domains that may be important to patients were identified as follows:

1   the process of communicating the clinical diagnosis

2   the specialist clinician's use of information and holistic therapies

3   the ability of patients to gain the information and contact they require

4   the patients' use of holistic therapies

5   the patients' emotional state (including depression)

6   the patients' access to and use of a patient support group.

The above domains were assessed in addition to the disease severity, as measured by Hoehn and Yahr stage and medication. The survey included a sample of over 1,000 patients with PD.

The first important finding of the study was that only 17.3% of variation in quality of life could be explained by knowing the disease stage and medication. With such a low percentage of quality of life accounted for by these assessments, other contributing factors were looked for. Another surprising finding of the survey was that 50% of patients had a Beck Depression Inventory (BDI) score above 10 and were, therefore, considered to be at least mildly depressed, although only 1% of patients considered themselves to be depressed. Furthermore, depression was significantly correlated with quality of life ($p < 0.001$). Although the results of the survey indicate that an increased BDI score and, therefore, depression is associated with reduced quality of life in patients with PD, the survey does not show that this association is causal. Consequently, it is not known at this time whether treating the patient for depression would have a positive effect on quality of life. This would be an interesting study to undertake in the future.

In the same survey (GPDS 2002), two other factors had small but statistically significant ($p < 0.05$) effects on quality of life. These were 'satisfaction with the explanation of the conditions at diagnosis' and 'current feeling of optimism'. When all three of the significant factors are known, 59.7% of the variability of quality of life between patients with PD can be explained.

It is particularly interesting that the communication with the patient at the time of diagnosis was significant. In the study by Peto *et al.* (1997), it was found that patients who were dissatisfied with the level of access to healthcare resources had lower quality-of-life scores than patients who were satisfied. The picture that emerges is one of a patient who has been given a devastating diagnosis and is then left to cope alone.

Conclusion

In a chronic, progressive condition such as PD, quality of life is the ultimate measure of the effectiveness of treatment. The likelihood of co-morbidity with depression should be considered and a holistic approach taken to the treatment of the patient with PD.

References

Brod M, Mendelsohn GA, Roberts B (1998). Patients' experiences of Parkinson's disease. *Journal of Gerontology B Psychological Science and Social Science* **53**, 213–222

Brown RG, MacCarthy B, Jahanshahi M, Marsden CD (1989). Accuracy of self-reported disability in patients with parkinsonism. *Archives of Neurology* **46**, 955–959

Bulpitt CJ, Shaw K, Clifton P, Stern G, Davies JB, Reid JL (1985). The symptoms of patients treated for Parkinson's disease. *Clinical Neuropharmacology* **8**, 175–183

Chrischilles EA, Rubenstein LM, Voelker MD, Wallace RB, Rodnitzky RL (1998). The health burdens of Parkinson's disease. *Movement Disorders* **13**, 406–413

Coleman RJ (1992). Current Drug Therapy for Parkinson's Disease. A Review. *Drugs and Aging* **2**, 112–124

De Boer AG, Wijker W, Speelman JD, de Haes JC (1996). Quality of life in patients with Parkinson's disease, development of a questionnaire. *Journal of Neurology, Neurosurgery, and Psychiatry* **61**, 70–74

Fahn S & Elton RL, members of the UPDRS Development Committee (1987). Unified Parkinson's Disease Rating Scale. In: Fahn S, Marsden M, Goldstein M, Calne DB (eds), *Recent Developments in Parkinson's Disease*, vol 2. New York: Macmillan, pp. 153–163

Finlay AY & Coles EC (1995). The effect of severe psoriasis on the quality of life of 369 patients. *British Journal of Dermatology* **13**, 236–244

Gill TM & Feinstein AR (1994). A critical appraisal of the quality-of-life measurements. *Journal of the American Medical Association* **27**, 619–626

Global Parkinson's Disease Survey (GPDS) Steering Committee (2002). Factors impacting on quality of life in Parkinson's disease: results from an international survey. *Movement Disorders* **17**, 60–67

Gotham AM, Brown RG, Marsden CD (1986). Depression in Parkinson's disease: a quantitative and qualitative analysis. *Journal of Neurology, Neurosurgery, and Psychiatry* **49**, 381–389

Gray A, McNamara I, Aziz T, Gergory R, Bain P, Wilson J, Scott R (2002). Quality of life outcomes following surgical treatment of Parkinson's disease. *Movement Disorders* **17**, 68–75

Guyatt GH, Feeny DH, Patrick DL (1993). Measuring health-related quality of life. *Annals of Internal Medicine* **11**, 622–629

Hely M, Chey T, Wilson A *et al.* (1993). Reliability of the Columbia scale for assessing signs of Parkinson's disease. *Movement Disorders* **8**, 466–472

Hoehn M & Yahr M (1967). Parkinson's disease: onset, progression and mortality. *Neurology* **7**, 427–442

Laitinen LV, Bergenheim AT, Hariz MI (1992). Leksell's posteroventral pallidotomy in the treatment of Parkinson's disease. *Journal of Neurosurgery* **76**, 53–61

Lang AE (2000). Surgery for levodopa-induced dyskinesias. *Annals of Neurology* **47**, S193–S199

Lindvall O, Rehncrona S, Brundin P *et al.* (1989). Human fetal dopamine neurons grafted into the striatum in two patients with severe Parkinson's disease: a detailed account of methodology and a 6-month follow-up. *Archives of Neurology* **46**, 615–631

Lyons KE, Pahwa R, Tröster AI, Koller WC (1997). A comparison of Parkinson's disease symptoms and self-reported functioning and well being. *Parkinsonism and Related Disorders* **3**, 207–209

Marr JA (1991). The experience of living with Parkinson's disease. *Journal of Neuroscience and Nursing* **23**, 325–329

Marsden CD (1990). Parkinson's disease. *The Lancet* **335**, 948–952

Pentland B, Barnes MP, Findley LJ *et al.* (1992). Parkinson's disease: the spectrum of disabilities. *Journal of Neurology, Neurosurgery, and Psychiatry* **55**(suppl), 32–35

Peto V, Jenkinson C, Fitzpatrick R, Greenhall R (1995). The development and validation of a short measure of functioning and well being for individuals with Parkinson's disease. *Quality of Life Research* **4**, 241–248

Peto V, Fitzpatrick R, Jenkinson C (1997). Self-reported health status and access to health services in a community sample with Parkinson's disease. *Disability and Rehabilitation* **19**, 97–103

Rajput AH, Uitti RJ, Rajput AH, Offord KP (1997). Timely levodopa (LD) administration prolongs survival in Parkinson's disease. *Parkinsonism and Related Disorders* **3**, 159–165

Riklan M & Diller L (1956). Certain psychomotor aspects of subtemporal pallidectomy for Parkinson's disease. *Journal of the American Geriatric Society* **4**, 1258

Schwab RS & England AC (1969). Projection technique for evaluating surgery in Parkinson's disease. In: Gillingham FJ, Donaldson MD (eds), *Third Symposium of Parkinson's Disease*. Edinburgh: Livingstone, pp. 152–157

Shindler JS, Brown R, Welburn P, Parkes JD (1993). Measuring the quality of life of patients with Parkinson's disease. In: Walker SR, Rosser RM (eds), *Quality of Life Assessment: Key Issues in the 1990s*. Boston: Kluwer Academic, pp. 289–300

Spencer DD, Robbins RJ, Naftolin F *et al.* (1992). Unilateral transplantation of human fetal mesencephalic tissue in the caudate nucleus of patients with Parkinson's disease. *New England Journal of Medicine* **32**, 1541–1548

Sprangers MA, Aaronson NK (1992). The role of health care providers and significant others in evaluating the quality of life of patients with chronic disease: a review. *Journal of Clinical Epidemiology* **45**, 743–760

Teulings HL, Contreras-Vidal JL, Stelmach GE, Adler CH (1997). Parkinsonism reduces coordination of fingers, wrist, and arm in fine motor control. *Experimental Neurology* **14**, 159–170

Ware JE & Sherbourne CD (1992). The MOS 36-item short-form health survey (SF-36) I. Conceptual framework and item selection. *Medical Care* **30**, 473–483

Wells KB, Stewart A, Hays RD, Burnham MA *et al.* (1989). The functioning and well-being of depressed patients. Results from the Medical Outcomes Study. *Journal of the American Medical Association* **26**, 914–919

Wendell RA, Houser RA, Nagaria MG *et al.* (1999). Chief complaints of patients with Parkinson's disease. *Neurology* **52**(suppl 2), A91.

World Health Organization (1947). *Constitution of the World Health Organization*. Geneva: WHO

Chapter 17

Future therapies in Parkinson's disease

Malcolm J Steiger

Introduction

The next decade will see the development of therapies for Parkinson's disease on a broad front. Present theories of the mechanisms of cell death associated with progression of disease have not yet led to an effective treatment. In time, a greater understanding of the mechanisms of genetic inheritance in some families and environmental co-factors will lead to prevention of the disease in those who are susceptible. Over the last 30 years we have witnessed the beginning of pharmacological manipulation of the denervated striatum with the use of dopaminergic compounds. The treatments currently available fall short of our expectations of best management. The quality of life of many patients prescribed symptomatic treatment regimens needs to be improved, particularly in those patients who have had the illness for 10 years or more, most of whom have developed impairment of postural reflexes, with increasing number of falls (Klawans 1986; Koller *et al*. 1989; Bonnet *et al*. 1987), disorders of speech, autonomic disturbances (particularly urinary urgency and urge incontinence), and increasing neuropsychiatric manifestations. The last are often destructive to the personality of the individual, affecting self-confidence and influencing the relationships of those who care for them.

Before considering treatment strategies that are currently in development, it is important to recognise therapies currently available that may be beneficial to Parkinson's disease patients, the effects of which are becoming better understood. In justifying the use of such potentially useful, though often expensive, medication, an important starting point is the socioeconomic impact of the disease.

The health economics of Parkinson's disease

In the UK the annual direct costs in 1992 of Parkinson's disease in UK was estimated at £383 million (Haycock 1994), although, in Germany in 1995, the direct medical costs were estimated at £1 billion (Dodel *et al*. 1998). The greatest cost was hospitalisation, with drug treatment being the next greatest. The treatment of patients with motor fluctuations doubles the cost. The average daily drug expenditure in Germany is £3.50 per patient, whereas in the UK this was estimated at 66p/day. However, by 1999, the costs in the UK of prescribing for Parkinson's disease had risen to £46 million, giving an approximate cost of £1.40/day (£510/year) per patient.

In the USA, the total cost to the family and society is £4,000 per annum (Whetten-Goldstein *et al.* 1997). The direct annual cost was £4,000 at < 65 years of age, rising to £9,400 > 85 years.

In younger patients the greatest single cost (11%) is drug therapy, whereas in the older patients the greatest cost is institutional care (with drugs 6%). The need for long-term care results in a net annual increase of £12,000 per patient (MacMahon *et al.* 2001).

Irrespective of the age of the patient, Parkinson's disease is often a devastating disease, costly to individuals, families, health and social agencies alike. In assessing the merits of any treatment strategy, a true understanding of the total cost of the illness is essential. In that way, rational prescribing will take into account the potential cost benefits of any new therapeutic intervention. Furthermore, an integrated care pathway involving adequately funded medical and social services becomes essential to improve total care. The use of nurse practitioners saves £300/year per patient (Jarman 1998), through:

- early detection
- a correct diagnosis
- prevention of complications
- delaying the need for complex care
- maintaining patients in their home environment.

Fundamental to the consideration of the pharmacological costs of Parkinson's disease is the appropriate use of medication. If effective, appropriate medication has an impact on total cost of care. Although the mean age at onset of Parkinson's disease is in the seventh decade, most of the published, double-blind, controlled trials have been on patients with a relatively younger age at onset (Mitchell *et al.* 1997; Clarke 2001).

What differentiates older from younger Parkinson's disease patients?

Parkinson's disease is more than dopaminergic-deficient disease. The differential effects of the condition in younger and older patients may be summarised as follows (Blin *et al.* 1991).

Younger Parkinson's disease patient

- There is a more severe and selective dopaminergic denervation.

Older Parkinson's disease patient

- Additional non-dopaminergic lesions.
- Greater progression of disease over time
- Poorer response to levodopa replacement therapy.
- Particularly problems of gait and balance.

Why do we not use more dopamine agonists in elderly patients?

It has been known for over 20 years that Parkinson's disease patients started on bromocriptine as monotherapy have virtually no dyskinesia or motor fluctuations compared with patients treated with levodopa (Rascol *et al.* 1979). Relatively few patients, compared with those on levodopa, can be sustained on agonist therapy alone. However, combination therapy of bromocriptine with levodopa, compared with levodopa alone, can produce comparable benefit, although with significantly fewer motor complications (Rinne 1989). Similar results were found by Montastruc *et al.* (1994).

A realistic aim in the next decade is to limit the onset and severity of dyskinesia in all age groups of Parkinson's disease patients, and to allow them to enjoy the benefits of dopaminergic therapy. The recently published 5-year study (Rascol *et al.* 2000) of ropinirole demonstrates the impact and tolerability of the long-term use of dopamine agonist monotherapy, with if necessary supplemental low-dose levodopa therapy to reduce the frequency and severity of dyskinesia. This group of drugs shares the ability to stimulate dopamine receptors. They have distinct advantages over levodopa therapy. They do not require metabolic conversion to exert their activity, and are therefore independent of surviving dopaminergic neurons. Individual agonists have different effects on dopamine subtypes, but all are active at the D_2-receptor. Perhaps most importantly, dopamine agonists do not undergo oxidative metabolism and therefore do not induce oxidative stress or generate free radicals. L-Dopa has a relatively short half-life (60–90 minutes) and therefore is thought to induce pulsatile stimulation of dopamine receptors. In contrast, dopamine agonists have a longer half-life and are likely to provide a more continuous stimulation of dopamine receptors. Also their absorption and transport into the brain are not influenced by plasma amino acids, unlike levodopa.

There have been relatively few studies of the use of dopamine agonists in elderly people (Mitchell *et al.* 1997). Possible explanations include the fact that elderly people have reduced drug metabolism, for example, of levodopa (Robertson *et al.* 1989) and a greater tendency to develop side effects (Joseph *et al.* 1995), and are likely to be taking multiple drugs. In many respects, the therapeutic goals of treatment are often different. Nevertheless, there are a number of studies suggesting that, in selected patients, dopamine agonists can be as well tolerated in elderly Parkinson's disease patients as in younger patients (Hindle *et al.* 1998; Appiah-Kubi *et al.* 2001). For example, the study by Shulman *et al.* (2000) demonstrated that, if one excluded patients with significant coexisting systemic disease, and/or cognitive impairment, 40–50% of elderly patients were able to tolerate and remain on agonist therapy for at least a 6-month period.

From the few published studies, it seems clear that prescribing of dopamine agonists in elderly patients should be avoided in those Parkinson's disease patients who have the following:

- history of dementia
- hallucinosis
- orthostatic hypotension
- significant systemic disease, e.g. ischaemic heart disease.

The data from these few studies of elderly patients contrast with the larger amounts of evidence from drug trials in younger Parkinson's disease patients. We need to be aware that such studies exclude a large group of Parkinson's disease patients from potentially useful therapy.

What causes fatigue in Parkinson's disease?

Fatigue is a common symptom in Parkinson's disease. Questionnaire surveys have emphasised fatigue as one of the three most disabling symptoms in Parkinson's disease (Friedman & Friedman 1993). Fatigue is a common symptom, with 25% of patients in a primary care clinic reporting fatigue as a major problem. Hoehn and Yahr (1967) stated that 2% of patients first presented with fatigue, whereas Karlsen *et al.* (1999) reported that 44% of Parkinson's disease patients had fatigue compared with 18% age-matched controls.

Most such patients were able to discriminate between the fatigue before disease and that after the onset of the illness. Yet, the present understanding of fatigue in Parkinson's disease 'is between non-existent and poor' (Friedman 1999). Friedman has stated that, only after attempting to dissect the myriad meanings of the term and then correlating the relationship with the clinical motor state and the psychological profile of the patient, can one achieve an understanding of the mechanism underlying the symptom.

Studies suggest that it is distinguishable from depression, with lack of self-esteem or feelings of hopelessness, and also with disease severity (Friedman & Friedman 1993). Similarly, van Hilten *et al.* (1993) found no association of fatigue between disease severity and anti-parkinsonian medication.

It is not clear whether fatigue relates to the neurophysiological changes involved in limb motor activity, as reported by Ziv *et al.* (1998), or a central symptom related to weariness of the mind. Ziv *et al.* (1998) concluded that, as muscle fatigue from a continuous isometric forearm flexion significantly improved after the use of levodopa, a central dopamine deficiency state might be proposed. Not only are the later stages of the disease associated with motor fluctuations, but also patients report changes in mood and concentration accompanying the changes in the motor state. To analyse this further it would seem to be necessary to correlate such fatigue symptoms with the 'on–off' motor state of the patient and the amount of levodopa-based therapy taken.

It is recognised that cognitive impairment is associated with fatigue (Sandroni *et al.* 1992), and therefore in any study it is important to exclude those patients with a Mini-Mental State Examination (MMSE) score of < 24 (Folstein *et al.* 1975). Dementia can often have a greater impact on the quality of the patient's life than the motor disability. It is important, therefore, to exclude such a variable because it may only confuse the origin of the patient's sense of fatigue. Furthermore, the recent study of Schrag *et al.* (2000b) concludes that the quality of life of the Parkinson's disease patient is not only influenced by the presence of cognitive impairment, but also determined by depression and disability, especially axial impairment.

The paucity of studies in Parkinson's disease should be compared with the studies of fatigue in multiple sclerosis (MS), where no definite conclusion has been reached about why this symptom should also be highly prevalent.

It has been estimated that up to 78% of patients complain of fatigue in MS (Freal *et al.* 1984). Krupp *et al.* (1988) reported fatigue in 28 of 33 MS patients, but also in 17 of 32 normal controls. There was no relationship with depression or degree of disability. Fatigue was the most common complaint in 80% of MS patients and the worst symptom in 40% (Reingold 1990). The study by Mainero *et al.* (1999) found no relationship between alterations in the blood–brain barrier and fatigue severity.

Furthermore, fatigue in MS is not related to clinical disease severity (EDSS), nor to the extent of abnormalities on magnetic resonance imaging (MRI) (Bakshi *et al.* 2000) or disease progression rates or number of relapses over a 2-year period (van der Werf *et al.* 1998). However, Kroencke *et al.* (2000) found a correlation of fatigue with disability and depression.

In a double-blind, placebo-controlled trial (Krupp *et al.* 1998), amantadine was significantly beneficial for fatigue independent of changes in sleep, depression or neurological disability.

Our understanding of which aspects of a patient's parkinsonism influences the quality of life is fundamental. Over the years, there has been developed reliable scales assessing the motor state, yet the non-motor aspects that significantly affect the individual patient and his or her partner or carer have not been well established. One might expect that the ability of the patient as assessed by an activities of daily living index might relate to the well-being of the patient. Is this the case? Any further studies of Parkinson's disease patients must incorporate activities of living and quality-of-life indices and those measures that assess the impact of the disease (and any treatment) on the well-being of the patient. Scales such as the PDQ-39 (Peto *et al.* 1995) (which assess eight health concepts: physical functioning, social functioning, physical role limitations, emotional role limitations, mental health, energy, vitality, pain and general health) and the SF-36 (Jenkinson *et al.* 1993) (which assesses the quality of life of PD patients) attempt to address these issues and need to be included (Schrag *et al.* 2000a).

The MS literature has given valuable insight into the biological nature of fatigue. The answer to this disabling symptom may not therefore lie in any distinct pathway or neurotransmitter. Its origin remains enigmatic, but an answer may relate to its associations with other variables that affect the well-being of the patient (such as motor activity, sleep, depression, etc).

Future strategies in parkinsonian dementia
Neuropsychological changes in Parkinson's disease

Although James Parkinson stated in *An Essay on the Shaking Palsy* that 'the senses and intellects remain uninjured', it is recognised that this is not always the case. The prevalence of dementia has been reported to be between 15% (Lees 1985) and 20–30% in randomly selected groups of patients attending hospital (Brown & Marsden 1984). If allowances are made for drug effects, and coexisting depression, intellectual impairment can still be identified with neuropathological confirmation *post mortem* (Hakim & Mathieson 1979; Jellinger & Grissold 1982).

The histological changes in Parkinson's disease include degeneration to cholinergic systems particularly in the neocortex and hippocampus, which demonstrate reduced choline acetyltransferase (CAT) activity. The more severe the degree of intellectual impairment, the greater the cortical cholinergic deficiency (Ruberg *et al.* 1982; Perry *et al.* 1986). Furthermore, the role of cortical cholinergic deficiency in the genesis of intellectual impairment is underlined by the fact that drug-induced cognitive impairment is more frequently seen in patients taking anticholinergic medication.

There are several similarities in the dementia associated with Parkinson's disease, compared with Alzheimer's disease. Both diseases show degeneration of cholinergic, noradrenergic and also the somatostatinergic neurons. Furthermore, the characteristic histopathological changes in Alzheimer's disease, of neurofibrillary tangles, senile plaques and granulovacuolar degeneration, may be seen in Parkinson's disease.

In Parkinson's disease, two types of cognitive decline are recognised. One is an Alzheimer's disease-type of dementia where cortical cholinergic denervation is accompanied by distinctive histopathological changes (Tomlinson 1984). The other is a non-Alzheimer pattern of dementia where damage is to cortically projecting cholinergic neurons unaccompanied by distinctive Alzheimer's disease-type histopathological changes. In both cases the basis for the dementia is neuronal degeneration, influencing cholinergic transmission (Nikano & Hirano 1984; Gibb 1989).

Clinical trials of anticholinesterases

The pathological similarities between the dementia of Alzheimer's disease and that of Parkinson's disease is recognised. Attempts were first made to arrest the progression of Alzheimer's disease with the use of a centrally acting non-competitive reversible acetylcholinesterase inhibitor, called tacrine. This drug is not available in the UK, but is licensed for use in Alzheimer's disease in France and the USA.

In 1992, Ott and Lannon published a study of the use of tacrine in Alzheimer's disease, which commented that mild features of parkinsonism were made worse by tacrine. This may be explained by the different mode of action of tacrine compared with the newer cholinesterases, particularly galantamine. Tacrine has direct activity on muscarinic receptors (Adem *et al.* 1990). It is this action that is likely to explain the exacerbation of the limb signs of Parkinson's disease, e.g. the worsening of tremor (Duvoisin 1967; Ott & Lannon 1992). Conversely, a study published in letter form in 1996 of the use of tacrine in Parkinson's disease patients with dementia (Hutchinson & Fazzini 1996) reported no significant deterioration in motor function. Tacrine (1,2,3,4-tetrahydro-9-acridinamine monohydrochloride) is a centrally acting non-competitive reversible acetylcholinesterase inhibitor. It acts both pre- and postsynaptically.

The newer-generation cholinesterases (donepezil, rivastigmine, galantamine) differ in their mode of action and pharmacokinetics. Unlike tacrine, galantamine (for example) is a competitive inhibitor. Furthermore, unlike tacrine, it is not related to the acridines, but is a naturally occurring alkaloid. Galantamine binds to acetylcholinesterase (AChE) less presynaptically than postsynaptically. The main therapeutic site of action is thought to be postsynaptic. The greater the cholinergic deficit in a particular area, the more cholinesterase inhibition will occur. Conversely, the more normal areas have less increase in acetylcholine.

The benefits of the more selective mode of action of the 'newer' cholinergic agents (rivastigmine, donepezil and galantamine) in their predominantly postsynaptic effects (and action on nicotinic receptors with galantamine) have resulted in the potential to use an acetylcholinesterase inhibitor in Parkinson's disease-associated dementia. A number of studies assessing the short-term impact of these newer agents (donepezil, rivastigmine and galantamine) in Parkinson's disease-associated dementia have been presented and published.

A randomised, placebo-controlled, double-masked, crossover study of donepezil in Parkinson's disease was performed by Aarsland *et al.* (2001). Fourteen Parkinson's disease patients with cognitive impairment (MMSE = 20.7 [3.3]) were studied. After 10 weeks, two patients dropped out (as a result of nausea and diarrhoea). Parkinson's disease severity did not change and the MMSE increased by 2.1 on treatment whereas MMSE decreased by 0.3 point on placebo ($p = 0.02$).

The open label study by Giladi *et al.* (2001), of 21 demented Parkinson's disease patients treated with rivastigmine, found similar results. After 12 weeks the 20 patients had an improved Unified Parkinson's Disease Rating Scale (UPDRS) by 3.9

± 1.9 (p < 0.03), and the Alzheimer Disease Assessment Scale (ADAS)-cog total score improved by 7.4 ± 1.9 (p < 0.005). Between 12 and 24 weeks, six patients stopped treatment because of side effects or lack of benefit.

In a further open label study by van Laar *et al.* (2001) of rivastigmine in 10 Parkinson's disease patients with psychosis, a significant improvement in psychosis (measured by BPRS > 20%) was recorded. MMSE improved 3–5 points, whereas the UPDRS improved from 40 to 35.

Although this review focuses on the dementia of Parkinson's disease, similar results have been shown in Lewy body dementia, e.g. the study by McKeith *et al.* (2000). In Lewy body dementia, clinicopatholgical studies demonstrate extensive deficits in cholinergic neurotransmission. Neocortical cholinergic activity is more severely depleted in Lewy body disease, compared with Alzheimer's disease. Postsynaptic muscarinic receptors are better preserved and more functionally intact compared with Alzheimer's disease (Perry *et al.* 1994; Lieberini *et al.* 1996).

In the randomised, placebo-controlled, double-masked study of 120 patients with Lewy body dementia (McKeith *et al.* 2000), at 20 weeks 63% of the patients showed a 30% or greater improvement from baseline on a neuropsychiatric inventory. Patients performed better on cognitive testing, particularly those sensitive to attentional component. Improvements were noted in 50% of psychiatric features such as apathy, indifference, anxiety, delusions and hallucinations.

In summary, anticholinesterases:

- may have a role in reducing hallucinosis in dementia associated with parkinsonism
- may slow cognitive impairment and increase alertness
- may be better tolerated than neuroleptic medication.

Cell therapy in Parkinson's disease

The relatively recently published placebo-controlled study of implanted embryonic tissue in Parkinson's disease patients has once again captured the interest of patients, scientists and clinicians (Freed *et al.* 2001). The development of severe dyskinesia in 15% of patients in the second year after surgery has raised questions about the efficacy of embryonic implantation surgery. Such is the interest around the world that it is unlikely to influence the search for treatment which offers the potential to reverse the course of a disease that remains relentlessly progressive. Growth of such technology will continue. For the present, implantation involving embryonic tissue is impractical for all but a minority of patients. Alternative sources of donor tissues must be found if transplantation is to become clinically useful for a large group of Parkinson's disease patients. Trials of adrenal medulla cells, for example, have been disappointing. Other therapeutic possibilities may include using cell lines derived from pluripotent human fetal or embryonic stem cells (Bjorklund & Lindvall 2000). The ethical debate surrounding such cell therapies is also testing the limits of science and technology legitimately playing a role in the relief of human suffering.

For most Parkinson's disease patients with severe disease, non-dopaminergic manipulation to reverse the abnormalities in basal ganglia circuitry responsible for dyskinesia is a distinct possibility in the next decade. This may lie in glutamate (N-methyl-D-aspartate or NMDA) receptor antagonists, opioid receptor antagonists, α_2-adrenergic receptor antagonists, or serotonin (5HT)-enhancing agents, e.g. adenosine α_2-receptors are preferentially localised on the indirect pathway and modulate dopamine D_2-receptors. α_2-Receptor antagonists have been shown to alleviate parkinsonian symptoms and induce much less dyskinesia, compared with levodopa-based therapies (Brotchie 1998; Stromberg *et al.* 2000; Bezard *et al.* 2001).

Knowledge about the interaction between the various neurotransmitters, in particular their influence on each other, requires clarification in order to predict the clinical effect reliably. Recently, there has been a resurgence of interest in amantadine because of its anti-dyskinetic effects induced by antagonising NMDA receptors (Luginger *et al.* 2000). NMDA-receptor antagonists in primates appear to reduce levodopa-related dyskinesia (Blanchet *et al.* 1998). At the present time, although there is no selective NMDA receptor antagonist available, amantadine can be tried, although its effects are not predictable in every patient.

The greater understanding of the mechanisms involved in basal ganglia circuitry has created the clinical trials of agents that, if successful, offer enormous potential benefit to the quality of life of the Parkinson's disease patient. If one can, for example, reduce the overactivity of the lateral pallidum and/or increase the activity of the subthalamic nucleus, then dyskinesia may be reduced and allow greater increases in the dose of levodopa preparations.

Parkinson's disease is not just a dopamine deficiency state. If we can also influence non-dopamine-responsive symptoms, we will create a greater impact on the quality of life and life expectancy of the Parkinson's disease patient.

Conclusion

Future strategies seek to recognise the broad impact of the illness. In addition to motor disability, cognitive impairment, balance, fatigue and other non-dopaminergic symptoms can have a great influence on the quality of life of the Parkinson's disease patient. Optimal therapeutic options may be viewed as initially costly, but increasingly the importance of the indirect costs of any treatment are being recognised. The socioeconomic costs of the illness need to be assessed in evaluating the merits of a new therapy. In an era of evidence-based medicine, improvements in design of clinical trials that include estimates of quality of life are essential. Such studies need to be more inclusive and address the impact of the disease in all age groups.

References

Aarsland D, Larsen JP, Janvin C (2001) Donepezil treatment in Parkinson's disease with dementia: a double blind, placebo-controlled crossover study. *Neurology* **56**, (suppl 3), A128

Adem A, Mohammed AK, Winbald B (1990) Multiple effects of tetrahydroaminoacridine on the cholinergic system: biochemical and behavioral effects. *Journal of Neural Transmission, Parkinson's Disease and Dementia* Sect 2, 113–128

Appiah-Kubi L, Nisbet A, Forbes A *et al* (2001) The tolerability and efficacy of cabergoline mono- or adjunctive therapy in elderly and young PD patients. *Parkinsonism and Related Disorders* **7**(suppl 1), s28

Bakshi R, Miletich RS, Henschel K (2000) Fatigue in multiple sclerosis: cross-sectional correlation with brain MRI findings in 71 patients. *Neurology* **54**. 1709–1710

Bezard E, Brotchie JM, Gross CE (2001) Pathophysiology of levodopa-induced dyskinesia: potential for new therapies. *Nature Reviews Neuroscience* **2**, 577–588

Bjorklund A & Lindvall O (2000) Cell replacement therapies for central nervous system disorders. *Nature Neuroscience* **3**, 537–544

Blanchet P, Konitsiotis S, Chase TN (1998) Amantadine reduces levodopa-induced dyskinesia in parkinsonian monkeys. *Movement Disorders* **13**. 798–802

Blin J, Dubois B, Bonnet AM *et al.* (1991) Does ageing aggravate parkinsonian disability? *Journal of Neurology, Neurosurgery, and Psychiatry* **54**, 780–782

Bonnet AM, Loria Y, Saint Hilaire MH, Lhermitte F, Agid Y (1987) Does long-term aggravation of Parkinson's disease result from non-dopaminergic lesions. *Neurology* **37**, 1539–1542

Brotchie JM (1998) Adjuncts to dopamine replacement: a pragmatic approach to reducing the problem of dyskinesia in Parkinson's disease. *Movement Disorders* **13,** 871–876

Brown RG & Marsden CD (1984) How common is dementia in Parkinson's disease. *The Lancet* 1262–1265

Clarke CE (2001) Dopamine agonist monotherapy in Parkinson's disease. *Current Medical Literature* **3**, 1–5

Dodel RC, Eggert KM, Singer MS, Eichorn TE, Pogarell O, Oertel WH (1998) Costs of drug treatment in Parkinson's disease. *Movement Disorders* **13**, 249–254

Duvoisin RC (1967) Cholinergic–anticholinergic antagonism in parkinsonism. *Archives of Neurology* **17**, 124–136

Fahn S, Elton RL *et al.* and members of the UPDRS Development Committee (1987) UPDRS: Unified Parkinson's disease Rating Scale. In Fahn S, Marsden CD, Calne DB, Golstein M (eds), *Recent Development in PD*, Vol. 2. Florham Park, NL: MacMillan HC Information, pp 153–164

Folstein MF, Folstein SE, McHugh PR (1975). Mini-mental state: A practical method for grading the cognitive state of patients for the clinician. *Journal of Psychiatric Research* **12**, 189–198

Freal JE, Kraft GH, Croyell JK (1984) Symptomatic fatigue in multiple sclerosis. *Archives of Physical Medicine and Rehabilitation* **65**, 135–138

Freed CR, Greene PE, Breeze R *et al.* (2001) Transplantation of embryonic dopamine neurons for severe Parkinson's disease. *New England Journal of Medicine* **344**, 710–719

Friedman J & Friediman H (1993). Fatigue in Parkinson's disease. *Neurology* **43**, 2016–2020

Friedman JH (1999) Enhanced fatigue during motor performance in patients with PD. *Neurology* **53**, 438–439

Giladi N, Shabat H, Benbunan B *et al.* (2001) The effect of treatment with rivastigmine (Exeleon) on cognitive functions of patients with dementia and Parkinson's disease. *Neurology* **56**(suppl 3), A128

Gibb WRG (1989) Dementia and Parkinson's disease. *British Journal of Psychiatry* **154**, 596–614

Hakim AM & Mathieson G (1979) Dementia in Parkinson's disease: a neuropathological study. *Neurology* **29**, 1209–1214

Haycock J (1994) *Meeting a Need.* London: Parkinson's Disease Society

Hindle JV, Meara RJ, Sharma JC *et al.* (1998) Prescribing pergolide in the elderly – an open label study of pergolide in elderly patients with Parkinson's disease. *International Journal of Geriatric Psychopharmacology* **1**, 78–81

Hoehn MM & Yahr M (1967) Parkinsonism: onset, progression and mortality. *Neurology* **17**, 427–442

Hutchinson M & Fazzini E (1996) Cholinesterase inhibition in Parkinson's disease. *Journal of Neurology, Neurosurgery, and Psychiatry* **61**, 324–325

Jarman B (1998) The Community Nurse Specialist Project. Conference presentation, British Geriatrics Society Special Interest Group Meeting

Jellinger K & Grissold W (1982) Cerebral atrophy in Parkinson's syndrome. *Experimental Brain Research* **5**(suppl), 26–35

Jenkinson, C, Coulter A, Wright L (1993) Short form 36 (SF 36) health survey questionnaire: normative data for adults of working age. *British Medical Journal* **306**, 1437–1440

Joseph CL, Siple J, McWorter K, Camicioli R (1995) Adverse reactions to controlled release levodopa/carbidopa in older persons: case reports. *Journal of the American Geriatric Society* **43**, 47–50

Karlsen K, Larsen JP, Tandberg E, Jorgensen K (1999) Fatigue in patients with Parkinson's disease. *Movement Disorders* **14**, 237–241

Klawans HL (1986) Individual manifestations of Parkinson's disease after ten or more years of levodopa. *Movement Disorders* **1**, 187–192

Koller WC, Glatt S, Vetere-Overfield B, Hassanein R (1989) Falls and Parkinson's disease. *Clinical Neuropharmacology* **12**, 98–105

Kroencke DC, Lynch SG, Denney DR (2000) Fatigue in multiple sclerosis: relationship to depression. disability, and disease pattern. *Multiple Sclerosis* **6**, 131–136

Krupp LB, Coyle PK, Doscher C *et al.* (1995) Fatigue therapy in multiple sclerosis: results of a double-blind, randomized, parallel trial of amantadine, pemoline, and placebo. *Neurology* **45**, 1956–1961

Krupp LB, Alvarez LA, LaRocca NG, Scheinberg LC (1998) Fatigue in multiple sclerosis. *Archives of Neurology* **55**, 435–437

Lees AJ (1985) Parkinson's disease and dementia. *The Lancet* **i**, 43–44

Lieberini P, Valerio A, Memo M, Pano PF (1996) Lewy body dementia and responsiveness to cholinesterases inhibitors: a paradigm for heterogeneity of Alzheimer's disease? *Trends in Pharmacological Science* **17**, 155–160

Luginger E, Wenning GK, Bosch S, Poewe W (2000) Beneficial effects of amantadine on L-dopa induced dyskinesias in Parkinson's disease. *Movement Disorders* **15**, 873–878

McKeith I, Del Ser I, Spano P *et al.* (2000) Efficacy of rivastigmine in dementia with Lewy bodies: a randomised, double-blind, placebo controlled international study. *The Lancet* **356**, 2031–2036

MacMahon DG (2001) Organization of services, concepts of management and health economics. In Playfer J & Hindle J (eds), *Parkinson's Disease in the Older Patient*. London: Arnold, pp 215–238

Mainero C, Faroni J, Gasperinin C *et al.* (1999) Fatigue and magnetic resonance imaging activity in multiple sclerosis. *Journal of Neurology* **246**, 454–458

Mitchell SL, Sullivan EA, Lipsitz LA (1997*)* Exclusion of elderly subjects from clinical trails for Parkinson's disease. *Archives of Neurology* **54**, 1393–1398

Montastruc JL, Rascol O, Senard JM, Rascol A (1994) A randomised controlled study comparing bromocriptine to which levodopa was later added, with levodopa alone in previously untreated patients with Parkinson's disease: a five year follow up. *Journal of Neurology, Neurosurgery, and Psychiatry* **57**, 1034–1038

Nikano D & Hirano A (1984) Parkinson's disease: neuron loss in the nucleus basalis without concomitant Alzheimer's disease. *Annals of Neurology* **15**, 415–418

Ott BR & Lannon MC (1992) Exacerbation of parkinsonism by Tacrine. *Clinical Neuropharmacology* **4**, 322–325

Perry EK, Haroutunian V, Davis KL *et al.* (1994) Neocortical cholinergic activities differentiate Lewy body dementia from classical Alzheimer's disease. *NeuroReport* **5**, 747–749

Perry RH, Tomlinson BE, Candy JM *et al.* (1986) Cortical cholinergic deficit in mentally impaired parkinsonian patients. *The Lancet* **ii**, 789–790

Peto V, Jenkinson C, Fitzpatrick R *et al.* (1995) The development and validation of a short measure of functioning and well-being for individuals with Parkinson's disease. *Quality of Life Research* **4**, 241–248

Rascol A, Guiaud B, Montastruc JL, David J, Clanet M (1979) Long-term treatment of Parkinson's disease with bromocriptine. *Journal of Neurology, Neurosurgery, and Psychiatry* **42**, 143–150

Rascol O, Brooks DJ, Korczyn AD *et al.* (2000) A five year incidence of dyskinesia in patients with early Parkinson's disease who were treated with ropinirole or levodopa. *New England Journal of Medicine* **342**, 1484–1491

Reingold SC (1990) Fatigue and multiple sclerosis. *MS News British Multiple Sclerosis Society* **142**, 30–31

Rinne UK (1989) Combination of a dopamine agonist, MAO-β inhibitor and levodopa – a new strategy in the treatment of early Parkinson's disease. *Acta Neurologica Scandinavica* **126**, 165–169

Robertson DR, Wood ND, Everest H *et al.* (1989) The effect of age on the pharmacokinetics of levodopa administered alone and in the presence of carbidopa. *British Journal of Clinical Pharmacology* **28**, 61–69

Ruberg M, Ploska A, Javoy-Agid F *et al.* (1982) Musarinic binding and choline acetyltransferase activity in parkinsonian subjects with reference to dementia. *Brain Research* **232**, 129–139

Sandroni P. Walker C, Starr A (1992) Fatigue in patients with MS. *Archives of Neurology* **49**. 517–524

Schrag A, Jahanshahi M, Quinn N (2000a) How does Parkinson's disease affect quality of life? A comparison with quality of life in the general population. *Movement Disorders* **15**, 1112–1118

Schrag A, Jahanshahi M, Quinn N (2000b) What contributes to quality of life in patients with Parkinson's disease. *Journal of Neurology, Neurosurgery, and Psychiatry* **69**, 308–312

Shulman LM, Minagar A, Rabinstein A, Weiner WJ (2000) The use of dopamine agonists in very elderly patients with Parkinson's disease. *Movement Disorders* **15**, 664–668

Stromberg I, Popoli P, Muller CE, Ferre S, Fuxe K (2000) Electrophysiological and behavioural evidence for an antagonistic modulatory role of adenosine A2a receptors in dopamine D2 receptor regulation in the rat dopamine-denervated striatum. *European Journal of Neuroscience* **12**, 4033–4037

Tomlinson B (1984) Ageing and dementia. In Hume Adams J, Corsellis JAN, Duchen LW (eds), *Greenfield's Neuropathology*, 4th edn. London: Arnold, p 98

van Laar T, de Vries JJ, Nakhosteen A, Leenders KL (2001) Rivastigmine as anti-psychotic treatment in patients with Parkinson's disease. *Parkinsonism and Related Disorders* **7**(suppl 1), S73

van der Werf SP, Jongen PJ, Lycklama a Nijeholt GJ *et al.* (1998) Fatigue in multiple sclerosis: interrelations between fatigue complaints, cerebral MRI abnormalities and neurological disability. *Journal of Neurological Science* **160**, 164–170

van Hilten JJ, Weggman M, van der Elde EA, Kerkhof GA, van Dijk JG, Roos RAC (1993) Sleep, excessive daytime sleepiness and fatigue in Parkinson's disease. *Journal of Neural Transmission* **5**, 235–244

Whetten-Goldstein K, Sloan F, Kulas E, Cutson T, Schenkman M (1997) The burden of Parkinson's disease on society, family, and the individual. *Journal of the American Geriatric Society* **45**, 844–849

Ziv I, Avraharn M, Michaelov Y *et al.* (1998) Enhanced fatigue during motor performance in patients with Parkinson's disease. *Neurology* **51**, 1583–1586

Index

Throughout this index, the abbreviation PD is used for Parkinson's disease. As this is the subject of the entire book, no references appear under 'Parkinson's disease', so the reader is advised to search under more specific headings.